UNDER THE INFLUENCE

Edited by Ana Miljački

Contents

The *Under the Influence* book is based on the eponymous symposium, which brought together scholars and practitioners of architecture in order to focus on one of the most anxious disciplinary topics: influence.

The symposium invited each of the participants to illuminate a single term—a disciplinary synonym for appropriation—and through that term, the specific strategies, historical, and disciplinary circumstances in which it is enmeshed. It was organized and hosted by Ana Miljački, and presented by the MIT Department of Architecture.

The book includes introductory texts by Mario Carpo and Nader Tehrani and discussions moderated by Ana Miljački, Amanda Reeser Lawrence, and Michael Kubo.

Postscripts

  Ana Miljački

P.S.
Ana Miljački

The Postscript convention stipulates its appearance at the end of a completed letter, statement or book. Its consideration is meant to take place after everything else one might have encountered and absorbed in the intended communication. This textual postscript and others included here before the Introduction reflect various types of anachronisms embedded in the book, both originally and in this republication by Actar. In this "copy" of the proceedings of the *Under the Influence* symposium, we included a few new pieces by the original participants in the event, refracted through and perhaps even prompted by the conversations we had together in 2012. These micro "postscripts" range from exhibitions on other architects' influences, through "reproductions" of various authored architectural ideas, to references to mythology, as well as resistance to the smooth Alibaba-ization of architecture via legal means.

Much new work on the question of copying and authorship has been produced since our event, the intellectual space around these topics has become far more crowded than it was in 2012. Many more of us are now examining forms of repetition and transformation, authorship, originality and unoriginality, as well as the contemporary condition of which that very examination is symptomatic. The *Under the Influence* symposium predicted the inevitability of all that. The speed of architectural (and all other) image flow has only increased since then, with no slowing down in sight.[1] A footnote in one of our conversations in 2012 has become a whole, full-fledged career.[2] There have been issues of *Mass-context*, *Perspecta*, *arq*, dedicated to *Repetition*, *Quote*, and *References*, respectively.[3] The "Fair Use" exhibition, which opened on the occasion of the symposium at MIT, has had another life as "Un/Fair Use" emphasizing the legal dimension of architectural copying and originality.[4] Architecture schools have reinvigorated their plagiarism clauses, in a Sisyphean attempt to appease individual student—and protect their own institutional reputations—while acknowledging the force of the trend to consume

1. Flow has been theorized by media and cultural theorists since the 1970s: Raymond Williams in *Television: Technology and Cultural Form* (London: Fontana, 1974), more recently David Joselit, *After Art* (Princeton: Princeton University Press, 2012), and Boris Groys, *In the Flow* (London: Verso, 2016), to name just a few particularly relevant works.

2. In the first panel conversation, Michael Meredith of MOS and Florian Idenburg of SO-IL discuss posts by Andrew Kovacs, whom they only really know at this point as the curator of the *Archive of Affinities*. Kovacs is now an established producer, critic and curator of architecture.

3. *Masscontext 21: Repetition*, 2014; *Perspect* 49: *Quote*, edited by AJ Artemel, Russel LeStourgeon and Violette de la Selle, August 2016; arq 95: arquitectura, diseño, urbanismo, Chile, *References*, April 2017.

and reproduce images of architecture. In 2016, the Victoria and Albert museum put on an amazing show at the Venice Biennale dealing with preservation and reproduction, "The World of Fragile Parts." Winy Mass (and his think tank the Why Factory, t?f) published a volume *Copy Paste* in 2018.[5] And even with all this attention, there may not yet be any definitive clarity on how the discipline of architecture and culture in general have reformulated the ethical, aesthetic and monetary values historically ascribed to originality, authorship or reproduction. There is, however, certainly more self-awareness about the anxiety, ecstasy and ambivalence these topics produce in the era of afternet, copyright, and twitch.

The *Under the Influence* event and record produced a momentary generational response on some of these topics in the form of an open, even confessional, conversation. The book in your hands presents transcripts of these conversations and presentations, as well as the textual and image references made in them. Preserving various specificities that were part of that historical moment and event (instead of adapting the jokes to suit the latest trends), it performs a polemical position on the value of a historical recording. In republishing this book, sending it into circulation again, we followed perhaps a naïve hope (though at least as old as the printing press) that saying things "for the record," at a specific moment in time is indeed the only way to resist the flattening force of the ever-swelling image and information flow. And while resistance to that flow may indeed be futile, in the end, we will at least have this copy to rely on.[6]

4. For this second rendition of the exhibition, co-curator Sarah Hirschman produced a series of interviews on the 1990 Architectural Works Copyright Protection Act in the US. The exhibition has been reviewed and has thus left a trace in Wired, Margaret Rhodes, "Architecture's Fine Line Between Stealing and Inspiration," Wired, October 2015, https://www.wired.com/2015/10/architectures-fine-line-stealing-inspiration/.

5. The Why Factory, *Copy Paste: Bad Ass Copy Guide* (Rotterdam: NAI010 Publishers, 2018)

6. I want to thank Meejin Yoon, now former Head of MIT's Department of Architecture, for encouraging the republication of this volume.

Florian Idenburg

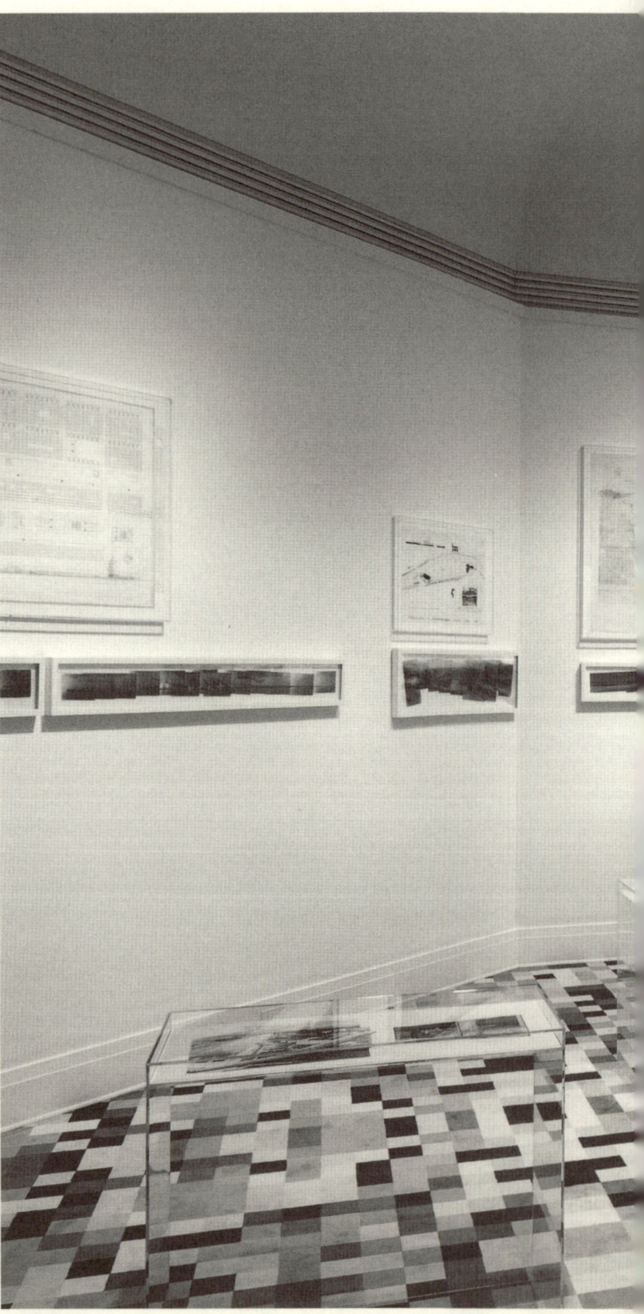

Postscripts — Florian Idenburg

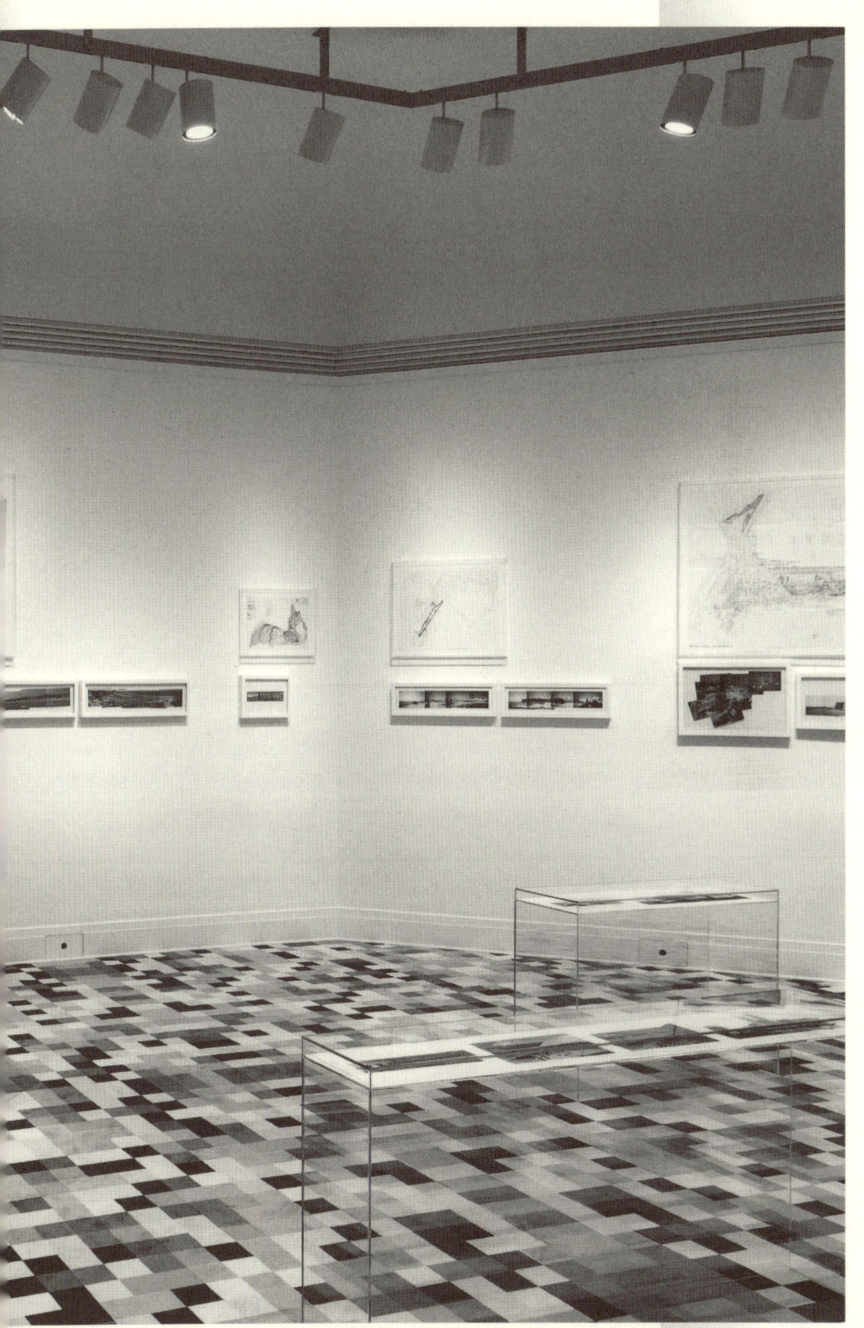

Michael Meredith & Hilary Sample

Maybe it was because of this conference. Maybe it was something we stumbled upon. Or maybe we noticed a lot of our former students making 3-D printed vases, doodads, and designer tchotchkes, then selling them online. Whatever it was, we wanted to be part of it. During spring of 2014 we started writing, designing, and making a series of so-called "Reproductions." They were fakes. We fabricated little absurdist stories about each piece. They were reflections on the architectural discipline. There was an obvious formula to them. The objects were all very minor, non-architectural, temporary, domestic, and decor things with short lifespans (with one or two exceptions). They were negations piled upon negations. We had a long list of things to make: candles, soaps, cutting boards, erasers, trivets... We didn't make all

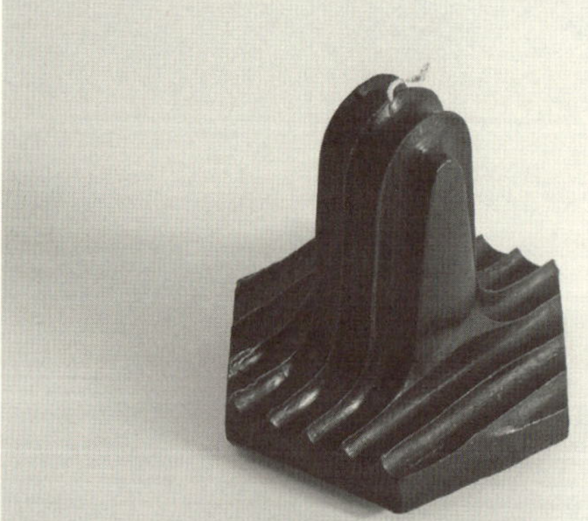

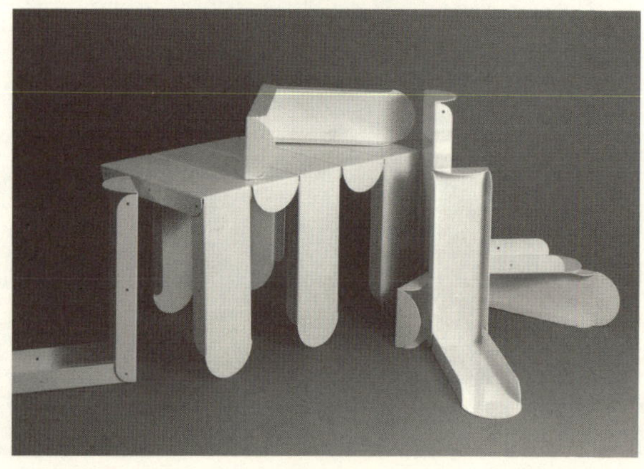

of them, but we made some. We wanted to play with
the relationship between real and fake, to play around
with disciplinary narratives and commerce, to play with
authorship, history, myth-making... But also, and maybe
most importantly, we simply enjoyed making things. It
was fun to make furniture or learn about making soap.
We liked the strange how-to videos on YouTube, exploring
different woods and the nice perfumed scents. Looking
back, it was important for us at the time. We drafted, set
up, and started a bunch of little projects that haven't been
executed. We reworked our website to include a shop.
We were ahead of our time. We sold things, until we sold
out. It was exhausting. We were even going to sell our
models, old sketches, and office trash online. But like
many things, we didn't get around to it yet. We became
distracted by something else along the way.

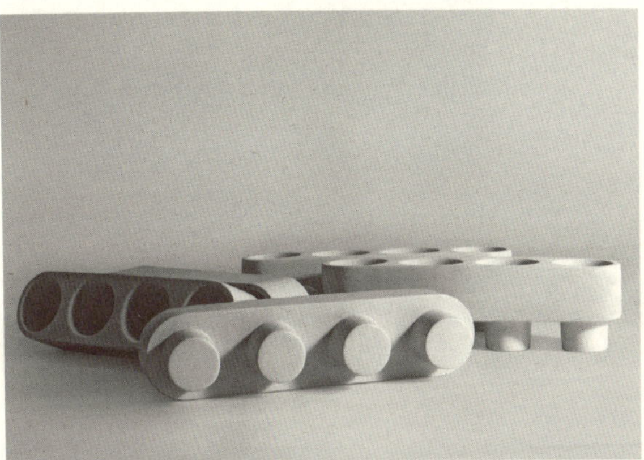

Reproduction No. 3
Aldo Rossi

Possibly a Vase
Material: *Porcelain,
Glaze*
Edition: *20*
Size:
3.25"x13"x3.5"
Price: *Sold Out*

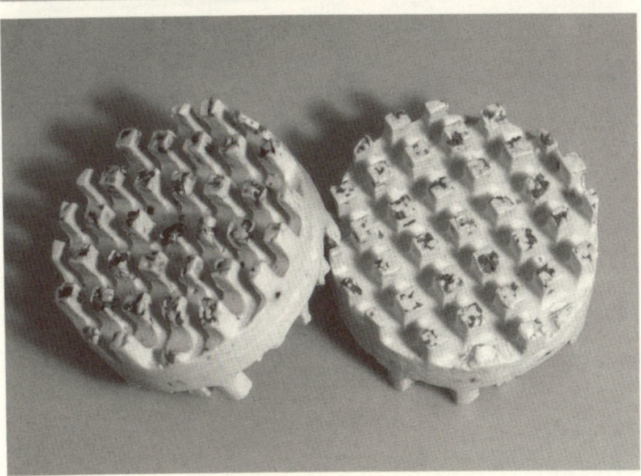

Reproduction No. 4
Lilly Reich

Soap No. 24
Material: *Soap, Oils*
Edition: *20*
Size:
4.25"x4.25"x2"
Price: *Sold Out*

Reproduction No. 5
Ray Eames

Utilitarian Stool
With No Design
Whatsoever
Material: *Oak, Oil*
Edition: *10*
Size:
14"x16.25"x16.5"
Price: *Sold Out*

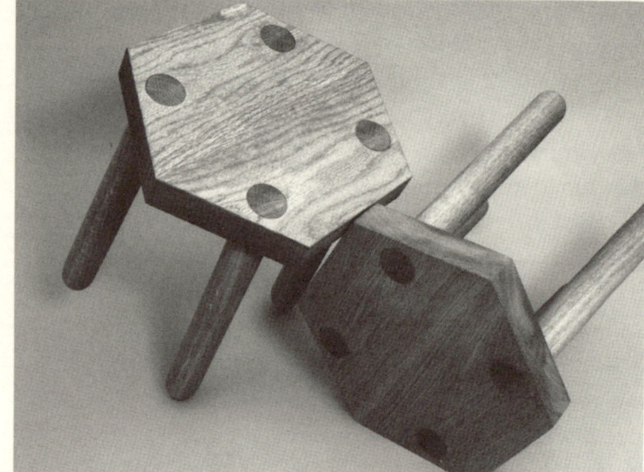

Reproduction No. 6
Ludwig Mies van
der Rohe

Average Soap Dish
Material: *Mahoga-
ny, Tung Oil*
Edition: *40*
Size: *5"x5"x1"*
Price: *Sold Out*

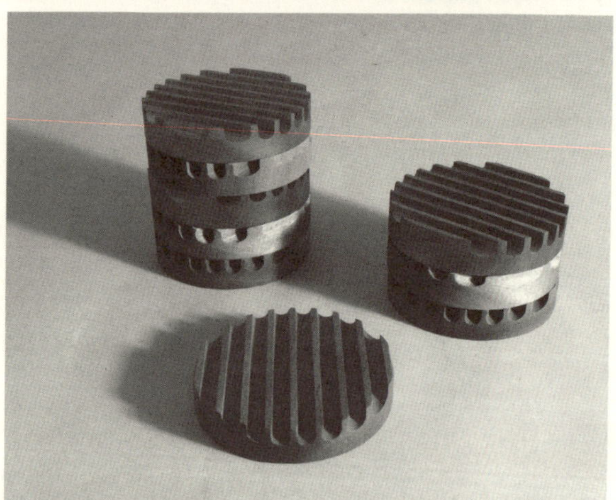

Reproduction No. 7
James Stirling

Coat-hook Thingy
Material: *Mirrored
Stainless Steel*
Edition: *50*
Size:
2.5"x2.85"x1.25"
Price: Sold Out

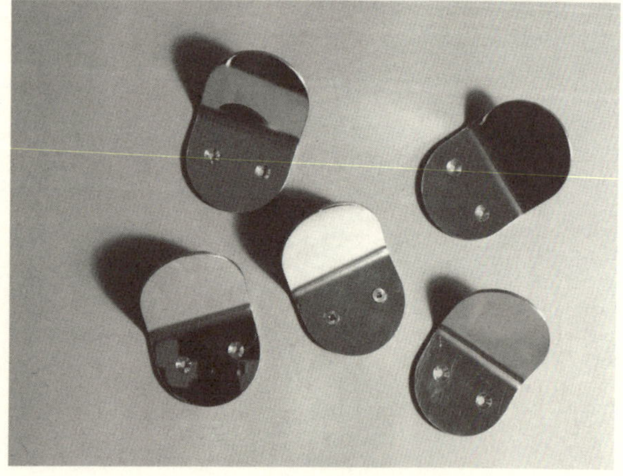

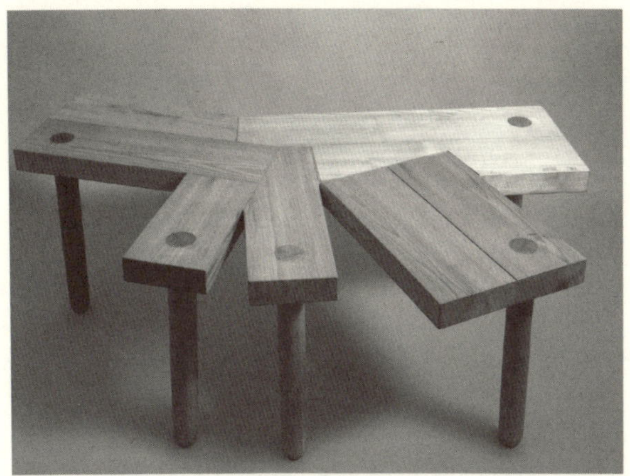

Reproduction No. 8
Gerrit Rietveld

Informal Plank
Bench
Variation No. 1
Material: *Oak, Oil*
Edition: *5*
Size:
3'10"x2'8"x1'6"
Price: *Sold Out*

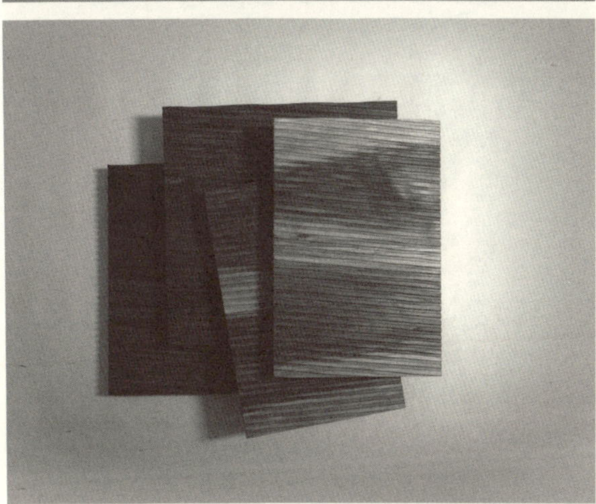

Reproduction No. 9
O. M. Ungers

Almost Positivist
Cutting Board
Material: *Ma-
hogany, Mineral
Oil, Linseed Oil*
Edition: *20*
Size: *12"x18"x1.5"*
Price: *Sold out*

Sam Jacob

A Very Small Part of Architecture resurrects Austrian Modernist architect Adolf Loos's 1921 design for a mausoleum for art historian Max Dvorák. Though never built, the image of Loos' design has haunted architectural culture ever since. Here the heavy dark and masonic form is recreated at 1:1 scale using a lightweight timber frame and scaffold net: A ghostly reenactment of an unrealised architectural idea.

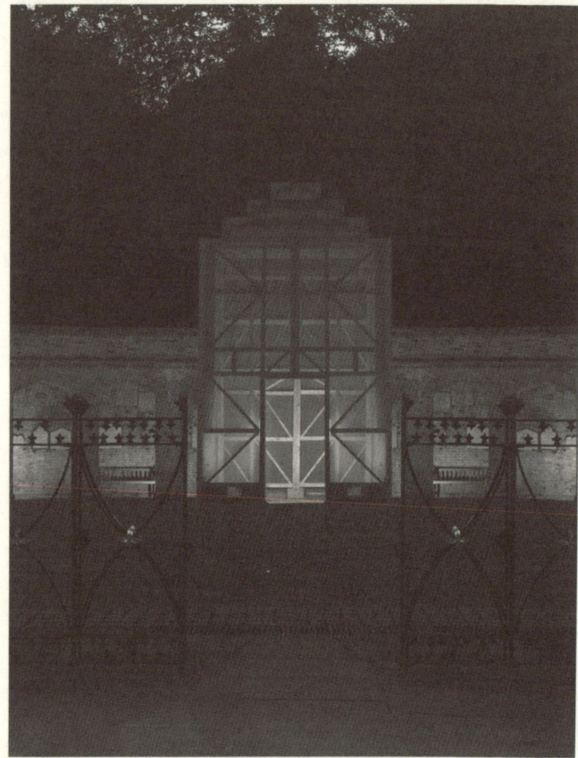

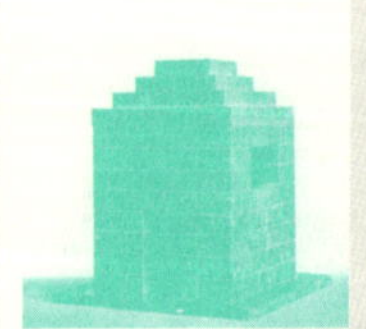

Reference:

Mausoleum for Max Dvorák, 1921, Adolf Loos

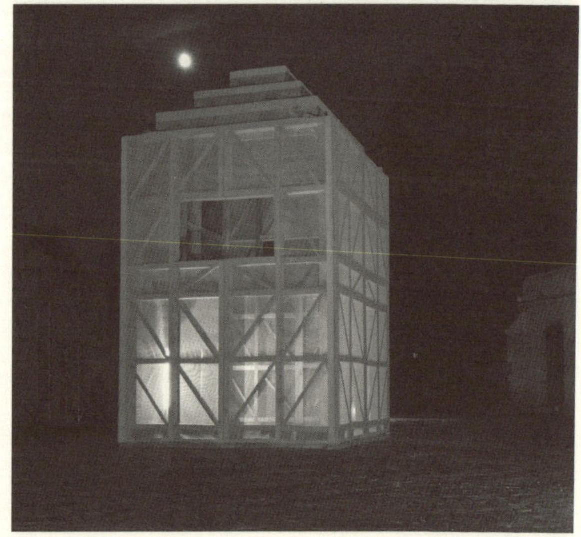

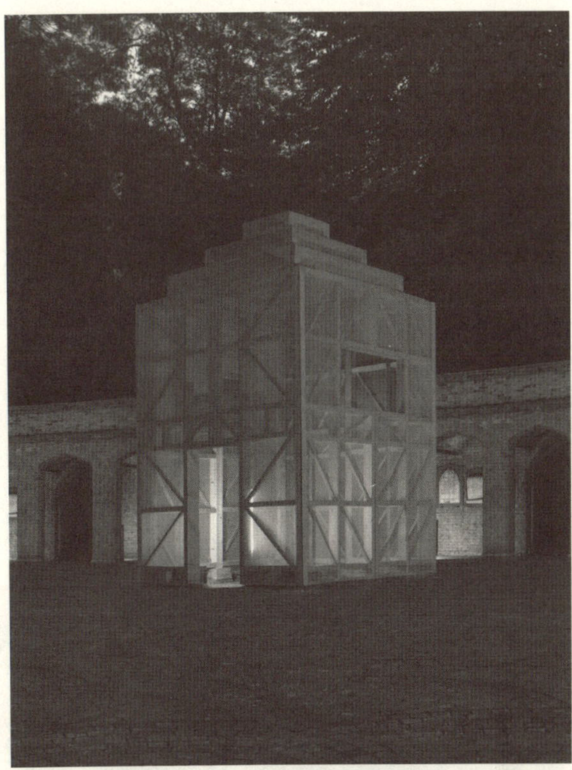

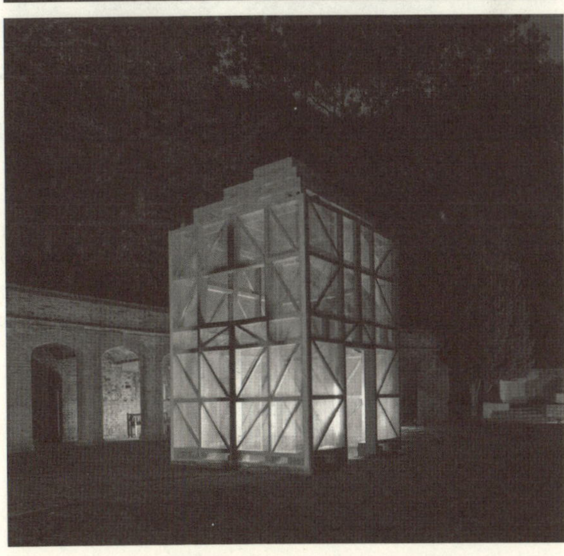

The project takes its title from Loos' essay *Architecture* (1910) in which he argues that "only a very small part of architecture belongs to the realm of art: The tomb and the monument".

Built within Highgate Cemetery, amongst the many monuments and memorials to the dead, A Very Small Part Of Architecture made a different kind of memorial. Not one dedicated to a person, an event or a moment in time, not designed to remember the past but instead to imagine other possibilities, altered presents and alternative futures.

Mariana Ibañez & Simon Kim

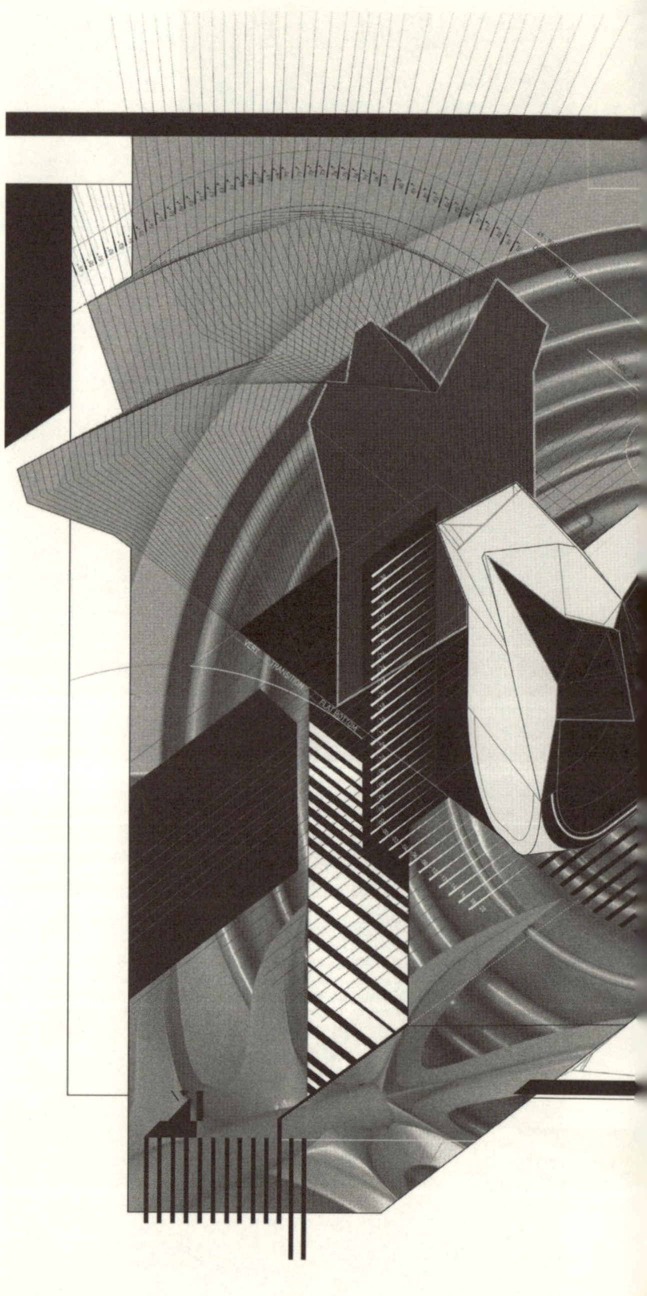

Postscripts   Mariana Ibañez & Simon Kim

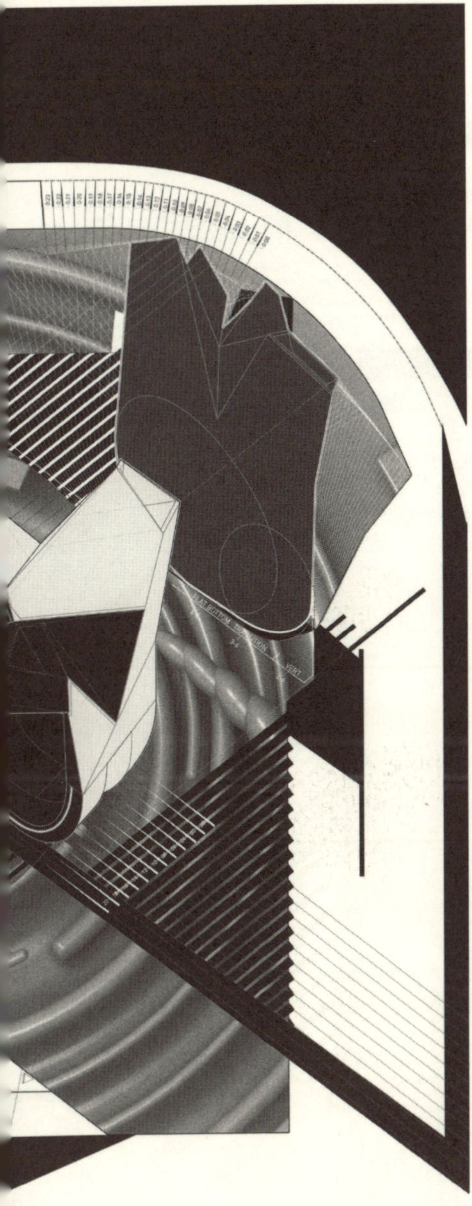

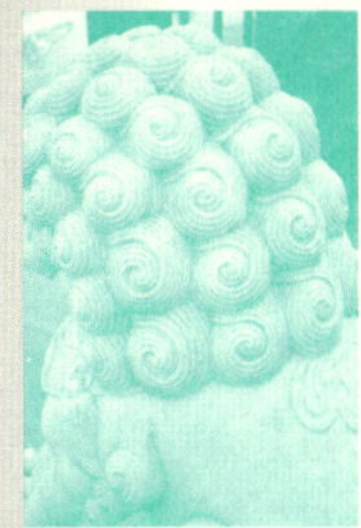

Reference:
Stone Guardian
detail

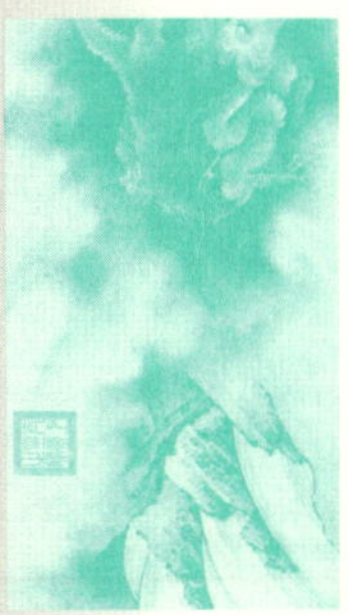

Reference:
Nine Dragons,
1244, Chen Rong

Urtzi Grau & Cristina Goberna

Subject: Image of "Fake Industries Architectural Agonism" for ▮▮▮▮▮▮▮▮▮▮▮
From: ▮▮▮▮▮▮▮▮▮▮▮▮▮▮▮▮▮▮▮▮▮▮▮▮▮▮▮▮▮▮▮▮▮▮
Date: 4/07/2017 12:36 AM
To: info@fakeindustries.org
CC: ▮▮▮▮▮▮▮▮▮▮▮▮▮▮▮▮▮▮▮▮▮▮▮▮

Dear Office "Fake Industries Architectural Agonism"

My name ist ▮▮▮▮▮▮▮ - architect and artist, Switzerland - and author of the ▮▮▮ Serie.
This morning I got several emails from colleagues - showing me your image for ▮▮▮▮▮▮ -
see below. I think I do not have to mention that your image is a "copy a paste" of:

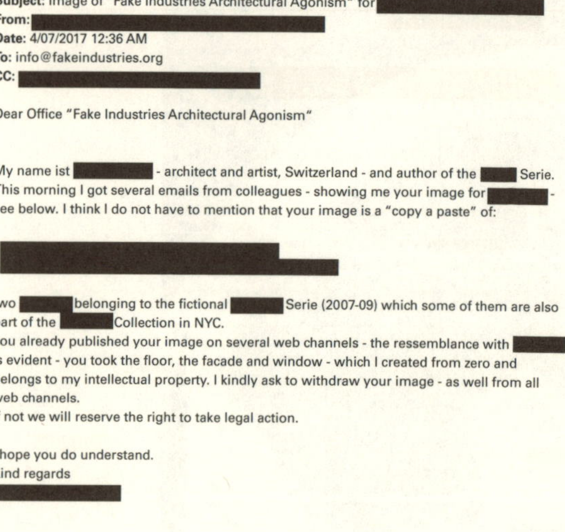

-
-

two ▮▮▮▮ belonging to the fictional ▮▮▮▮ Serie (2007-09) which some of them are also
part of the ▮▮▮▮ Collection in NYC.
you already published your image on several web channels - the ressemblance with ▮▮▮▮
is evident - you took the floor, the facade and window - which I created from zero and
belongs to my intellectual property. I kindly ask to withdraw your image - as well from all
web channels.
If not we will reserve the right to take legal action.

I hope you do understand.
Kind regards
▮▮▮▮▮▮▮▮▮▮

Dear Urtzi,

We have considered your response. Whether or not the image os legally 'fair use', the way that the setting is presented implies authorship by you. There is no explanation for the Jury: You could, for instance, have added a note that this was a borrowed setting to illustrate the type of exhibition the space would accommodate. You say that it was not your intention to replicate ▮▮▮▮▮▮▮▮'s museography, yet this is how it is interpreted by xxxxxxxxxx themselves.

We went to great trouble to highlight the importance that all competitors should respect any existing copyright for images used.

We will remove the image on the web site, obscure the image on the board and provide an explanatory note for the Jury.

Kind regards,

▮▮▮▮▮   ▮▮▮▮▮▮

Eric Höweler & Meejin Yoon

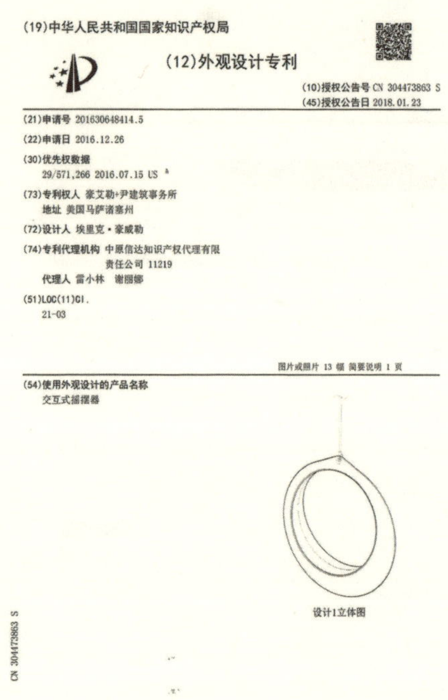

SwingTime produced a demand for the installation as a product. Inundated with inquiries as to whether the swings could be purchased, we began a two-year patent process for registrations in the US, China, and Europe to acquire some protection during the industrial design and product development phases.

While we waited for patent approval, reproductions of the installation were advertised both nationally and internationally. A quick search revealed vendors from both the US and China selling swings similar to our original design on Alibaba, and even using our own copyrighted images of our swings on Lawn on D to advertise their replicas. Widely known for fake goods, Alibaba has taken efforts to help curb false and faux listings. Just last year Alibaba upgraded its Intellectual Property Platform (IPP), a portal for uploading IP proof to address myriad infringement complaints, in an attempt to moderate their reputation for recurring IP violations.

Once official US and Mainland China patents arrived, we uploaded the proof of certificates to Alibaba's IPP. The

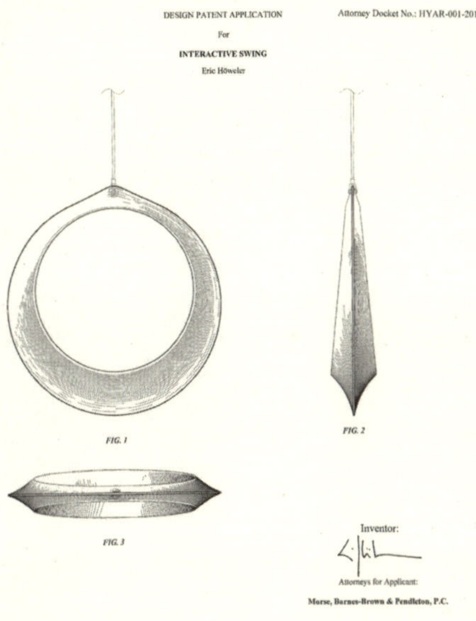

US patent was approved, and vendors were removed
from Alibaba. However the Mainland China patent was
rejected, requiring an additional Evaluation Report on the
Design Patent. For the images with registered copyright
on Alibaba, we provided a copyright certificate – and for
unregistered copyrights we uploaded copyright claim
statements with the corresponding photographs. These
actions removed most of the copyrighted images from the
platform, but not all. And vendors continued to replicate
the swings and sell them on Alibaba. So sophisticated is
the retail technology company's ability to track each computer, that our searches through the Alibaba website for
swings do not yield hits from the computer that registered
the initial complaint, however if searched from another
computer, many different companies are featured that
sell replicas of our swings, and some still using our own
images to sell them.

Introduction
Ana Miljački

UNDER THE INFLUENCE: INTRODUCTION[1]

"Does our appetite for creative vitality require the violence and exasperation of another avant-garde, with its wearisome killing-the-father imperatives, or might we be better off ratifying the ecstasy of influence—and deepening our willingness to understand the commonality and timelessness of the methods and motives available to artists?"

> — Jonathan Lethem, "The Ecstasy of Influence; A Plagiarism," *Harper's Magazine* (2007).

Influence is not easily quantified. It is elusive, even when we casually admit to it as we ogle images on the internet, or feel ourselves softening our resolve on an important issue in light of a beautifully crafted piece of rhetoric; or as the mass-media drone imperceptibly rewires some of our most fundamental desires.

The colloquial version of 'influence' that the title of this book is meant to conjure up in part should invoke the possibility of being high on hypars, having a bad trip on voronoi, or hallucinating in Hejduk's pastels. Or, if one is differently inclined, hypars can be switched with Blondel's remarks on History, voronoi with Tafuri's brand of Marxism, and Hejduk's pastels with kaleidoscopic diagrams of Ove Arup's simulations for the iconic building X. In all these cases, influence involves a kind of intoxication: both a matter of personal interests, obsessions and predilections on one end, *and* the surrounding disciplinary and cultural contexts on the other end. Getting influenced, then, is like getting the flu (influenza being indeed the etymological root of the term influence), which depends upon a circumstantial mixture of one's bodily predispositions and and the virus to which that same body has been exposed.

Though imagining discourse literally infiltrating our bodies as if we were imbibing a stimulating pharmacon while drawing or writing is fascinating for me personally, the aim of the symposium and the book is to expand our disciplinary language for dealing with appropriation beyond sensations of 'anxiety' or 'ecstasy' that it might indeed induce.[2] Techniques of appropriation and issues of

1. I want to thank: two Heads of the MIT Architecture Department, Nader Tehrani and Meejin Yoon for supporting Under the Influence symposium and books into existence and Michael Kubo and Amanda Reeser Lawrence for accepting and performing beautifully the task of moderating the discussions on February 23, 2013. I want to thank the participants for accepting the opportunity to contribute to the symposium and now the book. The Appropriation Research Workshop at MIT and my co-conspirator in that class, Sarah Hirschman, all did amazing work on the *Fair Use* exhibit, which opened on February 23, 2013 and lasted for three weeks. Kyle Barker held together the symposium organization and its graphic identity, and finally, Irene Hwang helped us package it all into the book you are holding in your hands.

2. See Harold Bloom, *Anxiety of Influence, A Theory of Poetry* (New York, NY: Oxford University Press, 1973), and Harold

Bloom, *Map of Misreading* (New York, NY: Oxford University Press, 1975), and also see Jonathan Lethem, "The Ecstasy of Influence. A plagiarism," Harper's Magazine, February 2007, accessed February 24, 2014, http://harpers.org/archive/2007/02/the-ecstasy-of-influence/.

3. Bloom's famous mid-20th century writings on originality in poetry marked a historical moment when the author as a type of subjectivity was becoming undone. Bloom came out in favor of a relatively strong version of that subject, in opposition to theorists like Michel Foucault and Roland Barthes . Lethem's characterization of the contemporary version of the same subject—the author of aesthetic products that range in media from text, through music to movies— relies on a self-consciously more fluid, multiple, and even distributed self. Voraciously appropriating pre-existing material, the contemporary poet creates by channeling and curating. The ecstasy of relational

individual and collective authorship, precedent, and originality are at the core of our discussions. This is precisely so not to accept influence as a mythologizing explanation of the movement of discursive and creative energies, but in order to engage the challenges posed to authorship both by Harold Bloom's work on the anxiety of influence and by Jonathan Lethem's perceptive and clever contemporary piece on the ecstasy of it.[3]

Until very recently the idea of architectural appropriation was so deeply intertwined with reductive definitions of postmodernism that it had become nearly impossible to theorize its disciplinary discursive function without conjuring up images of pastiche, both well and poorly executed. And yet, if we look beyond this recent chapter, an engagement with the past has long been understood as a legitimate and indeed requisite, aspect of the creative act in architecture. Appropriation is as much part of the architectural unconscious as the expectation of novelty. Narratives of appropriation allow us to understand the contemporary through its various historical lineages, both as specific lines of disciplinary inquiry (the content of appropriation) and understanding of the techniques of appropriation, their theorization, and the particular network of agents and circumstances they connect and traverse.

It is important to examine architectural appropriation now in part because our most recent reactions to postmodernism have made the pendulum swing away from any type of critical dialogue about it. Furthermore, while the field has been busy resisting discussing any type of referencing, many other cultural, technological, and legislative factors have in fact intensified issues of appropriation in contemporary aesthetic production across the disciplines and across the globe.

I want to highlight a couple of those particularly contemporary pressures. The inertia of Postmodern reality, or the belief, at least, that there are currently no collectively accepted, dominated lenses through which to filter history's lessons, and the various technological protocols, gadgets, and behaviors that network and disseminate facts and fictions of personal and collective importance have sponsored our era of flattened archives and instant historicization.[4] These, in turn, further support the superfast recycling of easily accessible visual material and the wikipedization of our *collective* explanatory imagination.[5]

While contemporary and historical information about architecture is now unprecedentedly easy to disseminate digitally, 'like,' and 'pin,' the discourse involving appropriation has become largely litigious. Simultaneously sensational and mysterious stories about architectural doppelgängers in China travel the web circles from Architizer to *The Guardian*. The same axis of popular architectural news is replete with the more sinister stories of the "you can advance my idea, but don't steal it or I will sue" variety. SHoP to Zaha, Zaha to "the pirates of Chongqing," first world architects to third world and sometimes back again.[6] However scandalized or amused the readers of these global disputes over intellectual property in architecture might be, far more curious than the relevant author's need to assert creative ownership is the way in which the copyright law, at least in the US, has rewritten the priorities of the discipline.

Although legal means for dealing with the ownership of ideas have existed for centuries, in today's globalized market, the rise of copyright mechanisms in various spheres of aesthetic and intellectual production scripts its own types of historical and political narratives. Installed in some form of practice only after the US accepted the Berne Convention for the Protection of Literary and Artistic Works in 1989, the Architectural Works Copyright Protection Act passed a year later comes with a specific (and for architectural instructors, possibly scandalous) definition of "Architectural Work." Under the Architectural Works Copyright Act, "originally designed" elements are protected, but functionally required ones are not.[7] Trying to illuminate the boundaries of legal protection for architectural works, the US Congress invited Michael Graves to testify as an expert witness. Graves differentiated between 'internal' and 'poetic' languages in architecture, with the former being "intrinsic to building in its most basic form—determined by pragmatic, construction, and technical requirements" and the latter being the poetic (which must be conceptually separable from the internal), was described by Graves as "responsive to issues external to the building" and incorporating "three-dimensional expressions of the myths and rituals of society."[8] If the internal and poetic languages are fused, the work

originality, or of belonging to a cultural continuum replaces the Modernist thrill of non-referential novelty.

4. Just as *Sixty Minutes* produces a history of the Cairo protests within two months of the uprisings, the collection of architectural blogs across the internet continually records for posterity a vast array of ideas without discriminating about their importance or quality too much.

5. Which is why we now need to protect and sponsor deep archival digging and cultivate rich explanatory historical writing more than ever before.

6. Comments on Zaha Hadid's design for Galaxy Soho and a possible lawsuit involved have appeared on a number of important architectural blog sites. See for example Oliver Wainwright's entry on his architecture blog for *The Guardian*, "Seeing double: what China's copycat culture means for architecture," accessed January 7,

2013, http://www.
guardian.co.uk/.
artanddesign/
architecture-
design-blog/2013/
jan/07/china-copy-
cat-architecture-
seeing-double,
or Guy Horton,
"The Indicator:
Architecture and
Crime," ArchDaily,
accessed January
25, 2013, http://
www.archdaily.
com/323161.

7. The language
here comes
from the AWCPA
directly. The actual
text of the legisla-
tion and commen-
tary are available
through the
library of congress
website, accessed
January 22, 2012,
http://thomas.loc.
gov/cgi-bin/query/
z?c101:H.R.3990.

8. Quoted in Daniel
Su, "Substantial
Similarity And Ar-
chitectural Works:
Filtering Out 'Total
Concept And Feel'",
*Northeastern Law
Review*, vol. 101, n.
10 (2007): 1865.

of architecture is not copyrightable. Even though this might seem unfair, it is meant to safeguard the space of "competitive invention" that copyright laws were initially designed to protect.

The key aim of the Under the Influence symposium was to migrate important topics from the sensationalist corners of the blogosphere onto a disciplinary center-stage. Particularly urgent among these are the definition of architecture thrown up by copyright laws, including its alarming distinction between signature (copyright-able) and utility (uncopyrightable), and the idea that in a discipline whose essence is defined chiefly in terms of historical lineages of ideas and techniques, one can now claim monopoly of use over any of them.

In the pages that follow, each of the participants of the symposium illuminate a single term—a disciplinary synonym for appropriation—and through that term, the specific strategies, historical, and disciplinary circumstances in which it is enmeshed. Following the organization of the event it indexes, the *Under the Influence* book takes on: Affinity, Allusion, Cliché, Collection, Doppelgänger, Replica, Revision, Color Sample, Side Effects, Signature, Thing Rights, and Vapor in three groupings of four, punctuated by transcripts of lively panel discussions that took place on February 23, 2013 at MIT.

               Ana Miljački

Contributor Bios

Mario Carpo is the Reyner Banham Professor of Architectural Theory and History at the Bartlett, University College London. Carpo's research and publications focus on the relationship among architectural theory, cultural history, and the history of media and information technology. His *Architecture in the Age of Printing* (The MIT Press, 2001) has been translated into several languages. His most recent books are *The Second Digital Turn: Design Beyond Intelligence* (The MIT Press, 2017), *The Alphabet and the Algorithm, A History of Digital Design Theory* (The MIT Press, 2011); and *The Digital Turn in Architecture, 1992-2012*, an AD Reader.

Alexander D' Hooghe PhD, MAUD, M.Civil Eng-Arch is a senior founding partner of the transatlantic design company ORG, and teaches architecture and urbanism at Massachusetts Institute of Technology (Cambridge, MA). He has directed the MIT Center for Advanced Urbanism, with a focus on large-scale contemporary design problems. D'Hooghe is internationally published, notably with *The Liberal Monument* (Princeton Architectural Press, 2010), and with numerous papers in journals across Germany, Israel, Spain, the Netherlands, Belgium, and the USA. With ORG, he focuses on the design and making of cities, with projects in New Jersey, New York City, Shenzhen, Bogota, Brussels, Ostend, Kinshasa, Ghana, The Hague, Reykjavik, South Korea, and Russia. Current major projects include the management and design of the conversion and capping of Antwerp's Ring zone, and the Regional Plan for the New York Metropolitan area (RPA). D'Hooghe obtained his PhD. at the Berlage Institute in 2007 with T.U. Delft, after achieving a Masters in Urban Design at the Harvard GSD in 2001, and a master in Architecture and Civil Engineering from the University of Leuven in 1996. He is a licensed architect in Belgium.

Cristina Goberna Pesudo is a practitioner architect, educator, and critic, and a founding partner of Fake Industries, Architectural Agonism (FKAA): an entity of "variable boundaries and questionable taste" that has received the AIA New York New Practices Award, and has been shortlisted for MoMA PS1, the Miami Design pavilion and the Guggenheim Helsinki Competition. Goberna completed her Bachelor Degree in Architecture at the University of Seville, Spain. As a Fulbright Scholar, she was awarded an MS in Advanced Architectural Design (AAD) and an Advanced Architectural Research Certificate (AAR) from Columbia University GSAPP. She is a PhD candidate at Escola Tècnica Superior d'Arquitectura de Barcelona (ET-SAB), and a PhD candidate in the program of Philosophy, Art and Critical Thought at the European Graduate School, Switzerland. Her writings have been published internationally, and exhibited at venues such as the Venice Bienniale, the Oslo Triennial, the Chicago Biennial, the Istanbul Biennial of Design, the MAXXI in Rome, the Guggenheim Museum, and MoMA. She has been on the jury of various competitions internationally, including Europan Norway (E13), and MoMA PS1 YAP (2018). Goberna has held the position of senior lecturer at UTS Sydney, Adjunct Assistant Professor at Columbia University GSAPP and Barnard College, and Visiting Professor at MIT. She is currently a Visiting Professor at Cooper Union School of Architecture where she coordinates the undergraduate thesis course, and a member of the New Museum Columbia GSAPP New Incubator Program in New York.

Urtzi Grau is an architect, director of the Master of Architectural Research program at the University of Technology Sydney (UTS), and a founding partner of Fake Industries Architectural Agonism (FKAA): an entity of "variable boundaries and questionable taste" that has received the AIA New York New Practices Award, and has been shortlisted for MoMA PS1, the Miami Design pavilion and the Guggenheim Helsinki Competition. Grau graduated from the School of Architecture of Barcelona in 2000, and was awarded Master in Advanced Architectural Design by Columbia University in 2004. He is currently completing his PhD at Princeton University with a focus on the 1970's urban renewal of Barcelona. Grau has previously taught at Cooper Union, Princeton University, Columbia University and Cornell University, and held the Cullinan Visiting Professor position at Rice University School of Architecture. His work and writings have been published in various international journals such as *AV, Bawelt, Domus, Kerb, Log, Plot, Praxis, Spam, Volume* and *White Zinfadel*, and

exhibited in a number of international venues, including
la Bienal de Buenos Aires, P! Gallery, RMIT Design Hub,
Shenzhen Biennale, Storefront, the Venice Biennale, and
0047.

Eric Höweler AIA, LEED AP is an architect, designer,
and educator. He is currently Associate Professor in
Architecture at the Harvard Graduate School of Design.
His design work and research explore the relationships
between architecture and building technologies with a focus on envelopes and material systems. Prior to forming
Höweler + Yoon Architecture in 2005, Höweler was a se-
nior designer at Diller Scofidio + Renfro in New York, and
an Associate Principal at Kohn Pedersen Fox Associates.
Höweler has been widely recognized for his innovative
and interdisciplinary work. He is author of *Skyscraper,
Vertical Now* (Rizzoli/Universe, 2003) and co-author of
1,001 Skyscrapers (Princeton Architectural Press, 2000).
Höweler received a Bachelor of Architecture from Cornell
University with the AIA Henry Adams Certificate in 1994, a
Master of Architecture from Cornell University in 1996.

Timothy Hyde is a historian of architecture whose
research focuses on the political dimensions of architecture from the eighteenth century to the present, with
a particular attention to relationships of architecture
and law. His most recent book *Ugliness and Judgment:
On Architecture in the Public Eye* (Princeton University
Press, 2019) explores episodes in aesthetic debates on
architecture and ugliness in Great Britain over the past
three centuries and reveals the ways in which architectural discourse participated in the legal formulations of
social techniques of the modern city. He is also the author
of *Constitutional Modernism: Architecture and Civil Society in Cuba, 1933-1959* (University of Minnesota Press,
2012) which examines the entanglements of architecture,
planning, and law in the years leading up to and following from the promulgation of a new Cuban constitution
in 1940. Hyde is a founding member of the Aggregate Architectural History Collaborative and is one of the editors
of the first Aggregate book, *Governing by Design*. Hyde's
writings have also appeared in journals such as *Log, El
Croquis, The Journal of Architecture*, the *Journal of Archi-*

tectural Education, *arq: Architecture Research Quarterly*, and *Thresholds*.

Mariana Ibañez is an Argentinian architect involved in practice, academia, and research. She is an Associate Professor of Architecture at the MIT School of Architecture and Planning and the co-founder of Ibañez Kim. Before joining the faculty at MIT, Mariana taught for eleven years at the Harvard University Graduate School of Design. She is an external examiner for the Architectural Association, and is on the awards jury of the Boston Society of Architects, the MacDowell Colony, and the Rotch foundation among others. As an academic and editor, Mariana's research focuses on the relationship between technology, culture, and the environment. Her recent publications include *Paradigms in computing*, (eVolo and ACTAR D, 2014), and *Organization or Design?* (a+t, 2016) . Mariana has a Bachelor of Architecture from the University of Buenos Aires and a Master of Architecture and Urbanism from the Architectural Association in London where she received thesis honors. After completing her graduate studies, she joined the Advanced Geometry Unit at ARUP before going to the office of Zaha Hadid, where she was the project architect for the London Olympic Aquatic Center among other projects. In 2006, Ibanez relocated to Cambridge and in 2012 co-founded Ibanez Kim with Simon Kim, a research and design practice. Her work has been exhibited at the Museum of Modern Art in New York, the MAXXI museum in Rome, and The National Art Museum in Beijing, with projects including work for the Smithsonian Museum in Washington DC, the Philadelphia Museum of Art, and the Biennale in Seoul.

Florian Idenburg is an architect and educator based in NYC. He founded the practice SO - IL with Jing Liu, and is currently a Visiting Professor in the Department of Architecture at Massachusetts Institute of Technology.

Sam Jacob is principal of Sam Jacob Studio for architecture and design whose work spans scales and disciplines from urban design through architecture, design, art, and curatorial projects. Recent projects include the V&A Gallery at Design Society, Shenzhen; *Fear and*

Love at the Design Museum; a new mixed use building in London's Hoxton; public realm design and cultural strategy for a South London market; and a landmark project for London Design Festival with Mini Living. Jacob's work has been published and exhibited internationally including at the Venice Architecture Biennale in 2016 and 2014 (where he was co-curator of the British Pavilion), *Spaces Without Drama* at the Graham Foundation (2017), Chicago, *A Very Small Part of Architecture* in Highgate Cemetery (2016), and the 2017 Chicago Biennial. Previously he was a director of FAT Architecture.

Simon Kim AIA is a registered architect in California and Massachusetts, Associate Professor at the University of Pennsylvania School of Design, and Director of the Immersive Kinematics Re-search Group. As principal of Ibañez Kim, he is interested in the augmentation of architecture and urbanism with active and emotive behaviors. As an architect and designer, Simon has been a producer and collaborator of several shows with artists, theater groups and performers such as The Dufala Brothers, Grace Kelly Jazz, Carbon Dance Theatre, and has produced and curated exhibitions at the Traction Gallery and the Slought Foundation. His work has also been exhibited at the ICA, Storefront, and MoMA. After completing the Design Research Laboratory program at the Architectural Association, Simon worked as a designer and project architect for Zaha Hadid and Frank Gehry. At MIT he worked with Bill Mitchell on modular, networked energy for buildings and landscapes, and was awarded a Master of Science. Simon has taught studios and seminars at Yale, Harvard, MIT, and the Architectural Association.

Michael Kubo is Assistant Professor of Architectural History and Theory at the Gerald D. Hines College of Architecture and Design, University of Houston. He was previously the Wyeth Fellow at the CASVA, National Gallery of Art, and Associate Curator for OfficeUS – the U.S. Pavilion at the 2014 International Architecture Biennale in Venice, Italy. Kubo holds a PhD in the history, theory, and criticism of architecture from MIT and an M.Arch from Harvard. His publications include *Imagining the Modern: Architecture and Urbanism in the Pittsburgh*

Renaissance (The Monacelli Press, 2019), *Heroic: Concrete Architecture and the New Boston* (The Monacelli Press, 2015), and *OfficeUS Atlas* (Lars Mueller, 2015). He is currently preparing a book on The Architects Collaborative (TAC) and the authorship of the architectural corporation after 1945.

John McMorrough is an architect and theorist. He studied architecture at the University of Kansas, where he received a Bachelor of Architecture, and at the Harvard University Graduate School of Design where he received both a Master of Architecture (with Distinction) and a PhD in Architecture. He has taught design and theory at Yale School of Architecture, Ohio State University, and the University of Applied Arts Vienna, among other institutions, and is currently an Associate Professor at the Taubman College of Architecture and Urban Planning, University of Michigan. His writing addresses the relationship between contemporary culture and design methodology, with treatments on architects' extended practices (in the form of buildings, but also in complementary media such as installations, films and other structured narratives). As a partner of studioAPT (Architecture Project Theory) he has worked on a range of projects at the scale of building (sets), situation (comedies), and the graphic (interiors). His theoretical writing and design work has appeared in numerous books and publications, such as *Perspecta*, *Thresholds*, *Log*, *Volume*, *Praxis*, *MAS Context*, and *Flat Out*.

Michael Meredith + Hilary Sample are the founding principals of the New York-based architecture studio MOS. An internationally recognized architecture practice, MOS was the recipient of the 2015 Cooper Hewitt, Smithsonian Design Museum National Design Award in Architecture, the 2010 American Academy of Arts and Letters Architecture Award, and the 2008 Architectural League of New York Emerging Voices Award. Individual works have similarly received numerous awards and distinctions, most notably: the 2015 Global Holcim Award for sustainable construction (Asia-Pacific Region), for Community Center No. 3 (Lali Gurans Orphanage); the cover of *Abitare* and an AIA NY State Award of Excel-

lence, for School No. 1 (Krabbesholm Højskole); the 2014
accession of both the firm's modular, off-grid House No.
5 (Museum of Outdoor Arts Element House) into The
Museum of Modern Art, Architecture and Design Collection; the acquisition of House No. 3 (Lot No. 6/Ordos) into
the permanent collection of The Art Institute of Chicago;
and the selection of Pavilion No. 4 (Afterparty) for the
2009 MoMA PS1 Young Architects Program. Recent
work includes: Store No. 2 (Chamber) in Chelsea, NYC;
House No. 10, currently under-construction; School No.
2, a competition proposal for the Institute for Advanced
Study Commons Building; and Housing No. 4 (Dequindre
Cut, Detroit). Recent and forthcoming publications, both
products of and surveys on MOS's work, include *Everything All at Once: The Software, Film, and Architecture of
MOS* (Princeton Architectural Press, 2013); *MOS: Selected
Works* (Princeton Architectural Press, 2016); *El Croquis
No. 184* (2016); *A Situation Constructed From Loose and
Overlapping Social and Architectural Aggregates* (AADR,
2016); and *An Unfinished Encyclopedia of Scale Figures
Without Architecture* (MIT Press, forthcoming).

Ana Miljački is a critic, curator and Associate
Professor of Architecture at MIT, where she teaches history, theory and design and directs the MArch Program.
Miljački was part of the three-member curatorial team,
with Eva Franch i Gilabert and Ashley Schafer, of the US
Pavilion at the 2014 Venice Architecture Biennale, where
their Biennale project, titled OfficeUS, critically examined
the last century of US architectural offices; their profes-
sionalization and their concomitant global contribution.
As part of that project she co-edited *OfficeUS Agenda*
(Lars Muller, 2014) *OfficeUS Atlas* (Lars Muller, 2015) *OfficeUS Manual* (Lars Muller, 2017). Miljački recently guest
edited *Praxis 14: True Stories*, and curated and produced
an exhibition on the role of copying and originality in
architecture, Fair Use with her students at MIT. Its latest instantiation, Un/Fair Use, co-curated with Sarah
Hirschman was presented at the Center for Architecture in
New York in 2015 and at UC Berkeley's Wurster Gallery in
2016. In 2018 she launched the Critical Broadcasting Lab
at MIT. Miljački is the author of *The Optimum Imperative:
Czech Architecture for the Socialist Lifestyle 1938-1968*

(Routledge, 2017), and the editor of *Terms of Appropriation: Modern and Architecture and Global Exchange* with Amanda Reeser Lawrence (Routledge, 2018). Miljački's writings have also appeared in journals such as *Log, Perspecta, Praxis, Thresholds, ARQ, MAS context.*

Amanda Reeser Lawrence is a tenured Associate Professor in the School of Architecture at Northeastern University. She received her PhD in architectural history and theory from Harvard University, her Master of Architecture from Columbia University and her BA (summa cum laude) from Princeton University, with a major in architectural history. Lawrence is founding coeditor of the architectural journal *Praxis: A Journal of Writing + Building*, an award-winning journal of contemporary architecture of the Americas. Her published books include *James Stirling: Revisionary Modernist* (Yale University Press, 2013), and *Terms of Appropriation* (Routledge, 2017), co-edited with Ana Miljački. Her work has been supported by the National Endowment for the Arts, the National Endowment for the Humanities, the Graham Foundation for Advanced Studies in the Fine Arts, the Paul Mellon Centre for Studies in British Art, the Graduate Society at Harvard University, and the New York State Council on the Arts.

Nader Tehrani is the Dean of the Irwin S. Chanin School of Architecture at the Cooper Union in New York. Nader Tehrani is also Principal of NADAAA, a practice dedicated to the advancement of design innovation, interdisciplinary collaboration, and an intensive dialogue with the construction industry. He was previously a Professor of Architecture at MIT, where he served as the Head of the Department from 2010-2014. As the principal and founder of Office dA, Tehrani's work has been recognized with notable awards, including the Cooper Hewitt National Design Award in Architecture (2007), the United States Artists Fellowship in Architecture and Design (2007), and the American Academy of Arts and Letters Award in Architecture (2002). He has also received the Harleston Parker Award for the Northeastern University Multi-Faith Spiritual Center (2002) and the Hobson Award for the Georgia Institute of Technology Hinman Research Building (2012). He was the William A. Bernoudy Architect in Residence at the American Academy in Rome in 2017/2018. Throughout his career, Tehrani has received eighteen Progressive Architecture Awards as well as numerous AIA, Boston Society of Architects and ID awards. For the past five years in a row NADAAA has placed in the top three design firms in the U.S. in Architect Magazine's Top 50 Design ranking.

Enrique Walker is an architect, and a Lecturer in Architecture at Columbia GSAPP where he also directed the Master of Science program in Advanced Architectural Design from 2008 to 2018. He has taught the decade-long series of studios and seminars *The Dictionary of Received Ideas*, the studio series *Under Constraint*, and the seminar series *The Ordinary*. As AAD program director, he also taught the lecture course, *Metropolis*, and launched the *Arguments* seminar and lecture series. In addition to GSAPP, he has taught at Princeton University, Cornell University, Barcelona Institute of Architecture, Tokyo Institute of Technology, Pratt Institute, and Universidad de Chile. His publications include the books, *The Ordinary: Recordings* (Columbia Books on Architecture and the City, 2018), *The Dictionary of Received Ideas / Under Constraint* (ARQ, 2017), *Lo Ordinario* (Gustavo Gili, 2010), and *Tschumi on Architecture: Conversations with Enrique Walker* (Monacelli, 2006). He has also published articles and interviews in *AA Files*, *Log*, *El Croquis*, *2G*, *Grey Room*, *Volume*, *Hunch*, and *Circo*, as well as in *The Building* (Lars Müller, 2016), *Conversaciones con Enric Miralles* (Gustavo Gili, 2016), *Bernard Tschumi — Architecture: Concept and Notation* (Power Station of Art, 2016), *After the Manifesto: Writing, Architecture and Media in a New Century* (GSAPP, 2014), *Luis M. Mansilla and Emilio Tuñón: From Rules to Constraints* (Lars Müller, 2012), *The Architectures of Atelier Bow-Wow: Behaviorology* (Rizzoli, 2010), *Office Kersten Geers David Van Severen: Seven Rooms* (Hatje Cantz, 2009), and *First Works: Emerging Architectural Experimentation of the 1960s and 1970s* (Architectural Association, 2009).

Ines Weizman is a Professor of Architectural Theory and Director of the Bauhaus-Institute for History and Theory of Architecture and Planning at the Bauhaus-

Universität Weimar. In 2015 she founded the Centre for
Documentary Architecture (CDA). Among her numerous
publications and exhibitions are the installation *Repeat
Yourself: Loos, Law and the Culture of the Copy* that was
presented at the Venice Architecture Biennale in 2012. In
2019 she will publish the edited book *Dust & Data: Traces
of the Bauhaus across 100 Years* with Spector Books.
Currently she is working on the exhibition of the CDA,
*The Matter of Data: Tracing the Materiality of "Bauhaus
Modernism"* which will be shown in 2019 at the Bauhaus
Museum Weimar, and in Tel Aviv at the White City Bau-
haus Center.

J. Meejin Yoon is an architect, designer, and
educator. She is currently the Gale and Ira Drukier Dean
of Cornell University's College of Architecture, Art, and
Planning. Previously, she was Professor and Head of the
Department of Architecture at Massachusetts Institute of
Technology where she began teaching in 2001. Yoon is
the co-founding principal of Höweler + Yoon Architecture,
a multidisciplinary architecture and design studio that
has garnered international recognition for a wide range
of built work. Her design work and research investigate
the intersections between architecture, technology, and
public space. Yoon received the New Generation Design
Leadership Award by Architectural Record (2015), the
US Artist Award in Architecture and Design (2008), and
the Rome Prize in Design (2005). She is the co-author
of *Public Works: Unsolicited Small Projects for the Big
Dig and Absence.* Yoon received a Bachelor of Architecture from Cornell University with the AIA Henry Adams
Medal in 1995, a Master of Architecture in Urban Design
with Distinction from Harvard University in 1997, and a
Fulbright Fellowship to Korea in 1998.

The Icon and Its Shortcomings:
In Defense of Discourse
(A Rose by Any Other Name…)
Nader Tehrani

In reading Mr. Jalil Takbiri's critical letter regarding the architectural work of Arsh, I was struck by a range of issues that I believe merit discussion—both in terms of current discourse, but also in particular to the Iranian architectural scene. As an extension of this critique, one should at once laud and challenge *Memar* for the publication of Takbiri's letter. Let us celebrate their role for creating this debate, but let's also not be innocent of their incendiary role. Are we to assume that they are acting in neutrality in the fueling of this critique? Does *Memar* not implicitly—if not explicitly—cast a shadow of morality over Arsh—maybe so much so that any response from Arsh would end up being read as defensive? For this reason, only a third voice can come to elaborate the intricacies of this debate—not in defense of Arsh, but in defense of architectural discourse itself.

In his letter, Mr. Takbiri makes significant charges, asking the authors of Arsh architects to acknowledge an alleged debt of authorship to the Kripalu Housing Project, authored by Peter Rose + Partners. There are a variety of reasons why this request is questionable, flawed in conception and ultimately completely at odds with the discursive nature from which architecture emerges. However, given the flagrant allegation, it merits discussion and elaboration, with details to accompany.

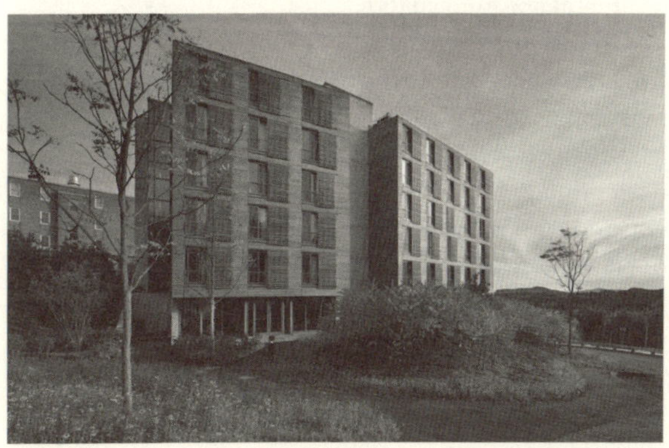

First, since both projects—by Peter Rose and by Arsh—were built in 2009, it would be unfair to assume that one of the two projects should, in some way, be in a secondary position to the other, or that one is somehow subservient in idea, concept and execution to the other.

Furthermore, it is not a huge leap to think that both are a manifestation of a zeitgeist—a spirit of explorations that, in fact, can be traced through a complex genealogy of projects over the past 20 years—from Switzerland, to the USA, and beyond. However, if one is so bold as to make such allegations, then why should we not assume that the project by Arsh preceded that of Rose?

Of course, to deny the similarities between the two projects would be to miss the 'potential' intellectual and critical alliances at work between the two architectures. It would also miss the notion that architecture emerges from a discourse that builds on itself, its techniques and debates as a stepping stone to its transformation. Do we not readily acknowledge that Oscar Neimeyer's Copan Building, Peter Zumthor's Archeological Shelters, and Herzog & de Meuron's Signal Box all share a common investment in the louver as the basis for shading, shelter, and architectural expression, while being significantly different in interpretation? Within this context, two historical debates loom large. The first debate is built on a myth of originality and the notion that there is a genius behind the work of art—free from cultural convention, from historical precedence, from public discourse or a social contract. This myth builds on the idea of originality and its links to authorship—an authority given to certain works of art, precisely to erase the very traces of its emergence from culture.

The second debate, by extension, is rooted in a productive article penned by Jorge Silvetti,[1] "The Beauty of Shadows"—the idea that architecture is a language built up on itself, with the ability to comment, critique and transform itself through form, through its materials and organization, what he termed 'criticism from within'. As an illustration of his argument, Silvetti cites the work of Giulio Romano's Palazzo del Te, describing its systemic alteration of the classical elements as a fundamental and critical challenge to a dominant system of representation—which by association is a challenge of the very social contract on which architecture rests.

Much of the critical work of post-modernity, which is lost in the amnesia of current discourse, has already trod this water with depth. Arguably, in post-modernism the re-appraisal of 'history' did not serve to give authority to the work of art, per se, but rather to incite a textual and

1. Jorge Silvetti, "The Beauty of Shadows," in *Architecture Theory Since 1968*, ed. K. Michael Hays, (Cambridge, MA: MIT Press, 2000) 266-282.

The Icon and Its Shortcomings: Nader Tehrani

intellectual conversation between works. In turn, this articulated the differences between classical scholarship on the one hand, and artistic or cultural production on the other: for scholarship, we still expect footnotes and acknowledgement today but we do not expect Umberto Eco's *The Name of the Rose* or Quentin Tarantino's *Pulp Fiction* to cite references at every turn, even though their inter-textuality is a central part of their intellectual project. In architecture, the work of Jože Plečnik, Robert Venturi, and Rem Koolhaas is built up on a self-conscious elaboration of the tenets of classicism, eclecticism, and the work of Le Corbusier, to name just three categories (I will leave it to the readers to align each architect with their realm of references), but we do not expect any of them to specifically footnote their sources; instead, we read into them, interpret them, and advance our own narratives, some of which even exceed the intentions of each author.

By reference to these debates, it would be necessary to do a closer reading of these two works, extracting from their details signs of commentary that display the kind of self-consciousness that differentiates architecture from 'building as usual'. There is little doubt that both works—by Rose and by Arsh—are exemplary. But the question is in what way? What questions do each pose? In what way does each project define the 'medium' and develop an architectural argument through its very material and detail systems as a vehicle? And do they belong to the same debate, or is there a possibility that despite their iconic similarity, that they may be part of varied species of arguments, as I will try to prove.

Peter Rose's building is built on an argument about the development of a screen that is at once respondent to environmental performance, but also an elaboration of a façade system that sets up a correspondent dialogue between the window and wall system both composed of a horizontal slat system. The sliding scrims on this façade set up a semantic equation between wall and window while sustaining the clarity of figure and ground, the 'difference' between foreground and background, load bearing wall and fenestration, transparency and opacity. To support this representation, the sliding scrims are disassociated with the plane of the façade, standing proud of it, as if to underline the artifice of the elevation.

The metal tracks supporting the scrim even protrude out, as if thin eyebrows over the windows. The wall remains solid, even if horizontally striated—a rhetorical flourish—while the window scrims are developed as a classic *brise-soleil*. The wood façade also responds to the bucolic nature of the site, attempting to 'soften' its presence in the New England landscape, as the author argues.

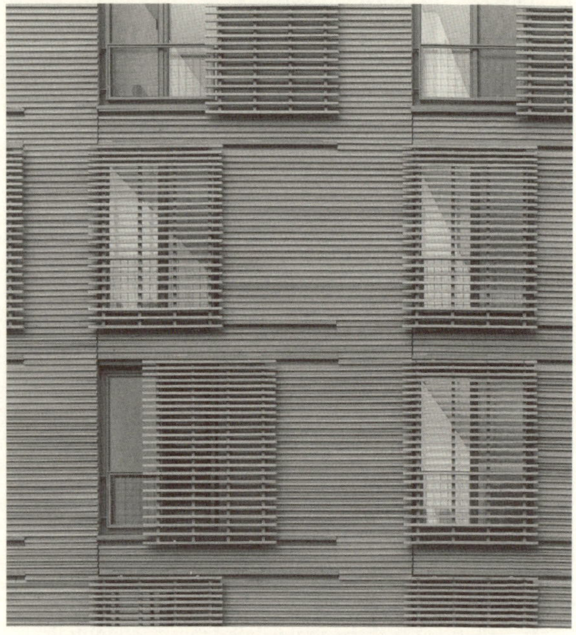

The Arsh building is similar to the Rose building in that it is built up of horizontal striations. This is, however, where the similarities end. If the Rose building maintains the stability of the figure-ground relationship, the Arsh building sets as its main agenda the very destruction of the relation-ship between figure and ground, opting for a de-stabilized field condition that simultaneously upholds multiple contradictory narratives in three dominant readings: the first a classical wall and window checkerboard pattern that challenges the very stability of structural trabeation, the second a solid scrim that supports the classical Modern interpretation of a *brise-soleil*, and thirdly, maybe the most scandalous of readings, a fluid, kinetic and shifting façade that blurs the relationship between figure and ground, foreground and background, structure and scrim, opacity and transparency. As the panels move over the façade, it produces a range of readings, from figure-ground, to figure-figure and ground-ground depending on the circumstance. Playing on the same kind of ambiguities of Alejandro de la Sota's Town Hall, the tension between solids and voids produces a depth of ambiguity that defies the singularity of reading of its classical antecedents. To complete this tension, Arsh develops a detail so deft, that it conceals the very technical mechanism that makes this all possible: the metal tracks are all suppressed behind the scrim, making the sliding screens flush with the fixed ones, opposing the two types of panels in absolute conceptual parity. Here, co-planarity is not to be misconstrued as a facile entitlement; to the contrary, it is both a technical and conceptual feat that defies the conventional aggregation of tectonic parts, and its rewards must be merited. In an environment where the technical elaboration of this facade is so critical, this comes as a radical inversion, an *a*-tectonic ruse that undermines every assumption we have come to expect of the idea of 'façade.'

If this were not enough, the setting of this project offers other readings that further enrich its design decisions. First, the horizontal striations are built up of a Kashan Travertine, a unique stone used in Iran in many venues, and thus already culturally encoded with a steeped sense of history, locality and association. The de-familiarization of this masonry unit through its de-materialization is central to the architectural argument, especially since the striations involve the provocation of a level of transparency in a culture where opacity, privacy, and a defensive posture have historically been essential to its architecture—a concept coined as *harim*. More recently in the past three decades, the social transformations unleashed by religious and moral codes have further underscored the fragility of the private realm—often now adopted as a refuge from the public realm, where the restrictions and the definition of individual rights are at odds with practices within private quarters. The rendering transparent of the private, thus, in this context takes on a more charged and critical overture, akin to the role of Islamic *Mashrabiya*, here not only serving as a veil of what happens within, but also a picture plane that reveals it.

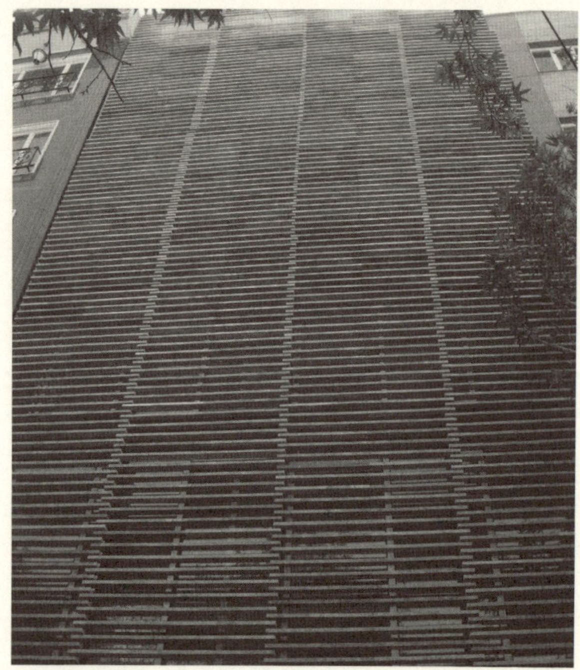

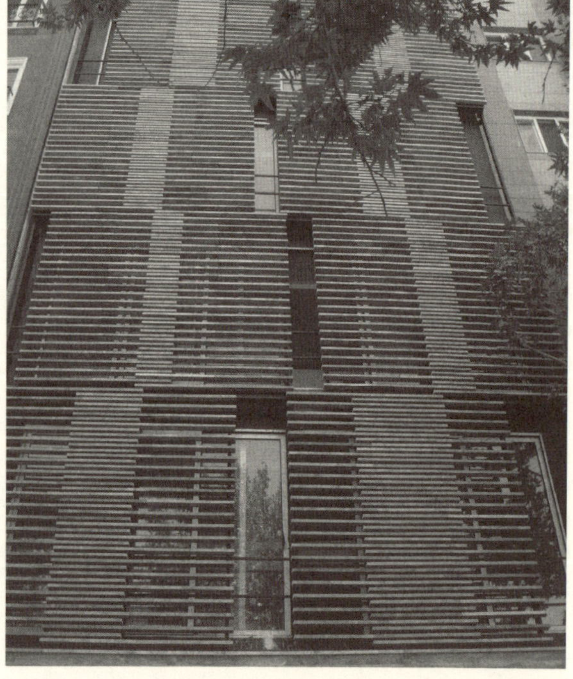

The Icon and Its Shortcomings: Nader Tehrani

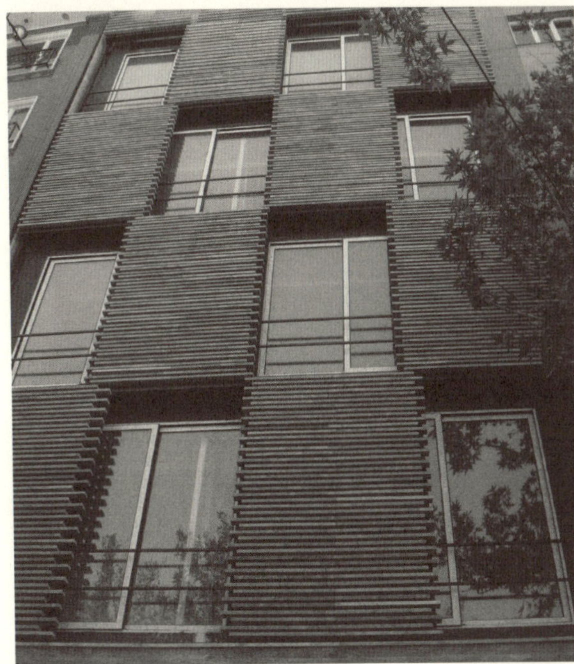

For these reasons, the works of Arsh and Rose, despite their iconic similarity, cannot be more different at a conceptual level—and this maybe points to another cultural predicament in which we find ourselves in this day and age. In a globalized world where communication, branding, techniques of Photoshop, and the commodification of images have come to overwhelm the more nuanced elaborations of disciplinary systems, arguably the role of the 'icon' has come to new heights. Most dangerously, it has come to compromise the very critical priorities of 'architects' themselves, eradicating all that is complex, intricate and at stake in the reading of architecture. If architecture and its representational systems have always produced a tension between the inside and outside, the 'type' and its façade, or the core and envelope, then this era has brought on an erasure of that very tension by simply eclipsing the tectonic and systemic nature between part-and-whole in the make-up of the icon.

Given the elaborations of these projects, it is comforting to write about two buildings of significant accomplishment; but to equate the two as if to suggest their

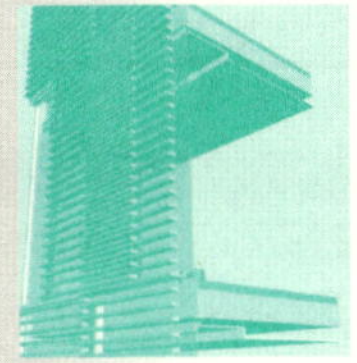

equity (or alliance) is to miss the very points on which these two buildings are conceptualized. After all, the Rose building is altogether another building type, with a radically different organization, mission, and level of sophistication. However, it is important to underline that the differences between the facades of these two projects, the object of contention, are not merely relative; the conceptual project undertaken by Arsh is, by definition, more difficult, complex and, hard to resolve. Maybe most troubling is a cultural dimension that reads through Takbiri's critique and falls into a classic trap: that for some reason, Rose's Western seniority somehow unquestionably trumps the youth and locality of the Arsh practice. Why is it that a young Iranian practice could not somehow unleash a critical piece of architecture that challenges the very institutions of the West? Is this an extension of the very inferiority complex (*oghdeh*) that Iran has come to be characterized by in all spheres, from the political to the cultural? Or is it a classical oversight that forgets that authority lies in the conceptual advancement of the discipline and not the assumed authority of its seniors? Let us not belittle the contributions of significant practices by succumbing to petty internal politics; instead, let us imagine the emergence of a discourse that is not only in dialogue with the West but also independent of it, charting inventive territory through the mechanisms of our own cultural instruments.

     Nader Tehrani

Topos, Stereotype, Cliché, Clone
Mario Carpo

This article was commissioned by L'Architecture d'Aujourd'hui more than ten years ago. Many things have changed since, but the main argument in this essay still stands and has been corroborated by recent developments in digital design theory. We now know, better than we could anticipate ten years ago that all digitally designed objects (media objects, and physical objects alike) are predicated on a new format of split agency, whereby one or more primary authors design the general aspects of a system and one or more secondary interactors customize it. Today this mode of composition is often called parametricism. Ten years ago we used Gilles Deleuze's and Bernard Cache's early definitions of the Objectile, or generic object. Regardless of what we call it, this mode of composition generates families of objects that share a common script, and this common script in turn generates visual similarities. Then, as now, and perhaps inevitably, the digital is based on similarities, not on identical replication; hence digital tools inevitably reenact traditional modes of imitation that the classical tradition has long nurtured and mechanical modernism had jettisoned. The digital notion of mimesis is closer to Cicero, Quintilian, and to Scholasticism than to Gropius and Mies.

TOPOS, STEREOTYPE, CLICHÉ, CLONE

The classical tradition has always practised and theorized the art of imitation. Tradition signifies transmission; we transmit rules and models, rules made to be applied, models to be imitated. For if a model is to be well imitated, it must be fully understood and the technique to reproduce it in a more or less creative manner mastered. But the history of architecture records two apparent exceptions to this pattern, which indeed did not derive from classical tradition, Gothic architecture in the Middle Ages, and the Modern movement in the 20th century.

For a 20th century Modern, the imitation of any given architectural model was anathema, since each project was a case apart that had to grow from its own programme—functional, technical, social or whatever— the scientific approach. Architects, with many Moderns among them, are known to have occasionally nurtured artistic ambitions. But the artist, in the Romantic tradition, is an inspired genius, whereas to copy—always considered as a servile act—is to be subject to mechanisms or constraint. As a result of this hybridization of the commonplaces of art and science, for nearly a century now a lot of architects have been engaged in imitation without ever saying so and at times without even knowing it.

I have vivid recollections of a so-called 'project' course in a faculty of architecture I shall not name, any more than the country in which it took place. For nine months, the course instructor droned on in a dark and somnolent room, before a screen where endless slides followed one after the other. All of them represented works by the same master. The commentary of our professor—quite a well-known figure at the time—consisted in a laconic and repetitive 'next,' this, of course, in reference to the following slide. After nine months of this treatment, in weekly doses, the course ended. What were we supposed to have learnt? No doubt, the idea behind it all, although nothing other than 'next;' at regular intervals was ever expressed, was that we would learn to appreciate, assimilate, and ultimately reuse some of these masterful and exemplary forms. But as I recall, the modes of this imitation encouraged in such an underhand manner were never the object of any critical discussion. The very notion of imitation was absent from our intellectual horizon. We knew that architects had practised imitation in the past, but they were bad architects. It was against them that modern architecture had been invented, based on programmes, technique, the scientific logic of the project. And so on and so forth—next.

Ancients and Moderns

Another consequence of this curious paradox, which consisted in removing from pedagogic discourse its most problematic, crucial and determining part, was that imitation, unjustly expelled from the creative act, reappeared in the act of interpretation whereby we busied ourselves looking for the 'influences' of one architect on another.[1]

This was a paper chase that consisted in discovering what the creator had hidden. The rehabilitation of the

1. Cf. James A. Ackerman, "Imitation," in *Origins, Imitation, Conventions* (Cambridge, MA and London: MIT Press, 2002), 125-143, in particular 135.

Topos, Stereotype, Cliché, Clone   Mario Carpo

classical notion of imitation began with post-modernism; quotation, a figure of imitation, reassumed its traditional role in the theory of the arts of design. More recently still, the theory and criticism of architecture—and its history too—have occasionally had recourse to categories of intertextuality. But what might be described as the instinctive hostility of most architects to imitation in any form has not diminished. In spite of the abundant critical discourse developed by the modern and contemporary visual arts on the themes of copying and reproducibility, architectural imitation is still considered to be a banal fault, a form of cheating, or just plain stupid; at its best an epiphany of kitsch or an expression of popular culture, which as such confers on the object an anthropological value.

Therein lies the big difference between ancients and moderns. The ancients, meaning almost all history, bar a few glorious decades in the 20th century, of which we cannot be entirely proud, always saw imitation and creation as inseparable, and on the subject of creative imitation they developed a plethora of philosophical speculations, theories, and methods for teaching.

Mimesis

Originally, mimesis meant to reproduce here and now the appearance of something that no longer exists or that exists elsewhere. This definition is in keeping, for example, with what is now known as virtual reality. The two great painters of antiquity, Zeuxis and Apelles, were famous for the realism of their paintings. Zeuxis painted grapes that were so lifelike that birds came down to peck at them. Apelles painted a horse so perfect that its image fooled even other horses. A rival of Zeuxis demonstrated his talent by painting a curtain that the master himself was tricked into attempting to pull aside.

Zeuxis also figures in another quaint story. He had been invited to a town, in what is now Southern Italy, to paint a picture of a goddess. Seeking inspiration, he asked to see some examples of local beauty. The elders sent him a selected group of handsome young men. Zeuxis protested. He was then allowed to see some girls. Finding none of them quite to his taste, he retained five of them as models. His painting was a fusion, a blend, an assemblage of features taken from all five, and it met with great success. But from the viewpoint of the theory of knowledge, this seemingly innocent tale suggests a major difficulty: if Zeuxis already had an idea of feminine beauty, why did he need to imitate real-life models? And if, on the contrary, he did not have an innate idea of beauty, how did he choose among so many incomplete individual manifestations of the ideal?

As we know, this conflict between realism and idealism has found different solutions throughout the ages. The realist solution postulates that things must be represented as they are; the idealist solution says they are to be represented as they should be. According to the second option, the act of imitation is based on the comparison and selection of several models to achieve a creative synthesis that surpasses and improves the originals. As for what modes and techniques are necessary to achieve this end, opinions have always varied.

Architecture is doubly an imitative art. In general, it imitates nature, or so classical theorists thought, who for centuries tried to explain what they meant by that. And more precisely, certain buildings imitate others. But to imitate a building, the architect must have seen it. If the model is on the corner of the street, it is easy to draw inspiration from it. But this is rarely the case. More often than not architects have had to compose working with technical media that reproduce more or less faithfully certain aspects of a distant or absent model.

Logocentric Imitation

The countless Mediaeval reproductions of certain sacred monuments of Paleo-Christian architecture have one thing in common that strikes us. Though designed as deliberate replicas of known archetypes, such as the Basilica of the Holy Sepulcher in Jerusalem, they are all very different from one another and from the original. In some cases, the only thing in common between the model and the copy is the geometry of the plan. In others, some dimensions or proportions coincide. This indifference to visual conformity has often been attributed to a presumed symbolic or abstract spirit, generously attributed to the culture of the Middle Ages.[2]

But we would have some difficulty making arguments like that stick concerning certain major works of the Quattrocento, such as the copy of the Holy Sepulcher of Jerusalem that Alberti built in the church of San Pancrazio in Florence (1456-1467). The dimensions (at a scale of 1:2) are the only thing that denotes direct knowledge of the original building. Alberti never went to Jerusalem. And it is highly unlikely that reliable technical drawings of the Holy Sepulcher were in circulation in Florence towards the mid-15th century. In fact, Alberti was imitating a building he had only heard of. He was imitating by ear. Descriptions can of course transmit some types of information better than others: words can easily state measurements or describe materials ('white marble', for instance); but to put forms into words—especially when the description is being made to someone who has never seen the work in question—is a risky business. This exercise, known as *ekphrasis*, was considered one of the most difficult of classical rhetoric.

Imitation in the manner of Alberti (and Mediaeval imitation in general) was logocentric because at the time architectural drawings were rare, of poor quality and very difficult to transmit. In the world of the manuscript, the word travelled better than the image, because the word could be recorded and transmitted with almost no error thanks to the technology of the alphabet, whereas no comparable technology enabled the reproduction and diffusion of drawings with any degree of exactitude.[3]

Scopocentric Imitation

The revolution of the printing press and the illustrated book changed all this. After the 1540s, thorough and reliable printed scale drawings of the best known works of ancient Roman architecture were sold all over Europe. For the first time architects had at their disposal precise graphic reconstitutions of the Coliseum, the Pantheon or Constantine's Arch, in plan, section and elevation (or almost), more or less precisely measured and drawn to scale. In principle, anyone so minded might build a perfect copy of the Pantheon, anywhere in the world (in Mexico, for example). But this is precisely what people did not do.

2. Cf. Richard Krautheimer, "Introduction to an Iconography of Medieval Architecture," in *Journal of the Warburg and Courtauld Institutes, V* (1942): 1-33. (Republished in *Studies in Early Christian, Medieval, and Renaissance Art* (New York: New York University Press, 1969), 115-130.

3. Cf. Mario Carpo, "Architecture in the Age of Printing. Orality, Writing, Typography, and Printed Images," in *The History of Architectural Theory* (Cambridge, MA and London: MIT Press, 2001), in particular, 42-56 and 119-124.

4. Cf. Mario
Carpo, "Metodo ed
ordini nella teoria
architettonica dei
primi moderni:
Alberti, Raffaello,
Serlio e Camillo,"
in Travaux
d'Humanisme et
Renaissance 271
(Geneva: Droz
1993) in particular
47-65.

5. Ibid.

The Renaissance culture of antiquity favored the practice of creative imitation and the identical replication of a known building was not seen as a type of imitation, but as plagiarism. The theory of imitation lay at the heart of humanist thought, and if rhetoric was its principal laboratory and literary composition its main field of experiment, Renaissance architects nonetheless took part in the debate more actively than is usually thought to be the case.[4]

According to one of the methods of literary imitation much in vogue in the 16th century, the source texts of the imitation had to be segmented and all their parts classified and archived before being reassembled in a new composition, formed exclusively of units or sections—words, phrases, locutions—of antique origin. This method was first developed to facilitate imitation of the style of Cicero. Curiously, the architects of the day adopted it and followed its example, as the illustrations of their treatises prove so eloquently. The key to this symmetrical process—the arrival point of deconstruction of the model and the departure point for recomposition of the copy—was the system of the five orders, the elements of a flexible and almost universal combinatory syntax that enabled any designer to build something new while imitating the old.[5] A composition might be absurd or fantastic, but insofar as each component was an attested and official part of the system of orders, the authority of antiquity guaranteed and supported the result.

Photographic Imitation

The monster of Doctor Frankenstein of the Renaissance theory of imitation, meaning the identical reproduction of an entire building, did not appear until late in the piece. The first known cases occur in the architecture of late 18th century English gardens. James 'Athenian' Stuart, better known as the author of the first scale drawings of ancient Greek monuments, which he began to publish in 1762, enjoyed a brilliant career as an architect by sprinkling here and there at different scales replicas of the octagonal tower of Winds and of the Lysicrates monument, which he himself had 'discovered,' so to speak, in Athens. In our day he would have been able to claim copyright.

Another exact replica of sad repute is that of the Log-

gia dei Lanzi in Florence, which thrones in the center of
Munich (Friedrich von Gärtner, 1841-1844). A reproduction
to the scale of 1:2 of Saint Peter's in Rome, designed for
Montréal in 1856, is outstanding in the annals of architectural facsimiles. Construction work began in 1868-1870
at a time when, because of the unification of Italy, the
temporal power of the Church in Rome was under threat.
The Catholics of Quebec no doubt saw in this an excellent
opportunity to remind the pontiff that their continent was
not necessarily an alternative to the Old World, but might,
on the contrary, become its ultimate refuge.

The topos of the last beach explains the fascination
for architectural facsimiles that marked the cities of North
America in the 20th century, from the famous Parthenon
of Nashville (1895-1897, rebuilt 1920-1931) to the Papy-
rus villa of Herculanum that housed the first museum
built by John Paul Getty in Malibu (1960-1974), without
forgetting Las Vegas.[6] The term 'facsimile' was introduced
to artistic discourse in 1823 by Quatremère de Quincy.[7]
According to the classical tradition, said Quatremère,
'facsimile' imitation, meaning the identical copy, was the
very negation of art. However, the exacerbated attention
and vitriolic censure that he dedicated to the subject were
premonitory signs of imminent change. How else can we
explain that at the same time as the notion of style (again,
a flexible language that allowed free expression within
a normative framework), the artistic culture of the 19th
century developed such a flourishing practice (for want of
a theory) of architectural facsimiles?

Since the 16th century, the mechanical reproduction
of drawn pictures—at first wood-cuts, then etchings,
etc.—had revolutionized architectural culture and the
method of the architectural project. But in the course
of the 19th century, photography introduced the notion
of a new technology for image production, the cultural
implications of which were to be just as important as
the technical spin-off. Unlike the drawn image, including
the perspective drawing, the photographed image was
in theory an automatic imprint of reality. The chemical
fixation of the projection formed inside the black box
was a mechanized mimesis. We have every right to point
out that random components, artistic or technical, enter
into every snapshot, but compared to, say, a perspec-

6. On 'topos of
the last beach,'
cf. Umberto Eco,
*Travels in Hyper-
reality*, trans. Wil-
liam Weaver (San
Diego, CA, New
York and London:
Harcourt, 1986)
1-59 and in particu-
lar 39. (First Italian
edition 1975).

7. Quatremère de
Quincy, *Essai sur
la nature, le but
et les moyens de
l'imitation dans
les beaux-arts*
(Paris: Treuttel et
Würtz, 1823) in
particular 93-94.

tive drawing, the photographic picture acquires an aura of objectivity. The photographic imprint is a standardized image: it is the same for everyone, everywhere. Like other optical technologies, just as widely diffused in the late 19th century, the projection of the same image onto a screen at real size seemed to guarantee precise reconstitution of the original. It was the principle of optical reversibility between nature and its representation that Alberti had postulated as early as 1436, in advance, as always, of the technology of his day. But by the late 19th century the automatically exact reproduction of the visual world was an established fact of Western culture.

If from that time on everything that we see could be duplicated as such, not verbatim, but *figuratim*, architecture could be, too. Unlike the drawn architectural image, which manipulates the observed object, analyses, and decomposes it, the photographed image of architecture reconstitutes the work in its entirety. Architects did just that. They drew by hand, as we have seen, projects for ideally photographic replicas of their chosen models.

And if we push this argument a little further, along the lines of the classical thesis, à la Benjamin, concerning the relationship between 'reproduction' and 'reproducibility', we inevitably conclude that certain architectural inventions of the Renaissance, such as the system of orders, were destined for the mechanical reproduction of the drawn image, while certain architectural inventions of the 20th century were no doubt designed with an eye to their photographed reproduction.

Algorithmic imitation

As we know, the mechanical reproduction of imagery, drawn or photographed, is now in direct competition with the electronic reproduction of digital imagery. But the initial consequences of this new technical paradigm seem to manifest themselves less in the domain of the documentary architectural image, or the representation of what is already built, than in the process of elaboration of the projected architectural image, or prefiguration of what the architect wants to build, which does not yet exist.

More than in architecture, it is in the domain of industrial design that the effects of this change are already perceptible. Everyone admits that all cars look alike today. This is not, or at least only partially, due to the fact that their designers copy or spy on one another. Quite simply, they use the same computer-assisted design software. To be more precise, there are three of four software families, and since each has its own logic, specialists can detect in the forms—curves, and especially in 'folds'—of vehicle bodies the type of software used to design them.

This is not the only thing in common between the design of automobiles today and the construction of medieval cathedrals. In both cases families of diverse and apparently anonymous forms bear a resemblance because they were generated by the same algorithms: geometric formulae in the Middle Ages and CAD/CAM software today. Ironically, one of the classical *topoi* of 'creative' imitation, which was supposed to emphasize the impalpable dimension of resemblance between the original and the copy, was the metaphor of biological reproduction. The well-made copy resembled the original in the same way as the son is the portrait of his father; everyone can see the resemblance, but no one can say precisely what it is. Both have a certain *je ne sais quoi* (*nescio quid*), something that is apparent but that cannot be defined.

Today we know that this *nescio quid* can be reduced to a listing of chromosome variants that scientists will soon be able to duplicate or manipulate at will. When we look at the 'folds' of two vehicle bodies that look alike, the *nescio quid* that they share is in fact the mathematical function which is their common logical matrix. It may be that computer-assisted design is approaching another form of imitation of which little has been said as yet, and which we shall no doubt have to examine carefully in years to come: the imitation of nature in its founding or morphogenetic act.[8]

8. Cf. among other theses of Greg Lynn, *Animate Form* (New York: Princeton Architectural Press, 1999).

Affinity
Alexander D'Hooghe

(IDEOLOGY AND) AFFINITY: ARCHITECTURAL HISTORIES AS CONVERSATION PARTNERS[1]

Innovation in architecture *today* is not only a question of introducing new technologies, materials, or even conceptual invention, but also a question of ideological consciousness. By ideological consciousness, I mean an awareness of the continuity of certain ideologies in architecture, articulated through aesthetic conventions and underlying belief systems that form lasting positions in an increasingly unstable society. These ideologies can easily span decades and connect into large lineages. Every new generation of architecture students wants to give meaning to architecture and urbanism by instilling ideals in them, most of which would address the alienations and destabilizations of modern society. However, these ideals are often similar across generations, and the formal orders we invent to further them can resemble one another, as well. Thus more often than not, though we may think we have invented a new position, we have really just added a line to an ongoing intergenerational conversation. Innovation then arises out of an awareness of our ideological position and, following from that, from our capacity to liberate ourselves from its constraints, or at least engage the conversation within which we are stuck with more precision and boldness.

Here is an example: There is a tradition in architecture obsessed with developing levels of complexity and variability found in nature, specifically in biology. From neo-Gothic architecture, to the *Jugendstil*, via the ornaments of socialist realism, to the complex mathematical patterns of post-war abstract art, to our current obsession with parametric design and complex 3-D prototyping, there is a great formal continuity in the production of complex non-orthogonal forms that display elements of growth, evolution, patterning, attempting to look like natural elements rather than dead material. This tradition shows a desire to make an architecture that is vital, organic, and ultimately critical of alienating, instrumental reason. As an industrializing society increasingly disconnected from nature, the amount of aesthetic projects searching to

1. This article was also invited for publication in the German Architecture Journal *ARCH+* for release in the first months of 2014, with the title: "Platform Architecture. Ideological Consciousness As a Form of Innovation".

reinstate its virtues increases. We could call this a lineage of organicism in architecture.

Constructing a map of lineages would be a herculean effort. Nevertheless, a diagram of such an effort could be found in the work of Georg Kateb. In *Utopia And Its Enemies* (1963), Kateb argues that our articulations of forms for a better world can be reduced to combinations of three vectors. Utopian forms are located in forms of nature, in forms of community, and in forms of progress. These forms can be seen as buttons that activate our imagination of a better place. In architecture and urbanism, Kateb's assessment translates to the forms and aesthetic conventions referring to the idea of nature (organicism), the idea of community (fabrics, weaves, small towns, monuments), or the idea of progress (acceleration, direction, buzz). Each of these vectors are symbolic arrows out of the present quagmire, born out of a profound sense of loss. When asserted as belief systems that allow us to plan the future, nature, community, and progress become ideologies. At that point, they become malleable in the hands of architects or urbanists. Each of these ideologies is paired with packages of aesthetics, tools, techniques and methods. Many of these have existed for over 200 years, if not more. Our supposed 'innovation' is nothing more than a conversation with our aesthetic-ideological ancestors, whose positions we have already implicitly adopted and whose work we are updating to current technology, current materials, and current demands of capital.

A design project then becomes a form of secondary literature. The corollary primary text here would be the collective body of drawings and literature that can be extracted as a family of resemblances within an identifiable lineage. If eloquent, over time one's own contribution gets added to the primary body.

Finally, such consciousness of ideology liberates the architect from imprisonment within any given lineage. It enables conversations with several lines and allows for the development of a body of work as a choreography of engagements and conversation with different partners. The possibility for innovation begins through the consciousness of ideology.

The Historical Lineage of the Empty Platform

What if creating complexity and liveliness is not a
task for architectural form, as in the organicist lineage
described above, but rather a reality of urban life, and if
we want to show complexity, all we have to do is stage
life itself? Such a project would not favor any kind of
specific utopian form in Kateb's taxonomy, but rather
produce the canvas onto which all possible dreams can
be projected by inhabitants and users. Is there a lineage
with formal consequences for this approach? There is. The
reference here is not Yona Friedman's utopian abstractions, but a more fine-grained attitude detectable in the
work of people like James Stirling, Louis Kahn, and Aldo
Van Eyck. In the below paragraphs, their position appears
to resolve a desire for absolute open-endedness with a
realization that such indeterminacy paradoxically requires
a strong formal and curatorial position by the architect,
to avoid a reduction of architecture to a mere piece of
technocracy, or infrastructure.

The post-war period witnessed a moment, starting with the work of John Weeks in the early 1950s and
ending shortly after 1973, when architects and urbanists
articulated a theory of built form as an open *structure*,
in principle capable of hosting almost any kind of *infill*.
Some protagonists argued for architecture to relinquish
its duty to make articulate aesthetic statements, and
instead offered what John Habraken called 'supports'
(1961)[2], not just for any function, but also for any ideology
or aesthetic to take over. This is commonly referred to
as structuralist architecture and participatory urbanism.
Structuralism considered the social and psychological
reality of the human world in analogy to language as a
complex system of relations without a center.

"The mental processes of man are the same everywhere, regardless of race and culture, regardless of the
apparently absurdity of beliefs and customs."[3] Architects
such as Aldo Van Eyck, Herman Hertzberger, John Habraken, Ralph Erskine, and others intuited that structuralist
thinking would unearth the authentic relations immanent
to human culture, and structuralist architecture would
build these relations. They hoped that, through scientific
inquiry, structuralist architecture could restore an organic

2. John Habraken,
*Supports: An Alter-
nate to Mass Hous-
ing, U.K.* (Tyne
& Wear: Urban
International Press,
2000). Reprint of
the 1972 English
edition. First
printed in Dutch:
*De Dragers en de
Mensen, Het Einde
van de Massa Won-
ingbouw* (Amster-
dam: Scheltema
& Holkema N.V.,
1961).

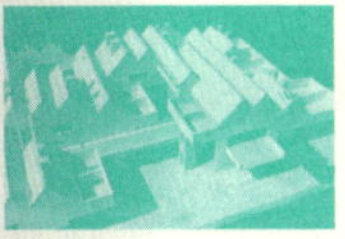

Reference: Kasbah
Housing Estate,
Piet Blom, The
Netherlands

3. Franz Boas, as
cited in *Forum*,
1959. Also noted in
Francis Strauven,
Aldo van Eyck
(Amsterdam:
Architecture and
Nature, 1998), op.
cit, 348. This quote
of the anthropolo-
gist Franz Boas
adorned the first is-
sue Forum in 1959.
It is a structuralist
statement par ex-

cellence. Aldo van Eyck, a self-declared structuralist appreciated the anthropology of Levi-Strauss, but his main sources were not Saussure (published only in 1972) or Levi-Strauss, but rather Franz Boas, Ruth Benedict, and Benjamin Lee Whorf.

social order and thereby eliminate the vicissitudes of architectural authorship.

The architectural outcomes of structuralism have enjoyed mixed reviews at best. Many structuralist buildings were shoddily detailed because the infill components (cheaply designed and built because they were thought of as only temporary) became a highly visible and enduring feature. In addition, several of these buildings lacked a conscious sense of composure, because they were indeed meant to be extendable.

In hindsight, we can argue that this lineage deliberately abandoned formal control and authorship, in order to allow for inhabitants to envision their own community. But if we were able to re-assert formal controls and authorship where necessary yet maintain ideological and functional open-endedness, we would be able to define a project for an architecture that has the capacity to host almost any of the three imaginations suggested by Kateb: "A building that is so neutral and indifferent to any particular wish image, whether based on nature, community, or progress, that it can serve as the projection screen for all of them."

We could then achieve a strict formal framework that is completely arbitrary to its potential functional performance and the ideologies and histories of its users, a frame that monumentalizes its own emptiness as a call for anyone to project their own desires again and again. Contrary to Aldo Rossi's architecture, such a project would emancipate the users from the history in which they appear rather than condemn them to eternal re-articulation of their typological essence.

4. Herman Hertzberger, "Tracing Dutch Structuralism," (lecture presented at Celebration of Berlage's 20 years, The Berlage Center for Advanced Studies in Architecture and Urban Design, Delft, The Netherlands , October 13, 2009), http://www.berlage-institute.nl/events/details/2009_10_13_tracing_dutch_structuralism.

"A generic structure that can be used for different purposes in time: that is the idea of structuralism."[4] Herman Hertzberger iterated a wider generational critique of the relentless and formulaic reproduction of post-war mass housing. Architects sought for the objective demands of architectonic form *beyond* immediate functionality. But while they were engaged in a disciplinary conversation, a breakthrough occurred in the pragmatic world of professional building services.

After World War II, technological devices in medicine faced an accelerated innovation curve and briefs for hospital buildings had to be systematically re-written and updated to account for new instruments and procedures. These changes shook up the much slower design process of the buildings that were to house the devices. Fast innovation cycles inspired the conceptual disassembly of the building as object into an accumulation of layers with different life cycles. John Weeks (1921-2005), architect and lecturer at University College London, designed several hospitals and researched their performance requirements. His work contributed to the re-conceptualization of the building not as an object, but as a series of layers with different life cycles. He specifically disconnected the permanent layer of the building, namely its structure and elevation, from any relation to the specific functional performance criteria required for the interior of the building. Weeks, with his partner Richard Llewellyn-Davies, worked for the Nuffield Foundation, which was tasked with the development of innovations in hospital organization, management, and architecture. Weeks published his findings as "Indeterminate Architecture" (1963)[5] in the periodical of the Bartlett School where he taught. He followed up with an article called "Endless Architecture" (1951)[6], which was accompanied its pragmatic counterpart, a book by Richard Llewellyn-Davies called *Building Elements* (1956).[7] In these publications, they articulated the structure-infill distinction for the first time.

"It was becoming difficult already in the eighteenth century to compose buildings to rule, even though functional requirements were less mechanically demanding than today and buildings, like institutions, were thought to be permanent [...] A building for an indeterminate brief cannot then adhere to a finite geometric control system. The ideal of unity through constant relationships cannot be achieved. Such a building will be geometrically aformal. What design rules, if any, are appropriate?

"[...]The fixed elements, then, were from the beginning the shape of the street system and the widths of the departmental buildings. The lengths of these were indeterminate[...]"

"Criteria for the design of the external skin of the building included the need for a column-free inner face which would enable partitions to be positioned freely... it was decided to use a structural mullion system [...] the mullions would then be used in numbers and clustered

5. John Weeks, "Indeterminate Architecture," *Transactions of the Bartlett Society* 2 (1963-4): 83-206.

6. Richard Llewellyn-Davies and John Weeks, "Endless Architecture," *Architectural Association Journal* (July 1951): 106 -112.

7. Richard Llewellyn-Davies and D.J. Petty, *Building Elements*, foreword by W.A. Allen, vol. 3 of Modern Building Construction series (London: Architectural Press, 1956).

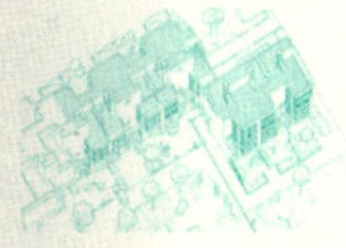

Reference: Diagoon Houses, Herman Hertzberger, The Netherlands

in a manner which related [only] to the mechanical load to be transferred [...] the loading condition dictate the appearance of the building [...]"

"All aspects of the design I have described have been affected by the requirement of indeterminacy. It has been a form giving and a unifying criterion. [...] The building I have described is, as was indicated, closely related in concept to urban design."[8]

Weeks thus sought to free architecture from conventional formal controls, proposing instead an indeterminate architecture disconnecting structure and function. He called this 'the loose fit' of form to function. He defined the structure as the permanent layer of the building. Other layers, such as walls or equipment, would have shorter life cycles. Weeks sought to express this indeterminacy in the elevation. In Northwick Park, he developed a system of structural mullions, but left the frequency and ordering capacity completely over to the engineers, himself refusing the responsibility for composition. The structure in Weeks' studies was either a system of shear wall panels, or a system of structural mullions.

Architects such as James Stirling and Ralph Erskine began to respond by composing different articulations of structure-infill. For Stirling, the building remained a composed object. In his campus of the University of St. Andrews, (1964-1968), structural mullions set up a repetitive order and free up the plan. Yet, Stirling still integrates the various building layers into a finite, authored object. Axes, proportions, platonic shapes, etc. continue to play a role in this composition. The building is complete, its architecture not unraveling into an endless pattern. The significance of this approach becomes clear in juxtaposition to that of fellow British architect Ralph Erskine. In Erskine's terrace housing in Nyttorp, Sweden (1955-1958), for instance, a repetition of structural shear walls forms the dominant expression. The overall plan suggests that the building should expand. Erskine's architecture effectively uses the structure-infill (S-I) concept to disassemble the building's objecthood. Weeks refers to the Smithsons as intellectual family, footnoting articles by them in both *Architectural Review* (London) and *Forum* (Amsterdam).[9] He and Llewellyn-Davies also built a stand devoted to 'indeterminacy' at the *This is Tomorrow* exhibition at Whi-

8. Weeks, "Indeterminate Architecture," 83-206.

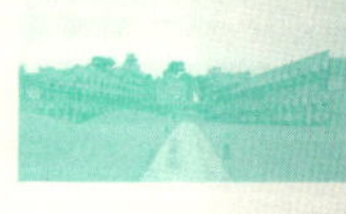

Reference: University of St. Andrews, James Stirling, Scotland

9. Weeks concretely refers, in "Indeterminate Architecture" to:

techapel in London in 1956. "Team 10 is of the opinion that only in such a way may meaningful groupings of buildings come into being, where each building is a live thing and a natural extension of the others."[10]

In the Low Countries, after the dissolution of CIAM in 1959, Aldo Van Eyck and Jaap Bakema developed the journal *Forum*. Van Eyck brought one of his students, Herman Hertzberger, on board as a member of the journal. Hertzberger, and later, on Piet Blom became the second generation of what came to be branded as 'Dutch Structuralism'.[11] This second generation of S-I completely destroyed the architectural object as an internally consistent geometric composition, replacing it with concepts of endless, pure structure. However, Van Eyck's own work never went quite that far. In the words of Francis Strauven, his main biographer, the 'shimmering of configuration' (*straling van het configuratieve*)[12], or the degree to which an aggregated structure was pregnant with an overall form, remained extremely important. Like Stirling, Van Eyck asserted the role of overall configuration and formal legibility as the end, with S-I as the means. Fumihiko Maki, another contemporary and potential Asian counterpart in S-I thinking, argued that various repetitive structural articulations should still result in an overall composition, which he called 'Master Form'. Structural parts are still parts to a whole. Van Eyck, Maki, and Stirling thus used structure-infill concept as a means to an end, or a unifying system to ultimately construct an object.

In hindsight, the structure-infill concept specified at least three distinct architectural and urbanistic positions. Van Eyck, Maki and Stirling coagulated open-ended structures into composed objects. Hertzberger, Erskine, Blom and others dissolved the object-background dichotomy in order to erect an endless structural order, in which joyful infill could take place using spatio-structural units like rooms.[13]

The elimination of subjective architectural authorship, considered an urgent necessity given the lack of legitimacy by the architect to define form on behalf of the public, holds together various threads of S-I thinking. John Weeks surrendered the elevations to the engineers; Piet Blom and Ralph Erskine denied their buildings elevations; and John Habraken and Lucien Kroll wanted the public

"Fix," *Architectural Review* (1960); and *Forum* 7 (1959).

10. Alison Smithson, ed., *Team 10 Primer* (Cambridge MA: MIT Press, 1974; first edition 1962; revised edition 1968).

11. Wim van Heuvel, *Structuralism in Dutch Architecture*, (Rotterdam: 010 Publishers, 1992).

12. Francis Strauven, *Aldo Van Eyck: Relativiteit en Verbeelding* (Amsterdam: Meulenhoff, 1994). Translated in English as *The Shape of Relativity* (Amsterdam: Architecture and Nature, 1998).

13. There is a much wider spectrum of authors in S-I we are not discussing for the purposes of this argument.

to build a pluralist patchwork elevation. But in eliminating the author as agent, they also reduced the presence of architecture to that of a semi-conscious aggregation of materials. The abandonment of this intellectual project, except for a few strongholds, such as the Massachusetts Institute of Technology deep into the 1990s, is the indictment of history. More than an intellectual refusal, a new generation may have turned its back on structuralist buildings' ultimate lack of precision in articulation, detail, and composition.

Today, almost two generations later, can we revisit this project? Is it possible to instill an optimism in architecture's capacity to contribute with its own means? Indeed, is it possible to accept architecture's limits (object-hood), its strengths (imposing an order), and its potentials (generous indeterminacy)? In other words, is it possible to work on a generation of monumental containers that are open-ended platforms, hosts for any belief system, while also being aware, because of what came before, that this effort requires a strong belief in the unavoidable formal articulations that architecture is doomed to contribute?

Platform For An Open Society, 2.0

The project for the food market in Brussels experiments with a modified platform concept. Broadly inspired by the earlier work of Stirling, Kahn and van Eyck, it attempts to radicalize the formal clarity and the openendedness of the platforms, floor-plates, and spaces conceived in the project.

An 8.2 m x 8.2 m concrete portico provides the key architectural definition of the project. The design of the construction joints obfuscates the reading of the portico as a summation of two columns with a beam on top. This reinforces the reading of the portico as an abstract formal frame.

In order to explicitly underline the fact that frames are not just structure but also form a cultural expression, they are designed as platonic shapes, in five different formal variations. A platonic shape is cut out of an imaginary 'full' concrete rectangle to constitute the overall frame form. There are five different such extractions, resulting in

                Alexander D'Hooghe

five different frames. The differences between them are arbitrary and have no functional or structural justification: they are pure form. Any association between the platonic shape defining the frame and functionality or structural need would destroy the premise of the project: to be functionally neutral, yet formally precise.

Most importantly, the portico's components are designed to be visible. Structuralism's structures were designed to disappear behind customized infill. To the contrary, the market project emblematizes the structural portico as the dominant form, both structure and finish at the same time, and performing as the largest scale-element in the building, thus asserting itself and creating the dominant reading.

A single frame connects to others in three-way or four-way intersections, resulting in a stiff grid of frames, stacked, juxtaposed. As a result, the portico becomes a three-dimensional formal system, legible both in the elevation, as well as in the interiors.

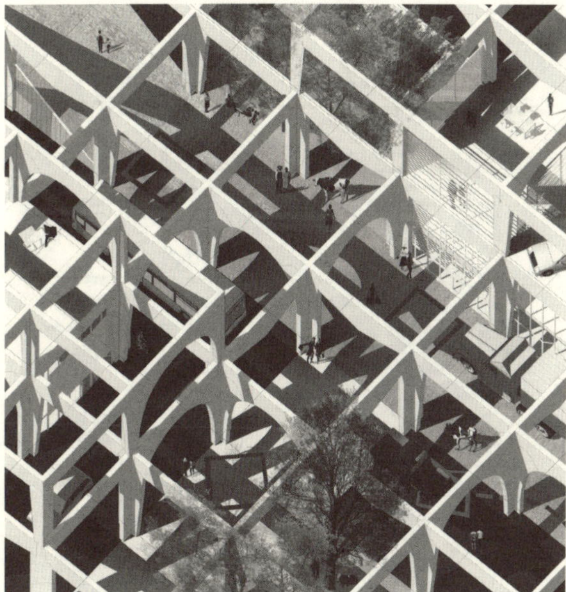

Image: Perspective view of market building concrete portico

Frame dimensions in plan allow everything from a parking grid, to residential units, to storefronts, to be realized. The sectional dimension allows for three shallow stories, or two higher commercial/civic floors, to be realized. Both plan and section of the frame assembly maintain the flexibility creed. However, no price is paid in formal decisiveness.

The version of the market project currently under construction includes market stands, butcher shops, a logistics docking area, a restaurant, and an urban farm. Earlier versions also included residential units and offices. Throughout a four-year process of design and programmatic changes, the system dimensions and forms have been refined to accommodate any of these scenarios. As a design tool, the portico has proven its flexibility in the design phase, but the ultimate purpose is to demonstrate the robustness of the formal system in reality, with changes being deployed after construction.

Finally, the urban context of this building is not coincidentally that of a vibrant immigrant district in Brussels, with a history of being a neighborhood for newcomers in the city. Historically a place of transition, it is a location per definition for shifting identities and reformulating of desires and utopias.

Image: Site plan of market building, Brussels, Belgium

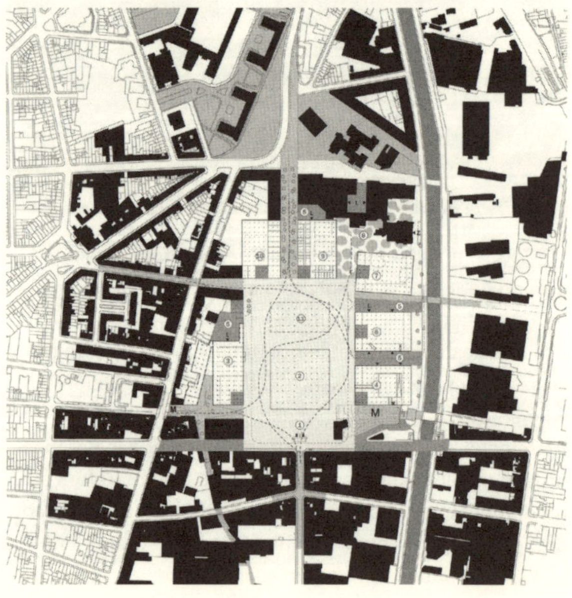

     Affinity   Alexander D'Hooghe

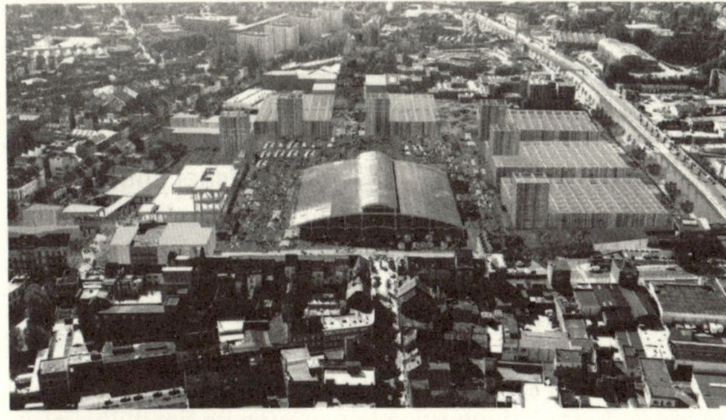

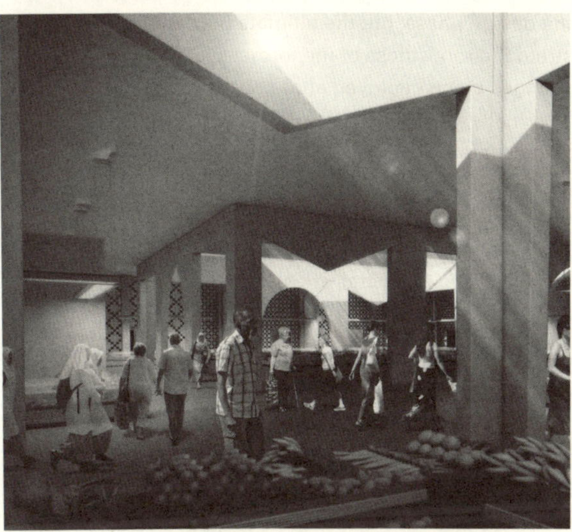

Today, many different constituencies find common ground here: from the butchers and their clients from surrounding farming communities; to immigrants from Africa and Eastern Europe; to bohemians and upper middle class citizens from Brussels and the European Union, who enjoy coming to the weekly markets in the area. Architecture here serves as a framework for each of these groups to define their own aspirations, and therefore as a monument to all. It seems that a redefinition and upgrade of the platform theory in architecture is the proper intellectual foundation for work in such a place.

Allusion[1]
Florian Idenburg

1a. Allusion establishes a contextual and cultural link, but rather than clarify meaning, it plays with it. With volume turned low, allusion disrupts an expected ideological framework. Rather than a joke to get, allusion is the promise of more.

1b. Allusion is playfulness. What looked like one thing could be another, too. It pushes back against the clarity of typology, and makes the canonical new.

1c. As a collage, allusion authors its own context, announces its loyalties, interests, legacies. But no one says it has to tell the truth.

1d. Allusion does not only clarify, it also bluffs. It is what Hitchcock called the "MacGuffin", an irrelevant plot device, but one that allows new ones to flourish.

1e. Allusion fails when it becomes a symbol, reducing a work to a one-liner. Heavy-handed allusion overcomes the work, becoming signage rather than intrigue.

0:00

Although less dominant than the use of the diagram, the use of allusions was part of the SuperDutch era, roughly the last decade of the twentieth century.

1:00

To understand the use of allusions in architecture in the Netherlands, it's important to understand the Dutch word for it. Allusion translates in Dutch as *zinspeling*. *Zin* translates as meaning and *speling* means play, and I think the notion of play is essential in thinking about this term. Other uses of reference, such as quotation or citation, are about clarifying things. But allusion is not about clarifying anything: it's actually much more about a subtle sort of hinting at something. The success of an allusion doesn't come out of its clarity, but out of the way you are able to disguise it within a project. And what is interesting about allusions is that they actually activate the discourse. It is about people being able to 'get it', and others not 'getting it', or the promise of discovering.

2:00

Allusions allow subtlety and reactivation of the histories that we share. They can be a very useful instrument pedagogically speaking, as well.

4:42

It was during my second year of studies that OMA's Kunsthal was built. The building raised an incredible amount of discussion in the Netherlands, as I'm sure it did here, as well. Everybody was sleeping with *S,M,L,XL* under or as their pillow. Through this book we started to understand the subtlety, or the value of strategic use of allusions and references. We see Villa Dall'Ava—and what's that other building (the Villa Savoye)—as obvious references in the Kunsthal pointing to the Modernist's work and its routing, while the structural solutions for the building invoke non-linear thinking as well. This project contains allusions to architecture that falls within the canon and, at the same time, includes allusions to a type of vernacular. A certain type of critical regionalism in the Kunsthal project is also very much about alluding to certain pasts, for example 'de dijkwoning,' the house on the

1f. Inasmuch as allusion is a form of representation, a relationship between a signifier and a signified, they simultaneously belong to a new work. The critique of OMA's work as a kind of mannerism (itself allusion), also allows their articulated volumes and surfaces to be collaged together.

1g. Allusion is embedded in the new. Citation without new content is either a collage or a copy. It is the friction between what seems to belong to one framework, and what belongs to another. The subject of allusion is not the sample but the twist.

1h. Rather than nurture unlimited meanings, allusion instead has the capacity to dispatch with the obvious. It peels back dominant images to allow secondary ones to interact. The subject of the allusion, paradoxically, is never the subject of its use.

1i. Allusion both produces the canon, and replaces it.

dyke, and other more regional things. This is a nautical area, the Rotterdam harbor, hence the round windows, and the corrugated plastic, which Rem himself said alluded to the slums of Calcutta. In the Kunsthal, multiple allusions, or a series of references, become a conflation, where the layering up of a series of cross-cultural references becomes so dense that it starts to produce a narrative in its own right.

This allusional type of thinking had a big impact on young practitioners, and I want to draw at least a loose link between architecture and the concurrent influence of rap music in the Netherlands. First there was grunge, and then came rap. Nas came out with *Illmatic* in 1994, and the notion of sampling, and remixing, and copying, and pasting, and collaging into something new was very much happening in Dutch architecture schools, as well. For example, two young Dutch architects, Marc Maurer and Tom Frantzen, coined 'MC-Architecture', which was really about appropriating rap strategies. They developed a design technique explicitly using architectural 'sampling.' In their graduation work, which was a full re-mix of OMA, they drew from Kurt Schwitters' *Merzbau* and from El Lissitzky. Most importantly, their attitude was hardly an isolated one at that time.

The notion of referring and alluding at least partly explains how Villa VPRO turned into a really big dispute about authorship. Rem very clearly accused MVRDV of taking their design from the OMA Jussieu Library scheme. Interestingly, he was being sued at this very moment by a student architect for allegedly copying the Kunsthal. Remembering the importance of allusion for at this time allows us to complicate the general understanding of the Dutch '90s.[1]

9:40

And then increasingly, the Dutch style developed into the one-liner, the single diagram, and I think it lost some of its richness, the richness of this conflation of allusions. I've argued elsewere that I think that, in Milstein Hall, Rem starts to allude to his own work. I think of Milstein Hall as a complete conflation of previous OMA ideas and projects assembled together in a single building. You can think of the elevator, which is a room, in relation to the Bordeaux House; the concrete landscape may be referring to the

1. And I learned on the morning of Under the Influence symposium that Sam Jacobs' father was the judge in this case.

Educatorium; and the truss, I think, can be read as a literal
reference to OMA's previous work.

10:50

I'm very drawn to the subtlety of certain allusions and the
notion of drawing these certain affinities with history

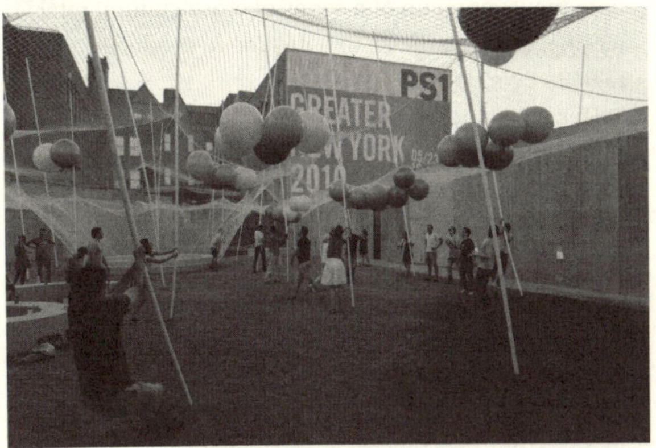

in our work. This is our scheme for Pole Dance, for PS1,
and there are some obvious allusions here, but, at the
same time, we tried to turn them around. So where this
is kind of a dystopian scheme, (non-stop city), we tried
to turn it around in a very hyper-playful and elegant dynamic system. The idea of Pole Dance, for example, had
to respond to something for MoMA, the treasurers of the
legacy of the Modern movement. We wanted to play with
this notion of Modernity, but weaken its structures. So we
considered the Bauhaus dance by Oskar Schlemmer,
the 'Pole Dance,' and there is obviously the referral or

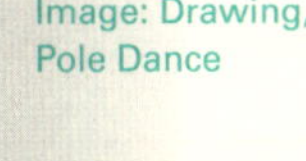

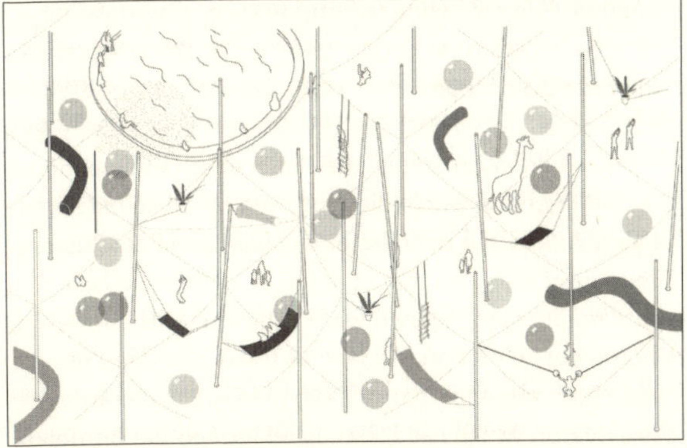

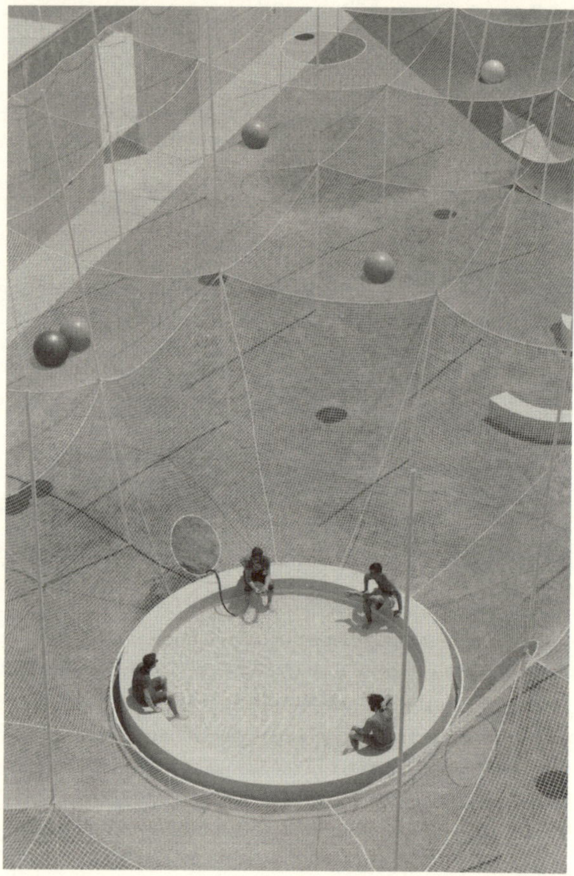

the reference there to the relationship between body and structure. But other elements we needed to speak about, for example sustainability, in this proposition, was the notion of collapse, which is embedded in the system, the notion of us being responsible for our own environment, and not a sort of top-down structure. There was the notion of game, alluding to the notion of play, and these balls are there to suggest a certain balance, but at the same time they alluded to the game for which rules do not exist.

There was also the notion of elasticity, and the fact that we can create our own environments, and I think there were also ideas of Aldo Van Eyck's playgrounds, and other ways in which we activate our outside urban space.

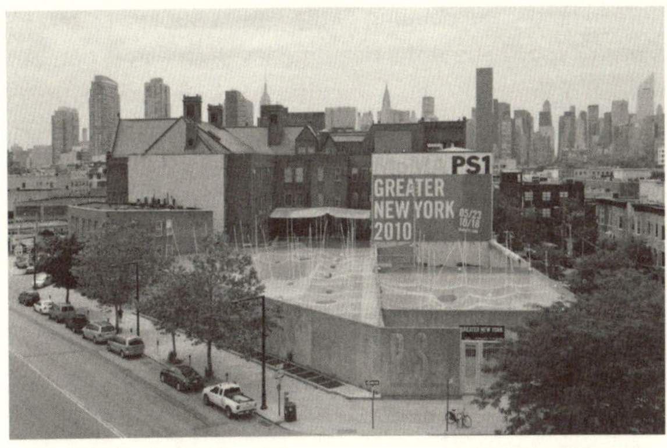

Image: Pole Dance installed on MoMA PS1 rooftop

These are pictures we found online of a sort of spontane-ous appropriation of the scheme. There were people who saw this as something very different than what we had anticipated. The group Body and Pole approached us to do a true pole dance, led by a national champion at pole dancing. So I think, here was something that—and I had to think about it yesterday when we spoke about the open work—in many ways was an open work where we placed something that was an infrastructure people could appropriate and work within. It also became something that we weren't even sure what it would become while we were working on it because it really was appropriated in many different ways. I do think though that we remained the author, and that it was not some sort of co-authored thing. Allusion similarly does not become co-authored, but instead becomes a new thing.

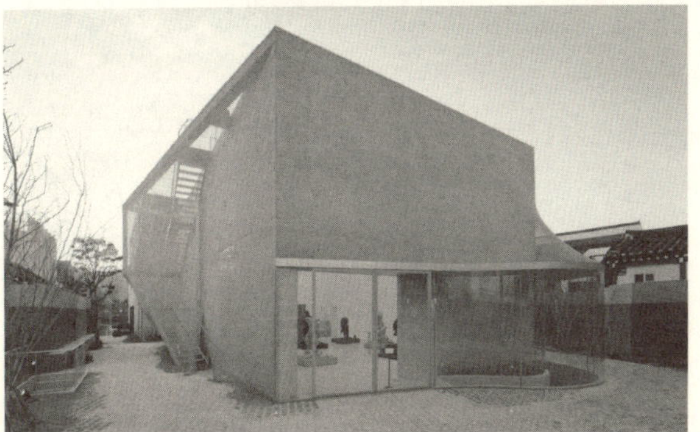

Image: Kukje Gallery, SO-IL, Seoul, South Korea

When speaking about Kukje Gallery to our client and to the historic committee in the area, we described a

Korean landscape painting of the site as our key inspiration. We spoke about the beautiful layering that is part of Korean or Asian painting: the diffusion of the space, the lack of hard lines, and the way our building fits within its surroundings. But that narrative is not entirely complete. We were also interested in the building's architectural diagram, whose source can be found in the Nakahechi Museum by Kazuyo Sejima (1997). The Kukje Gallery emerged from a process of cleansing or disguising its source diagrams. We shrink-wrapped the base diagram, hiding it behind a soft skin. At the same time, it's winking at hyper-digital geometric architecture. Our building is very low-tech. We hand-welded half a million rings together in a Chinese village.

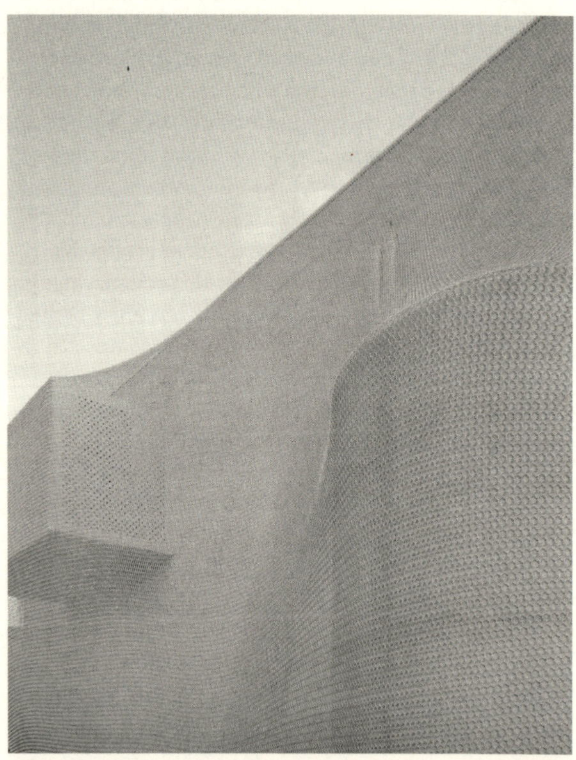

For the Shenzen and Hong Kong Biennale curated in 2011 by Terrence Riley, the curatorial provocation included producing The Street in direct reference to Paolo Portoghesi's *La Strada Novissima* featured at the inaugural

(1980) Venice Biennale. The Street included twelve teams of architects all engaged in thinking about façades. As a response, we wanted to play with the column, which was very much part of Paolo Portoghesi's work. At the same time we wanted to think about depth as a critique of contemporary skin fetishism. So the notion of the colonnade became operative. Although the plan alludes to a certain spatial symmetry, once you enter its space, it no longer works the way it looks like it would. We triangulated all the elements that made up the colonnades, and they were detailed in both marble (with its obvious allusions), and in veneer—a Miesian detailing of the pure veneer—of mirrors and marble. Once you enter the space it becomes an endless, very diffused, illogical space. One journalist called it a 'new nature,' a characterization about which we had never thought.[2]

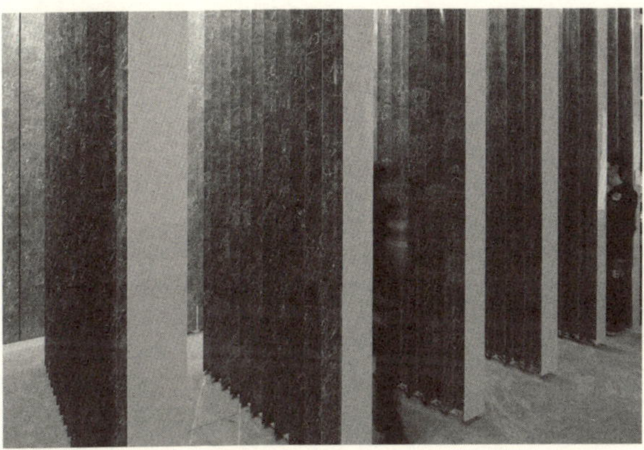

2. My 'mother' (Kazuyo Sejima) told me: "basically... we do not refer." Well, this is a quote from her Lecture at Columbia University GSAPP delivered in 2002.

Image: The Street, Shenzen and Hong Kong Biennale, 2011

0:00

It's a pleasure to take part in this event with so many friends who have critically contributed to the project I am presenting.

0:40

The project is called The Dictionary of Received Ideas, and was launched in 2006 as a series of design studios and seminars, which I claimed would last a full decade. So the project is still ongoing. The aim of the Dictionary is to examine *received ideas* (or clichés) in contemporary architectural culture. The project is based on an unfinished project by Gustave Flaubert, which was called *Le Dictionnaire des idées reçues*, and which has been translated into English in a number of different ways: *The Dictionary of Accepted Ideas, The Dictionary of Received Ideas,* and *A Dictionary of Platitudes*. Flaubert seems to have started this project when he was only a child. As he writes in a letter to a friend at the age of nine, he decided to write down the stupid remarks uttered by an old lady from Paris who would visit Flaubert's parents in Rouen. The project was fully defined by the time Flaubert wrote *Madame Bovary,* and it entailed recording in the form of a dictionary all the clichés and ready-made phrases that people repeated *ad nauseam*. Flaubert called his book the *Encyclopedia of Stupidity*. Many of the characters in his novels are in fact victims of those clichés. (*Madame Bovary,* for instance, is arguably the victim of the cliché of romantic love). Flaubert worked on this project throughout his life. At the time of his death, the project remained. It is believed that Flaubert planned to use this dictionary as a sort of epilogue to the also unfinished novel *Bouvard et Pécuchet.*

3:00

As the last task of their series of failed enterprises in the various fields and practices at the time, two scriveners return to the only thing they knew how to do well: that is, to copy what other people had written, and transcribe *Le Dictionnaire des idées reçues.*

Interestingly, Flaubert's was a project of appropriation. He planned to write his book without composing a single line, with the exception of a preface. The book would only include material that was already out there, repeated by everyone and coined by no one. Flaubert's aim was to block the reader, who would be afraid to speak, for fear of using one of the clichés contained in the book.

As I mentioned, the project remained unfinished. Only a few entries have survived, which have been collected into a small book. The interesting thing about these entries is that Flaubert provided a term, and a description, but the description (more often than not) was in fact an instruction, things that you had to do or say, prompted by the term. Most of the platitudes have been somehow lost over time. But some are still current. Hotels are always good in Switzerland. [audience laughs]. I must add that we consider a cliché to be well-defined once it triggers a grin or a laugh, the agreement that a cliché is in fact a cliché.

6:00

The plan of The Dictionary of Received Ideas is to record over a period of ten years all the clichés that haunt our architectural design culture. We address precisely the material that has not been historicized, hence restricting the project to the past decade: in other words, clichés recent enough to haunt everyone's work without their being conscious. Not the allusion, the citation, or the witty comment, but that of which you are not aware, what goes through the work almost unnoticed. So in that respect, the project is as Alexander [D'Hooghe] was mentioning, a project of consciousness, not unlike traditional psychoanalytical therapy. The project is not about novelty, but about becoming aware. Awareness might eventually transform the way in which we do things.

We have relied on two definitions of the cliché. The often-used definition of the cliché is an idea that, following recurrent, use is depleted it of its original intensity. But in addition, we have defined the cliché in a slightly different way, in order to change the question. We also understand the cliché as a solution to a problem that has outlived the problem. The problem is no longer there, but the solution still lingers.

7:42

For example, in early spy films, villains usually had

two recurrent attributes. On the one hand, villains spoke in British English. This is still recurrent today. On the other hand, villains usually caressed cats. Interestingly enough, if you go back in history, you might speculate that the reason for this operation was that a director planned to introduce the villain at the beginning of the film, but without showing his face. So the director would frame the cat on his lap. The villain would appear, but his face would be left out of the frame, without looking unnatural. Arguably, this function has been lost. But films still have villains caressing cats for no reason, or for whatever other reason.

9:32

The goal of the Dictionary is to examine and to record all the design operations and conceptual strategies that are recurrent in our contemporary architecture culture. To that end, we produce two kinds of documents. On the one hand, we propose users' manuals, which, not unlike Flaubert, simply tell you what to do, step by step, in order to use a certain cliché in a project. On the other end, we propose genealogies of projects in order to situate the cliché within a certain history. That is, lineages of the inventions that were coined, and subsequently exploited and abused while also discarding their original function.

So, as opposed to, let's say, what Florian presented, this case of appropriation implies distrusting the material you use. In fact, these are clichés, and will take you in a direction you already know, and, which entails no promise. So you must misuse them, or *divert* them. They can become an ally precisely by being an opponent. Denise Scott Brown used to quote a line she heard from Louis Kahn: "you must hate it, hate it, hate it, until you love it."

Of course, this project was not formulated out of nothing. It was actually the by-product of a previous series of studios and seminars called *Under Constraint*, which I taught right before for ten consecutive semesters. The goal of that series was to examine the use of self-imposed constraints in architecture to open up alternative avenues of designing. It was again based on a literary precedent, in this case the work of Raymond Roussel, Raymond Queneau, and Georges Perec. It was also based on the Oulipo group, which set out to use mathematics in order to explore potential forms of literature. Those studios tested the use of constraints that are voluntary, and therefore arbitrary, so could potentially open up alternative ways for design, and, insofar, as they were voluntary, would disappear as the work appeared. Not unlike a scaffolding, as Raymond Queneau would say.

14:00

That studio series attempted to stage a conversation with the process-based studios that worked upon the notion of the diagram. In fact, we advanced a critique of prevalent design methodologies at the time, one based on inscribing a starting point, and following a prescribed series of steps towards a product. In other words, instead of exploiting the accidents triggered by the process, those design methodologies were concerned with validating outcomes. That is, they were defensive. They appropriated a number of techniques from the avant-gardes to stabilize, rather than to destabilize. In fact, the process had as a goal to exclude judgment. In our case, the starting point was arbitrary, so you could only assess what you had designed by looking outside the rules of the game, or by inscribing the work within a certain history. In that respect, I strongly identify with what Alexander mentioned at the beginning: that you understand your work by virtue of establishing lineages.

Interestingly enough, the outcome of using self-imposed constraints was not an alternative starting point for design, but the awareness of your design assumptions. (A critique of the diagram was admittedly one of the goals.) With a self-imposed constraint, you undermine your own abilities—as a writer, as a designer—and might in turn trigger a finding. You might become aware of the way in which you do things, then speculate on the way in which you could potentially do things.

In other words, the lesson of these studios was that in designing under self-imposed constraints you could become aware of the clichés wo which you resort. So I decided to start a new series of studios and seminars, which would operate in reverse, and begin by examining clichés. This is the project I have been working on since. It implies, on the one hand, charting the clichés we resort to and proposing manuals for their use, and, on the other, treating those manuals as 'found objects,' and using them or misusing them as design tools. That is, transforming those clichés into constraints. I will unfortunately not have the time to develop this last point. I will wrap up simply by saying that the Dictionary is a work in progress, and will soon be published as a collection of one hundred entries.

Collection
Michael Meredith

I just want to apologize to everyone who was there.
I meant to say something incredibly meaningful about
contemporary culture and about how we think about
architecture today, and instead I just showed a bunch of
pictures. The night before, I downloaded them into my
computer's 'My Pictures' collection, a digital landfill of
stockpiled images. At the time, they just seemed so much
more interesting and less work to explain. I don't even
like those pictures anymore. Well, not most of them.

I wasn't thinking clearly. Tumblrs have become a hab-
it, a late-night drug of choice: browsing, scrolling, caressing beautiful images with my disembodied cartoon hand.
I'm still recovering from those washed-out photographs
of buildings, floating casually next to half-dressed Italian
(maybe German?) models. Nobody seems to mind the
disjunction. They're not shocking. If anything, they have
a strangely soothing filmic quality: a mood, a familiar
sensibility of a 1980s sun-drenched Caribbean that never
really existed. The sound track would have an abundance
of reverb. Sitting in a dark room, watching the constant
stream of images grow upwards from the bottom of my
screen, they seem like an endlessly renewable resource.

There are pictures of our buildings next to graphic experiments, next to books, next to shoes, next to pixelated
animated gifs, next to pink ceramic coffee mugs, next to
new wave album covers, next to dead plants. I feel like
everyone has already seen them by now. Our work feels
out of place to me in that context, but there it is. As estab-
lishment figures in our field lament the end of plans and
the end of the discipline, everyone else is staring blankly
with their headphones on, scrolling through a dizzying array of images. Architecture casually floats on our screens.
It used to be about getting more work built or about being more relevant to culture; at present, it's about getting
more 'likes.'

Over the past century, architecture has recast and
repositioned itself through the representational media
of painting, photography, and digital modeling. Now, it
has to contend with Google searches, collecting, and the
phenomenon of image repositories like Tumblr, Pinterest,

1. Leo Steinberg, "The Flatbed Picture Company," in *Other Criteria: Confrontations with Twentieth Century Art* (Chicago: University of Chicago Press, 2007), 55-92.

Images: Image wall at MOS office

Instagram, Flickr, etc. Thinking about this eventually led me to return to Leo Steinberg's essay," The Flatbed Picture Plane," in which Steinberg considers Robert Rauschenberg's painting as a process of "world-making."[1] Rauschenberg's images accumulate on a horizontal rather than a vertical flatbed, resulting in painting's "eroding plane" and a new mode of representational legibility. Rereading the essay, it seemed to relate to how a reconsideration of architectural representation needs to take place.

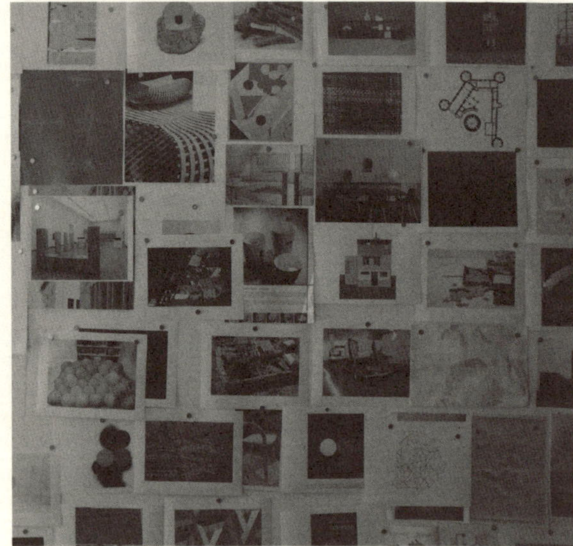

The visual act of collecting images has confused the intentionality, specific legibility, or 'meaning' of architectural representation to such a degree that plans and sections no longer have an orientation: they're just images. Everything has become flat. Inevitably, 'flat' comes across as Pop, Post-Modern or global, etc. But my use of the word isn't supposed to be ideological: it's just a reference to Steinberg's essay. The qualities of flatness and fadedness, like a Rauschenberg combine, have to do with the fleeting nature of architectural reception and production, which, in turn, translates to how we look at and make architecture. It's the current state of the discipline.

The stakes of image formatting should not be brushed off as simply a formal concern. There is nothing simple about it. As David Joselit has argued, formatting, defined

     Collection   Michael Meredith

as, "the capacity to configure data in multiple possible ways," becomes more pressing in our current age than discussions of medium-specificity.[2] For Joselit, format is as much a political issue as an aesthetic one, because the decision to present data as information presents an ethical dilemma in terms of what data is presented and how it is framed as intelligible, worthwhile, or important.[3] The shift in emphasis occurs not on the level of production, but on how we frame or format images.

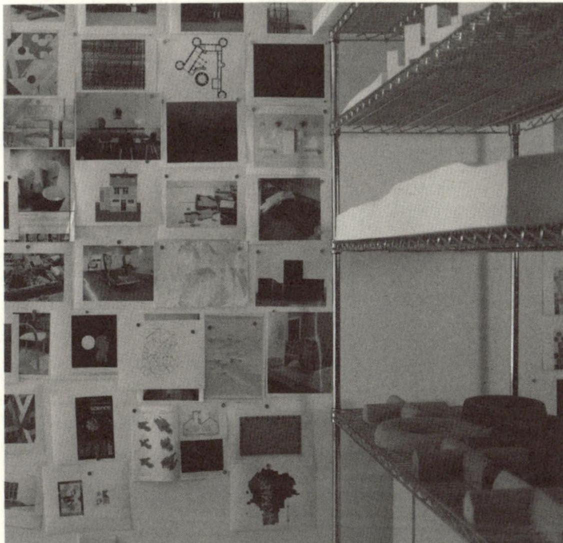

This connects to how the fundamental relationship between aesthetics and politics has been understood in architecture historically. It is, in some ways, more straightforward and more complex than questions of format alone. The primary project of architecture is the construction of subjectivity: a collective identity, an individual identity, or both. This facet of architecture's disciplinary power has empowered activist do-gooders and navel-gazing celebrity formalists alike, and it's what architects and their clients both wrestle with in design. Architecture, like art, presents itself as a value system, and those of us who care enough to discuss and fight for it use it as such.

The omnipresence of imagery and their formats has enabled images to be appropriated by anyone and every-

2. David Joselit, "What to Do with Pictures?," *October* 138 (Fall 2011): 82.

3. Joselit writes, "In digital economies, value accrues not solely from production—the invention of content—but from the extraction of meaningful patterns from profusions of existing content. As the term "data mining" suggests, raw data is now regarded as a "natural," or at least a naturalized, resource to be mined, like coal or diamonds. But unlike coal and diamonds, with their differing degrees of scarcity, data exists in unwieldy and ever-increasing quantities—it is harvested with every credit-card transaction, click of a cursor, and phone call we make. This reservoir of tiny, inconsequential facts, which is sublime in its ungraspable enormity, is meaningless in its disorganized state. Since such data is both superabundant and ostensibly trivial, what gives it value are the kinds of formats it can assume, which may be as wide-ranging

as marketing profiles and intelligence on terrorism. Such a shift from producing to formatting content leads to what I call the "epistemology of search," where knowledge is produced by discovering and/or constructing meaningful patterns—formats—from vast reserves of raw data, through, for instance, the algorithms of search engines like Google or Yahoo. Under these conditions, any quantum of data might lend itself to several, possibly contradictory, formats." Ibid.

one. Through the act of selecting, grouping, and tagging, we can project and create cultural and/or personal identities. In this way, everyone is a designer. Everyone has aesthetic affiliations and affections. Architecture is part of this widespread culture of collecting and curation. We are all collectors and curators of stuff. Our stuff defines us.

Curating, however, should not be synonymous with collage. Right now I think we are in a moment of curation that is distinctly different from previous collage models of the '80s and so on. Collage is a collection of fragments, with the emphasis on the seams, the frayed edges, the inconsistencies between pieces. It is surrealist in nature. Collage laments the fragmentation of the world, and the impossibility of the whole. Contemporary curation, on the other hand, is based on analogy and a unifying resonance. It collects wholes and celebrates their coexistence. If you like this, you will also like this. Tumblr bases itself on this model, and so does Amazon. Images maintain their identity and integrity within a collection, a universe made of tiny aesthetic planets, producing a simultaneity where discrete elements are flattened out. To use an architectural analogy, they function as windows into self-contained and simultaneous worlds.

Image: Image wall at MOS office

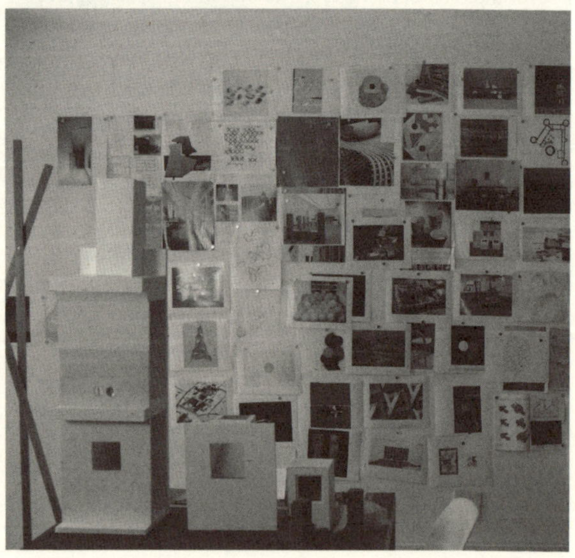

This erasure of difference exists everywhere. The quote-unquote market is fabricated around the assumption that people like to hang out with people who have the same interests, enjoy the same music, like the same food, share the same values, and debate these values within mutual references and pleasures. Likewise, the niche and genre system of contemporary art and architecture constructs camps that ultimately share ontological views. At best, architecture is a series of clubs that anyone can join, and within each of these clubs, value systems seem safe.[4] Once you construct the field through niches, the avant-garde narrative of difference and shock is harder to achieve since 'shocking' is just another one of these groups. Although difference exists everywhere, any antagonism, friction, or political position produced by this difference is neutralized, and thus marginalized within each niche.

The problem with architecture today is that some of these aforementioned clubs are more popular than others. Only a select few seem to be able to identify with an architecture that goes beyond basic necessity or the status quo and approaches something that aspires to be more polemical, symbolic, or critical. The upshot of this is that the discipline has lost its dependence on generating narratives, which has, in turn, invalidated traditional methods for analyzing and evaluating work beyond practical concerns. Despite the differences that are ubiquitous in the field, we struggle to articulate and discriminate between these differences because we no longer seem to place value on having a vocabulary to clearly distinguish camps and their agendas.

People used to discuss architecture through orthographic plans and projections, but now architectural ideas circulate mainly through images: photography, film, diagrams, and renderings. I used to think that photorealistic rendering devalued plans and sections, and perhaps it has, but it has become our disciplinary linguistic currency. Everyone engages architecture through photographs, and has for the past century and a half, but we now use renderings to produce photographs before we produce buildings. This has caused a definite shift in the way we look at architecture. Previously reserved for communicating ideas to clients, renderings have now become the

4. The clubs I'm thinking of are typically what I would consider 'medium' conditions of architecture: Math-nerd Geometric Formalists, Earnest Brooding Materialists, Urban Programmists, Political Activists, Erotic Phenomenologists, Parametric Pattern-makers, Silly Cartoonists,etc…

medium through which architects engage with buildings.

Architecture's playing field has eroded. The proliferation of images brought on by ever-changing technologies has fundamentally changed our relationship to architectural production and to architecture as a form of cultural practice. A culture that privileges the analogical flatness of a more or less routine model of curation over the antagonistic manifestos of ideological difference, newness, and so forth is dismantling previous value systems. Our failure to articulate these shifts has estranged us from the specific attributes of architecture as a medium. In order for architecture to propose meaningful difference in its state as a mashed-up discipline, we need to re-imagine how the apparatus of the Internet can function as a platform for a new format of architectural practice, one that may wholeheartedly reject these earlier polemical models without eschewing all semblances of meaning, ethics, or politics in the process. This would entail delving into a more critical examination of the current wave of curation that has overtaken us. We need to develop a more specific vocabulary to articulate the micro-differences that exist in the ways in which images are generated, talked about, and managed, and their resulting effects. Once the operations of collection and curation are understood as an extension of the architect's toolkit, I think we will be able to reassert a sense of agency for the discipline, to reclaim a kind of disciplinary specificity that seems to have been otherwise lost in the stockpile.

     Collection   Michael Meredith

**PANELISTS:
ALEXANDER D'HOOGHE,
FLORIAN IDENBURG,
MICHAEL MEREDITH,
ENRIQUE WALKER**

0:00 Michael Kubo: As I had hoped when I saw the four terms included in the panel, there are a series of themes and continuities that track nicely across the presentations. For the sake of efficiency, I will set out a question for each of you and we can go from there.

For Alexander [D'Hooghe], I want to deal with the question of ideology with which you started. For you, ideology re-actualizes history. Ideology appears at the moment when history becomes a burden and collapses onto us, when we encounter myths that we don't fully understand. Yet ideology and history are usually discussed in precisely the opposite manner. Ideology is what we inherit and what burdens us, whereas telling history differently has the capacity to free us. In fact, you leveraged history in your presentation in just this way. All of you deliberately introduced historical elements as potential liberating devices, appealing to them in order to construct new lineages in which you then placed yourselves. That method—for example, Alexander, the way you showed the work of Cedric Price and Herman Hertzberger—has itself become a canonical procedure in architectural discourse. You declare up-front that your first act involves curating a genealogy of affinities that allows the audience to situate you and your work, to receive and interpret it in a particular way. I would like you to discuss this idea of affinities as you have set it out here, as opposed to your idea of myth, the burdensome thing that limits you. How do you see the difference between these two?

Florian [Idenburg], I have a similar question in relation to what you proposed as the confessional mode of your presentation, but which ended up as being not so confessional. Having offered us a confessional as the setup, you proceeded with a lecture about a particular historical moment in the 1990s in Holland. You claimed that while the SuperDutch moment came to revolve around the diagram, there was initially a play of allusions operative within it that was gradually forgotten. Once this play of allusions fell out of it, the remaining discourse ended up coalescing around the topic of the diagram, becoming much less robust as an historical moment for that reason, and eventually ending. Are you framing your work as a recapture of this elusive moment? That would again repeat the method of identifying a genealogy for yourself and saying: "This is a history of things which are good or interesting, and I am now the inheritor of this lineage." This strikes me as a positioning argument rather than as a confessional statement.

I would also like Enrique [Walker] to take on this question of the diagram, which came up in both Florian's and Michael Meredith's talks, as well. The diagram has been circulating through all of these presentations. Enrique, in your project, you use the question of the cliché to first identify the diagram as the thing that has become burdensome, overwrought, mythologized. But you want to invert these negative readings, to work that diagram, that cliché, to the point where you can push through it—hate it, hate it, hate it until you love it, but now in a different way. I wonder if you have a position on Florian's framing of the diagram as forming the center of a certain discourse, but which can also end that discourse past a certain point.

Having declared at the outset of the conference that we don't want to discuss influence in terms of anxiety, there has been a certain kind of anxiety tracking through this panel. There is a tension between the notion of the imprisonment or burden of history on the one hand, and of its liberating potential on the other hand. Leveraging historical things or the data that surrounds us can be a way of breaking out of a certain set of constraints. We could try to place each one of you on that line.

So my question for Michael Meredith would be, how does one do that? You seem to have anxieties not just about the ways that you accumulate and consume information, but also about how information about your own work gets inserted into that cloud of data, in spite of yourself, without you wanting it to. If the first three presentations were all about strategies for crafting a deliberate project using historical references, building yourself into that history and that history into your own work, then

Michael, you are suggesting that we have to contemplate the other side of that procedure, which creates a vapor trail around whatever one does, in order to control the way that data slips into the stream. This gets back to Mario Carpo's discussion from yesterday about the Google world in which data is generated beyond our ability to control it. What do we do if that leaves us outside of the mode in which all of us are accustomed to giving presentations about our deliberately crafted programs? Michael, you seem to suggest that these programs run in some sense without us and that we don't matter much within them.

7:12 Alexander D'Hooghe: I enter architecture through the urban project. Two main representations of any urban project are the urban plan and the perspective, which contain typically a few buildings, public spaces, and some form of nature. The burden, the imprisonment, the incredible sadness that overcomes one when seeing one master plan or perspective after another, the endless repetition of the same few ingredients. Nature, community, and progress form a triad of dominant myths, which are basically childlike dreams about things that will make our world better, recur with their assorted aesthetic apparatuses. Insofar as I and my office enter architecture through the urban project, our work is in part at least an attempt to find ways to get beyond that. An urban plan has to appeal to and please many people. It's not just for one private client, you have to appeal to a large and diverse audience. Whether that means that the urban plan has to be reduced to an utterly depressing banality or not is a question I'd like to address through architecture, and by engaging with other histories that might allow for a way out. So the depression, or the heaviness of ideology and myth, have to do with these three main terms that structure almost any urban project, of which we have to get out.

8:54 Kubo: I want to pick a little more at this question of breaking out, because it seems that you are now reverting to the notion of ideology as something that constrains and limits. So ideology and myth are now what burdens one to repeat inherited or received ideas for urban plans, for example. But when you introduced ideology and affinity in your presentation as a setup for your own work, you used them in exactly the opposite way from what you are saying now. Your reading of the 'ugly big box' you showed as a kind of secretly realized Potteries Thinkbelt, for example, is what allowed you to avoid simply repeating the big box and produce a plan which internalizes both the historical precedent and the present condition. Isn't that procedure the opposite of the argument you are now making about ideology?

09:56 D'Hooghe: But we are still condemned to the big box, or some variation of it. Given the fact that both vanguard's and mass-market commercial procedures lead to the same result, it's something you can't escape from. From the acceptance comes a certain potential playfulness.

10:30 Florian Idenburg: I'm going to share something else that might contribute more generally to what we are talking about. OMA's Kunsthal opened twenty years ago, and I recently had to write a piece for a magazine revisiting the building from the contemporary perspective. In re-looking at it, and in part because I didn't fully understand it during my student years, I realized that it allows for complex and layered readings, which far exceed, and cannot be captured by the way we consume architectural information today. I think Michael Meredith and I are very similar. We at SO-IL also have an archive full of images that we consume voraciously. Today, when we absorb architectural images in a matter of seconds, a project like the Kunsthal, if we slow down to contemplate its complexity, seems impossible to exceed. The rise of diagrammatic architecture is obviously coinciding with the rise of the way we are consuming architecture through imagery. I was nostalgic thinking about Kunsthal. How could we reintroduce as rich an architectural language and intelligence as that? So this may be one anxiety, or wonder, or desire I have. Alexander speaks about the construction of myths, which I am interested in, but at the same time we work much more intuitively. Our work is not constructed so self-consciously. It absorbs all these various elements that surround us and in some way influence us.

12:20 Idenburg: While I was in Japan at SANAA, we won the competition for the New Museum. The design initially was overly diagrammatic. One box, one shift, one

               Moderator: Michael Kubo

program—a very clear but 'ugly' building. We spent a substantial effort essentially disguising the clarity of that diagram. In the process, I realized that there were things to be said that are not always, or only, direct and obvious, things that can allude to meaning beyond them and invite for multiple readings. This is something that we at SO-IL are interested in now: layering and introducing different references. Also, my partner, Jing Liu, is from China, and brings completely different things than I do to the table. We are not forcing a referential mess at SO-IL, it just sort of happens.

13:49 Kubo: I wonder then how we should take the message that you ended on by [Kazuyo] Sejima, in your last slide: "basically we do not refer." Are you setting up this idea up for a fall? It seems now that you are saying it is impossible not to refer. In the simple sense, we refer to things all the time. I want to pick up on something that Michael Meredith brought up, as well: the tension between wanting to reintroduce allusions into one's work and the alternate idea that allusions creep into things whether we want them to or not. No matter how deliberate one tries to be, they exist in and of themselves, beyond our control, to the point that one can say with a straight face: "basically we do not refer," even though that's patently false in practice. So what was the meaning of that last slide?

14:56 Idenburg: That was irony, basically.

15:10 Michael Meredith: I have a question for Enrique. For years I have been hearing about this project, The Dictionary of Received Ideas. And it always sounds amazing to me. As you were presenting it, I was thinking, one, I can't wait to see it (you're always sort of hiding it) and, two, when you talk about your hopes for it, I wonder if you are trying to recreate conditions for a type of modernism—an environment for cultivating a Shklovsky-esque Russian formalism. When you say you are trying to make your students "write a novel without the letter E," how do you save it from becoming another cliché? Or, can one escape the cliché nowadays?

16:04 Enrique Walker: You don't escape. I will try to answer Michael Kubo's question while answering Michael Meredith's as well. I think the whole project is one of awareness, and not one of novelty. First, you're aware of what's haunting your work, and it's important to mention that this is only a studio project, and has to do with the way in which students design. When I started doing this project, I was interested in doing what Flaubert intended, which was blocking everyone. In other words, you show so much of what's around that any producer is immediately paralyzed; most of the things one would usually resort to are out of bounds. So instead of presenting a sort of catalogue of sensibility, as in say the "Parallels Between Art and Life," which is sort of a "These are a Few of my Favorite Things" catalogue, you produce precisely the opposite. So these collected clichés then are a number of things that are there being purposefully depleted, which makes it possible to use them, and work on them—as long as one is conscious of the fact that they have been depleted.

17:20 Meredith: But do you think that still holds true today? Because it assumes that the intent of the author is to produce novelty to begin with. Let's say nowadays, maybe, that's not the intent—that the archive, and the endless imagery may be just part of the stream of images, as opposed to somehow really different from it.

20:00 Walker: The project of clichés is not really a search for novelty. It instead recognizes a very straightforward argument, that there are a number of design arguments that are simply solutions to certain problems.

20:12 Meredith: But to feel blocked by the cliché, to feel that frustration, you must already have the desire to exceed the cliché.

20:22 Walker: Right. Well, but I think the question of newness is somehow unavoidable, because as soon as you re-engage (even) a cliché, it turns into a different thing. So the question is one of awareness. In that respect, I think the cliché project is very psychoanalytical. It doesn't promote a cure, becuase there is no cure, simply awareness. Through awareness, you can say, "Look, I will work with this cliché," but as soon as you do, and you understand it as a cliché, you inevitably misread it and misuse it, because you are aware of the fact that you have to use it to a certain end. So the whole point is a very traditional question of understanding design as proven by problems.

I like to describe the function of cliché via the story

               Moderator: Michael Kubo

of wine bottles that used to be laid down horizontally to keep their corks wet. As soon as the cork was made of plastic, the procedure of laying the bottles down horizontally no longer needed to happen, but this continued to be the way the bottles were handled. It is not a question of novelty, "Let's arrange the bottles in a different way," but basically understanding that design techniques address specific problems. As soon as the problem is no longer there, you have to formulate other design operations. I am interested in defining design operations as strategies. Strategy may be the most abused word of the '90s, but a strategy is really the way in which you approach a given problem—though it was never that back then.

21:58 Idenburg: But it can also be the opposite if the cliché actually becomes useful again. I think this notion of novelty versus appropriateness is very interesting. The fact that maybe something didn't work at a certain time, but now it becomes appropriate again, which is maybe what Alexander is also arguing: that some typologies become appropriate again, or can be reinterpreted anew.

I was also wondering, does everyone look at Archive of Affinities? Is that something that everybody 'Tumbles'? Do you know Archive of Affinities? The Tumblr, Andrew Kovacs at UCLA....

22:58 Meredith: He had this big change recently where he started to insert his own work into it. And I don't know if that's a good move.

23:03 Idenburg: Well, Andrew Kovacs of Archive of Affinities researches archives. He travels to Eastern Europe to copy old archives and then feeds his found images to the web as direct responses to new, contemporary projects. So as soon as MVRDV shows their Jakarta proposition, he starts to feed some sort of Ukrainian archive from 1930s to say that it has already been done. So the archive is in this case a defense mechanism, which pushes out clichés as a response to their contemporary variation.

23:45 Kubo: But that's what I mean by "the moment of revelation." When you go through your Tumblr and get to the [Frank] Gehry house and say, "maybe all of our house work comes out of the Gehry house and we never knew it," you are suggesting that architectural ideas and influences are actually residues that have accumulated and densified, and that there can be a moment when they suddenly jump out of the archive and "hit" you. This hit comes with the revelation that the idea wasn't new, but you weren't aware of that fact because it was embedded there as a residue and could not be called out as anything else. Enrique's project is about playing up that loop of revelation in a more explicit way.

4:25 Meredith: At one point, though the archive was a kind of academic project, it was a thing that was policed. Now the archive is outside. I gave Andrew [of Archive of Affinities] a copy of *Log* that had I worked on, and he said "Oh, how many copies do they produce of this?" And I said "Oh I don't know, it's like two or three thousand," and he said "You know, I got 10,000 hits yesterday on my blog." The archive now is outside of the policed space of the academy, and I think that's an interesting moment for all of us. I think part of our job now—one that we are not accomplishing so well, and I include myself here—is to construct new narratives and new meaning. It is just not happening. You could do it through the historical mode, but I don't think enough people are really dealing with the contemporary, even the contemporary via the historical.

25:58 Meredith: Sam [Jacob], you wrote recently for Dezeen (you're now like the Dezeen critic) something about the incontinence of Photoshop. I just saw a pink square, with your head, and "Sam Jacob says Photoshop incontinence is everywhere." And I thought, that's interesting, but I still don't know how you get out of that one.

26:20 Sam Jacob: So I've got this new job as a columnist on Dezeen, which is obviously a very important role. And I decided that my first column would be about how terrible Dezeen is and all it has done to us. I was saying that Dezeen is incontinence, endless vomit of stuff, but it is constipated at the same time. It's as though everything is falling out at the same time but nothing can move on simultaneously. And I didn't know what to do about that, and I didn't offer any solution to it, but we have to accept that that is how we consume architectural culture, design culture, and so on. And this mode of architectural culture is nothing like going to the museum,

            Moderator: Michael Kubo

or reading a magazine, it is no longer anything like what it has been historically.

Then the question is what do we do, now that that incontinence is the format: a press release, which gets regurgitated onto the front page of a website, for maybe a day max, and then it's gone. In some ways, I think the key issues is to consider how one constructs images. Imagery operates in that environment while successfully representing other issues as well. So maybe that's the multi-valent reading that you were talking about Florian, which can operate as "Oh my God, wow!" as you scroll past for two seconds, but on the other hand is also a complex building that will be there for many years.

There's no point in resisting the 'Dezeen-ification' of architectural culture, there's no way you're going to succeed if you can't get your work on Dezeen. But at the same time, if it is consumed by the culture, it won't survive anyway, because the voracious appetite of digital communication will eat you up. So you have to both be able to provide this realm of architectural communication with the meat it wants to eat, but give it enough gristle that it doesn't get completely digested.

29:00 Kubo: Anyone else?

29:12 John McMorrough: I want to just thank the panel. I think that the A through C grouping [Affinity, Allusion, Cliché, Collection] may be the most coherent. The talks really related quite well. You could sort of divide the table, between the "know your sources to overcome them" half [D'Hooghe, Walker], and the "always forgetting to make new" half [Idenburg, Meredith]. Maybe it is just the way that Ana [Miljački] has set up the conference, but the framework of each of the discussions in this panel has been about authorial strategies. And I wonder if there are ways in which the affinity, or the allusion, or the collection might have another valence if you were to examine them through the lens of reception, or possible audience: that is not an audience of designers, or the disciplinary drawing room about which we talked today. So when you talk about the clichés, Enrique, a cliché in architecture within the last ten years is fascinating, because those clichés are probably not built in the period in which they generate their cliché.

So I'm wondering what is the sense of audience here?

Would these clichés play out differently, as you imagine them, when received by an audience outside of the field?

30:45 Walker: I appreciate the question. And I am particularly interested in the reception within the field. I'm obsessed with the question of rebuilding the discussion within the field, which is why I am interested in this conference. As you rightly said, the clichés proliferate through other media besides buildings. But the project I am working on right now is restricted to the field of architecture and indeed the authorial problem of how one designs.

31:30 D'Hooghe: To Enrique's point, the most interesting thing about Dezeen and the proliferation of imagery is that it really does exhaust the ability to ever be new. Whatever you do is already captured by the virtue of the 450 by 700 pixel image, which does not propel you forward to some kind of vanguard victory. You can't innovate, it's no longer possible. But actually that brings a really big question. It was really important for designers, and for designers' egos, to propel work forward. So if that falls away—if you cannot innovate, if you cannot be new, and if you can't differentiate yourself—what is the purpose of design?

32:19 Meredith: I want to revisit one thing about the cliché project: it may produce self-awareness, which we all try to do as teachers, but it doesn't produce a value system. It's hard to come out of it saying something is better or worse. You've produced awareness, you can say, "that's more aware, or less aware," I guess, but you can't really judge. If all of a sudden we judge projects only through intent, we might end up really off the mark, because that's not how the rest of the world is judging them. Dezeen, for example doesn't care so much about intent. So I think this is the most pressing issue: we still have to produce an appropriately contemporary value system.

Doppelgänger
Sam Jacob

DOPPELGÄNGER

The term 'doppelgänger' is a term Ines Weizman and I have been using in our research at the Architectural Association into the strange world of architectural copies.[1] The doppelgänger is different from a straightforward copy. It's a myth. It's the story of your own double walking amongst us, someone who looks and acts just like you. It's the story of the effect that this doubled version of yourself has on the world. In Dostoevsky's novel *The Double*, for example, the doppelgänger brings such psychic collapse to an otherwise humble and ordinary clerk, such confusion over identity, meaning, authenticity, such doubt, and then despair, that the poor 'original' is destroyed.[2]

The myth runs that encountering your doppelgänger presages your imminent demise. And that's why it seems to have such resonance within the discipline of architecture. The idea, the threat even, of the copy is such an apparent anathema that it seems to signify the death of many of the things we value within the core of architectural culture: authorship, identity, truth, authenticity, for example.

But, of course, a counterargument runs that copying is central to architectural culture. Historically, copying was the means by which architecture became a language, and was disseminated, as well as created.

Nonetheless, the architectural copy is nowadays characterized as an enemy of progress, as inauthentic, as *pastiche*, as fake, as a dead end of invention, with originality being the prized goal of architecture. The point is that there are other, more productive ways of thinking of meeting your doppelgänger than death.

These ideas about the power of the copy, the significance of the copy, and how the copy has become something in and of itself was explored in a project for the 2012 Venice Biennale titled The Museum of Copying.[3]

It takes as its start point the Villa Rotunda, the Ur Example of the architectural copy, both the result and the source of copying. The Villa Rotunda itself is composed of copies, of references stuck together to create a new typology. Its bi-symmetrical plan can even be read as reflecting itself, so that its total form is made up of copies of itself.

1. http://pr2013.aaschool.ac.uk/research-clusters/architectural-doppelgangers/

2. For a digital version of The Double visit: http://en.wikipedia.org/wiki/The_Double_(Fyodor_Dostoyevsky_novel)

3. http://fffff.at/the-museum-of-copying-by-fat-at-venice-architecture-biennale/

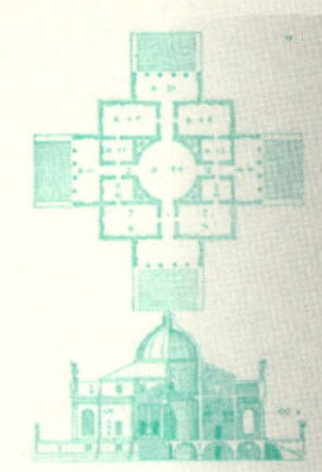

Reference: Original Villa plans (http:// en.wikipedia. org/wiki/Villa_ Capra_%22La_Ro- tonda%22)

4. http://sketchup .google.com/3d warehouse/search? q=villa+rotunda&s typ=m&scoring=t& btnG=Search

It's a building that has been copied again and again, often within the historical canon of architecture, and often in ways that have helped project architecture forward. In England, for example, it became a way of the English Baroque taking hold in the form of Chiswick House. The Villa then displays the way a copy both refers to the past, and also projects culture and propels it forwards.

For the project, we became interested in other kinds of copies of the Villa, especially Google's 3-D Warehouse where we found a whole range of amateur SketchUp Models of the Villa Rotunda.[4] The models vary wildly in accuracy, skill and resolution.

The model we downloaded had been, at that time, downloaded about 20,000 times. This is in itself a strange idea, that 20,000 copies of a digital copy of the Villa were sitting on hard drives around the world.

And of course, it's significant that it was a shareware model, which has its own kind of legality in relation to copying. So importantly, our starting point was not only a building designed by somebody else, but a model of that building made by a third party.

This source set a tone. Throughout the project, we were interested in an idea of process as concept, of developing a way in which the project's fabrication could relate directly to the act of making a copy.

Running through the process is the idea of transmission: the fact that you take one thing and, as you move it to another media or another technology, from digital to physical, it both loses a certain amount of information and gains something else through the process.

The installation comprised two parts. First, a CNC mold of a quarter of the Villa was routed into polystyrene blocks from the original model. The blocks were resin coated and assembled to form the mold. Then a cast was taken by spraying expanding polyurethane foam into the mold.[5]

The installation acted as a visible documentation of the process. In its fabric, we could see how Palladio was transmitted to the SketchUp model, how the digital model was transmitted to physical form, and how the mold was transmitted to the cast. Together, the elements displayed the process of manufacturing the copy, each part displaying the transformation of the subject by the process.

5. http://www.fash- ionarchitecture- taste.com/2012/08/ villa_rotunda_ redux.html

     Doppelgänger   Sam Jacob

The arrangement of cast and mold displayed qualities of positive and negative, interior and exterior. The Villa's form was only faintly echoed in the outside of the mold, with its steel framing, fiberglass coatings, and air-vent pipes. The inside of the mold was entirely accurate yet inverted, the exterior surface of the Villa turned inside out.

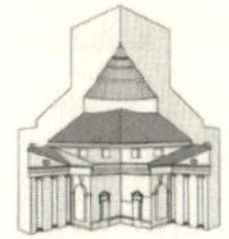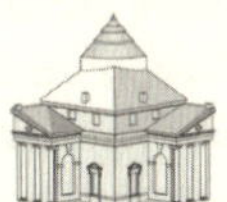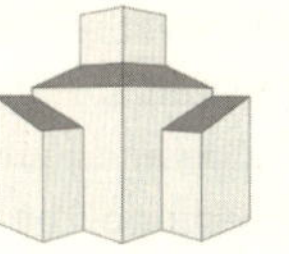

The exterior of the cast displayed its fidelity to the Villa, while its interior resembled a gloopy cave, a record of the spraying process that produced the cast.

The arrangement talked about the transformations of the elements themselves: playing with strange versions of symmetry and reflection, inverting interior and exterior. Columns, which are usually solid, structural things, became the opposite in the mold; they became absences.

You walked from the exterior, which was an exterior, to an exterior, which is an interior, to an interior, which is an exterior, and so on. All of the parts of the process were laid out in front of you at a visceral, experiential scale.

There was a quality in the installation's 'quartered' state that also referred to Palladio's drawing of the Villa, that sectional elevation where you see outside and inside simultaneously. The project, then as a representation of the Villa, also mimicked the original representation of the building.

Though it was ostensibly a copy of the Villa Rotunda, it was also a copy of many other things. There was an element of Aldo Rossi, of David Greene, of Archigram's spray polyurethane houses, of the amazing cross-sectional model of San Carlo alle Quattro Fontane all present in the project. The Villa Rotunda might not have been the content of the project at all, but rather the form. It could be argued that it was about something else entirely: about the way all architecture is saturated in reference, precedent, and, yes, copying, too.

Through projects like this, I think we refute the disciplinary anxiety over the copy. For example, the making of a copy is far from shallow, or easy. It demands first that you look incredibly closely at the subject that you wish to copy. The copy is a product, a physical object, that embodies the knowledge and understanding of the thing you've been looking at.

We can also say that the manufacturing of a copy is a project in and of itself, separate from its source. How you copy something becomes a technical issue, a site, often of innovation. There's an amazing story about a Rolex watch seized at Hong Kong customs. Customs officers opened it up and found that the inside was entirely made from bamboo. The technical ingenuity to make a working Rolex out of bamboo is of course way more valuable, way more 'original' than the original.

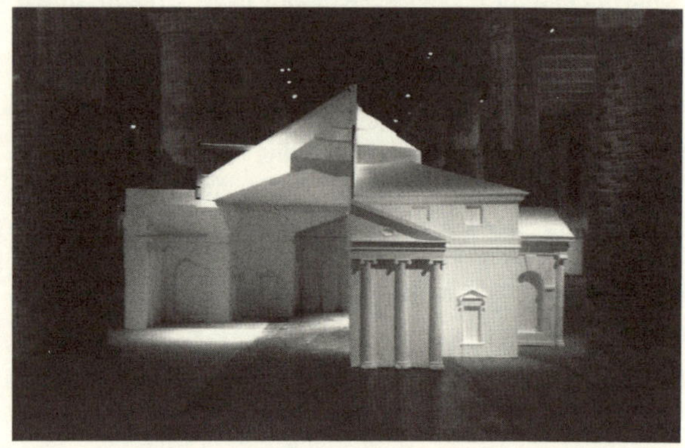

Image: Installation view of Villa Rotunda full-scale cast and mold models

The desires that motivate the production of a copy rewrite the meaning of that object. Take Villa Rotunda: every time it has been copied, it has taken on a different meaning, become a representative of a different culture. These differences become encoded into the replica. Which means the copy can be both exactly the same and radically different from its source. The copy can carry a whole set of ideas not present in the original. In this process of transformation, the copy can act as a cultural response, something that gains new political and ideological meanings.

My last point is something that perhaps explains part of the fear of the copy. Copying is dangerously fertile. Indeed the etymology of the word copy takes us back to cornucopia, the horn of plenty from which an endless flow of produce emerges. We could also think of the mold in its definition as a matrix: that is, to say, as situation or

surrounding substance within which something else orig-
inates. This has biological resonances, too, of the womb
and of formative cells. If the copy then is a fertile flow, we
can understand the fear it generates, or why, for example,
we need controls in the form of legal protections that
help guard against the rapacious nature of the copy.

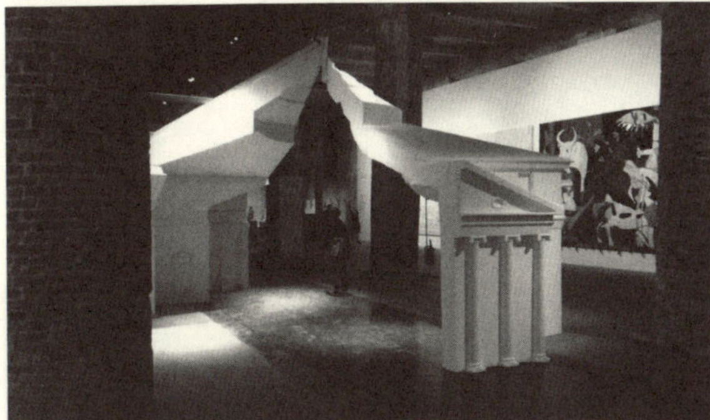

Image: Installa-
tion view of Villa
Rotunda full-scale
cast and mold
models

Replica
Cristina Goberna
& Urtzi Grau

0:00 Cristina Goberna

The concept of *replica* for us bears a double-meaning: it designates both a literal reproduction of a preexisting work and, in Romance Languages, the word denotes a response to a previous statement.

Urtzi Grau

The double meaning of the concept of replica has potential implications in the production of architecture, in architectural pedagogy, in the legal status of architecture, and in the conceptualization of public space. Can we reproduce a work of architecture that already exists and, by doing so, put forward a new position? In other words, can we produce *agonistic copies*?

Goberna

In what follows, we present four hypotheses about the possible implications of agonistic copies and four examples through which we have tested their effects.

1:06 Grau

First hypothesis (and bear with me, because the drama of doing a series of lectures about copies is that they start to look alike): we can use appropriations, blueprints, camouflage, carbon copies, clones, confidence-men, cons, copies, counterfeits, couples, deceits, deceptions, decoys, delusions, détournements, disguises, doubles, doppelgängers, duplicates, duplicities, duets, emulation, facsimiles, fakes, falsifications, forgeries, frauds, generics, illusions, imitations, impersonations, likenesses, look-alikes, mash-ups, masks, masquerades, mirages, mirror images, mock documentaries, models, monkeys, montages, mystifications, objet-trouvé, palimpsests, para-fictions, parallels, parodies, parrots, pastiches, phonies, photocopies, re-appropriations, recycling, reenactments, remakes, remixes, replicas, reproductions, satire, shadow plays, Siamese twins, similarities, simulacra, smokescreens, subtitles, transcriptions, translations, tricks, twins, and voice-overs to produce architecture.

As with any other creative discipline, architecture is subject to a regime of originality. Yet, operations that rely on already produced forms such re-appropriation, détournement, objet-trouvé, mash-up, or para-fiction, which are well known critical tools in a wide range of artistic productions, remain unobserved and even taboo in architecture.

1:47

In fact, while imitation and reproduction are the obvious root of the last 20—not to say the last 600—years of excess of architectural shapes, the field has resisted openly embracing copies. In so doing, it has hindered its potential. To intentionally copy entails a radical reformulation of architectural imagination. It allows for a renunciation of form-making, since form is defined a priori, in order to focus on architectural knowledge yet to be discovered.

2:21

We have tested this notion in our practice and will describe a specific example that was part of an exhibition (invoked earlier in the Symposium): the portion of the Biennial in Shenzhen a year ago, titled The Street, and curated by Terence Riley. It was an incredible exhibition, first of all, because one could witness how architects have smoothly moved from a serious interest in the façade to a critical embrace of the possibility of not having façades at all. We discovered that our proposal was answering the curatorial provocation, but doing it by chance. We were initially interested in producing a façade that was not ours, but a re-use of someone else's.

3:31

We chose to take the façade of a building that had been demolished a few months before: the façade of Ai Weiwei's studio in Shanghai. We found people in China who provided us with some of its pieces, and we exhibited them. In the exhibit, the façade not only blocked the possibility of seeing what was behind it, but it was also not our own. It worked as a replica: that is, a literal reproduction and as a clear answer to the curatorial provocation. It was simultaneously an original façade in the exhibition of façades a political response to the demolition of Ai Weiwei's studio by the Chinese government.

Goberna:

Second Hypothesis: replicas are operative in architectural pedagogy. When we talk about 'agonism', we are invoking Chantal Mouffe's "Artistic Activism and Agonistic Space", and transposing to architecture her conclusions about contemporary art.[1] For instance, in order to produce architecture that can possibly instigate dissidence

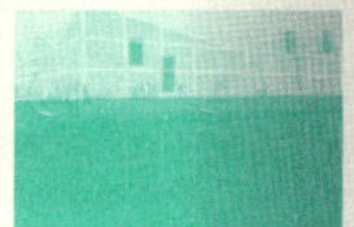

Reference: Ai Weiwei's demolished Shanghai studio. (http://www.foreignpolicy.com/articles/2010/11/08/the_party_goes_on)

1. See for example, Chantal Mouffe, "Artistic Activism and Agonistic Spaces" *Art and Research,* vol 1 & 2 (Summer 2007), accessed January 22, 2014, http://www.artandresearch.org.uk/v1n2/mouffe.html.

Replica

Cristina Goberna
& Urtzi Grau

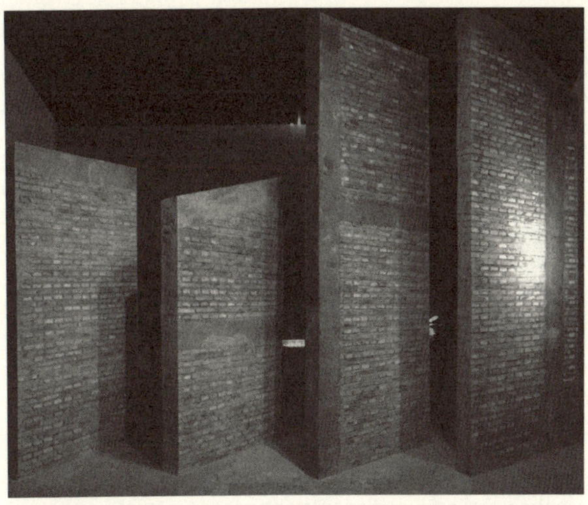

or resistance, we should avoid the formats used by the avant-gardes at the beginning of the 20th century and the neo-avant-gardes of the '60s. That is, the rejection of past and current conditions is necessary in order to propose a new order of things.

5:17

The avant-garde model is no longer relevant as we know its production has been eagerly absorbed, neutralized, and banalized by the market. To get to an architecture that proposes any kind of resistance, we cannot negate the present or the past. An architecture of resistance should not be antagonistic, but agonistic, and it should not propose something new, but always copy.

6:03

We apply these principals in architectural pedagogy. In one of the first lessons that we teach, students learn, through a high number of short exercises, to construct a critique, to highlight specific polemics that certain buildings raise, and to design corrections for these questions to be unveiled, intensified, or solved, establishing, by doing so, agonistic discussions about current architectural conditions. The second point challenges the notion of originality, with the students copying existing city analysis and buildings. In other words, the students are confronted with the idea of *Agonistic Copies*, that is, with the possibility of raising currently relevant architectural questions through copying.

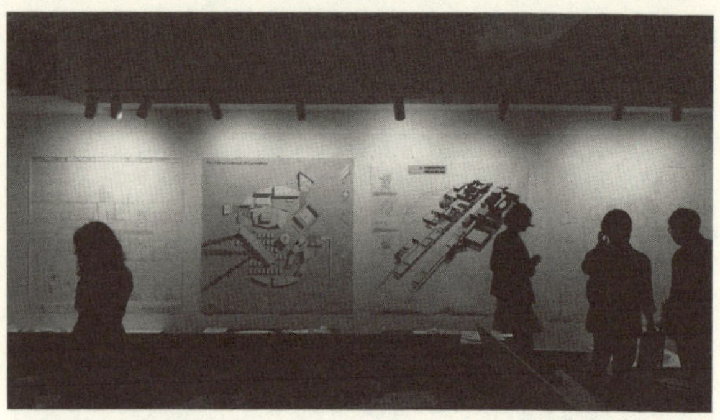

6:53 Grau

Third hypothesis: architecture is probably the creative field in which the flow of knowledge is less regulated.

In distinction from other creative fields, the use of architectural knowledge remains mainly unregulated. Architectural plagiarism, quotations, or paraphrasing have neither clear definitions nor legal repercussions. However, the inclusion of architecture in the USA 1999 Copyright Act—or the more recent case in 2007 in which Santiago Calatrava successfully sued Bilbao's municipality because it changed one of his bridges by adding a pedestrian pathway without his permission—is endangering this condition of architecture.

Preserving the open status of architectural property in the field, requires exploring legal protocols and defining operations of copy that won't stop the flow of architectural knowledge. Intellectual property has not yet been defined legally in the field of architecture, but we are in the position to do that right now and are exploring ways to do so.

For example, for a competition we just won in Medellín [Colombia], the new National Velodrome, we found a pretty simple solution. We are basically building a massive public square. As you probably know, Medellín is undergoing a massive renovation of its environment. After the recent dark years of drug trafficking, any new offering of public space is immediately taken over and occupied by Medellín's citizens. When we were asked to build and design a velodrome, we decided to devise a massive cantilever that would essentially define a public space. Its temporary façade would appear only in order to enclose the building during periods of competitions. The rest of

Cristina Goberna
& Urtzi Grau

the time, the square simply would have an apparatus on the top. Its roof structures would take the form of basic masts holding up compression rings, which would also be held in tension by cables.

But it was important for us to design these elements so that we could simultaneously define a velodrome and give the city the right to use or misuse the masts and reproduce them throughout the city. This technology includes a climatic system, illumination, and a series of technological devices that intensify and potentially produce public space. We thought that we should allow the city to reproduce the mast element, but, at the same time, do it in an orderly way. So, we are in the process of trying to sign the contract to define this design as some sort of creative commons, a design that the City Hall will be able to reproduce.

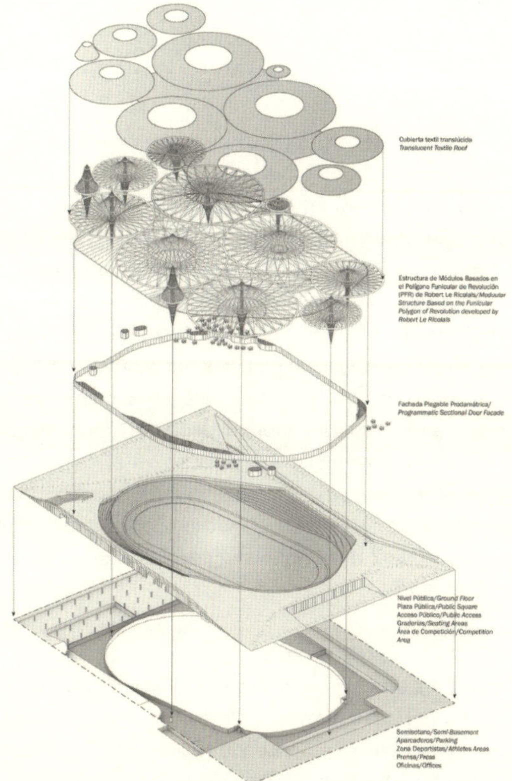

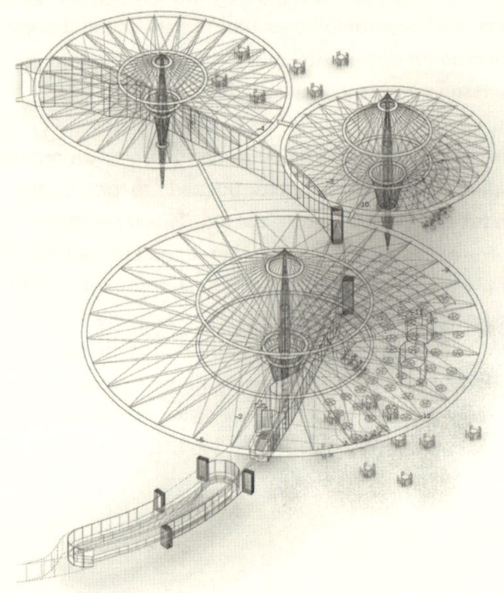

Goberna

Fourth hypothesis: replicas are instrumental in the construction of public space.

When we talk about public space, we talk about *agonistic public space*. Agonistic public space is not a space of comfort; it's not a space for enabling consumerism, it doesn't foster any kind of consensus; it is not designed as a 'nice' space for the well-being of the citizens; it doesn't need to have good intentions; it is not motivated by the desire to do the right thing or create a better city. An agonistic public space should unveil what is repressed by the dominant consensus and should give voice to what is silenced by the prevalent hegemony. It is a space that includes latent polemics and creates friction and discomfort, a space that does not make people contemplate but hopefully think.

11:34

So the construction of an agonistic public space involves the architect as a public intellectual, someone who, through giving certain information to the citizens, offers them tools to practice the ancient art of *replica*, enabling thus their transformation from passive observ-

Cristina Goberna
& Urtzi Grau

ers to active agents, because, quoting Chantal Mouffe, "contrary to what neo-liberal ideologists would like us to believe, political questions are not mere technical issues to be resolved only by experts."[2]

12:04

We applied the idea of the construction of an agonistic public space and the need to recover the role of the architect as a public intellectual to our publishing and editorial activities. We were invited to edit an issue of *The New City Reader*, the newspaper of the Istanbul Design Biennial.[3] The theme of the Istanbul Design Biennial was 'Adhocracy.' One could interpret Adhocracy to mean a network of designers dedicated to working with open sourcing, refusing mass production, and ultimately making products that are not market driven. Yet the institutional framework of the biennial could be understood as the betrayal of the very concept of Adhocracy. We wondered what an open source process was doing in a museum for which you had to buy a ticket. We asked, could we display processes without transforming them into exhibition objects?

13:15

In response to our own question and to the Biennale invitation, we edited *The New City Reader* No. 8, titled "Adhocracy: An Obituary," inviting every designer that had work exhibited in the biennial to write a very simple set of instructions of how to copy or replicate his or her

2. Ibid.

3. *The New City Reader* archive is available online, http://newcityreader.net/ (last accessed on January 22, 2014).

Image: Unfolded issue of *The New City Reader* plastered to public wall as 'billboard' piece by the public. We worked with a publicist to design a campaign using the unfolded pages of our issue of *The New City Reader*. Finally, we organized a global network of people interested in pinning up our 'billboards' on the streets of Istanbul, Los Angeles, New York, Madrid, Sao Paulo, Cartagena, Rotterdam, Madrid, and many others. Thus, our campaign presented the instructions for reproducing works from the Istanbul Design Biennial to the citizens of each of these cities.

& Urtzi Grau

Replica

Cristina Goberna
& Urtzi Grau

Revision
Amanda Reeser Lawrence

STIRLING SEEING AGAIN

On the one hand, to revision suggests an improvement or a correction—think of revisions to a text, in which the argument is made more clear, or the language more smooth. Yet to revision also suggests an illicit or problematic violation of the past. The revisionist historian has manipulated the facts to her own aims or according to her own biases, obscuring the truth.[1]

In all cases, the act of revision acts violently and decisively on a chosen past. Unlike copying or mimicry, in which the original must remain more or less intact or at least recognizable in the later version, with revision comes an expectation that the original is deformed or altered somehow.

To revision, then, is not simply to change, but to 're-see,' to fundamentally reconceptualize and reconsider.[2] Once we see again, it seems, we must reimagine.

British architect, James Stirling (1924-92), was one of post-war Modernism's most accomplished and provocative revisioners.[3] Stirling's was a complex formal game in which he looked to the past as a means to generate an unprecedented present. Rather than identifying or legitimizing his 'sources,' this paper instead explores the *way* in which Stirling brought forward the past in order to see it again—in other words, in the act of revision.

Correcting

Stirling's first commissioned project, the Flats at Ham Common, completed in partnership with James Gowan in 1958 in an upscale London suburb, is one of the most clearly identifiable revisions of Stirling's career. The revision is directed at Le Corbusier's Maisons Jaoul, completed just the year before.

When published images of the two buildings are compared, their similarities are apparent, if not striking: a façade organized by horizontal bandings of exposed concrete floor slabs, infilled with load-bearing brick walls; an overall arrangement of low-rise, detached cubic buildings on a long, narrow site; and even such specific details such as the U-shaped pre-cast concrete gargoyles. [Img.1]

1. This text is itself a triple revision. Firstly, a revision of the talk I gave at the Under the Influence symposium documented in this publication— smoothed over, thinned and then thickened a bit—but maintaining the same structure and general argument. The talk was a revision of portions of my book *James Stirling Revisionary Modernist* (New Haven: Yale University Press, 2013), particularly Chapters 1 and 3. And finally, the book was a revision of my doctoral dissertation *Remaining Modern: The Architecture of James Stirling, 1955-77*, completed at the Graduate School of Design at Harvard University in 2007.

2. "The revisionist strives to see again, so as to esteem and estimate differently, so as then to aim' correctively.'" Harold Bloom, *Map of Misreading.*

3. An aside that would might otherwise be inconsequential emerges as perhaps prescient in light of our investigation of Stirling's revisions: sometime in the

mid-1960s, at the moment his international reputation began to ascend, Stirling began stating his birth year as 1926, though in fact he was born in 1924. Nearly all subsequent accounts of his work and life—with the exception his careful biographer Mark Giruoard and old friend Colin Rowe—continue the postdating.

Image 1: Ham Common, James Stirling. Image courtesy of the CCA.

4. James Stirling, "Garches to Jaoul: Le Corbusier as a Domestic Architect in 1927 and 1953," *Architectural Review* 118 (September 1955): 145–51. As scholar Mark Crinson has noted, Stirling deliberately chose his own photographs of the building in its unfinished state, with site debris, construction ladders, exposed wires—though by that time finished photography would have been available—as a means to highlight its "crude" and unfinished quality and place it in greater contrast to Garches. Mark Crinson, "L'Architecte

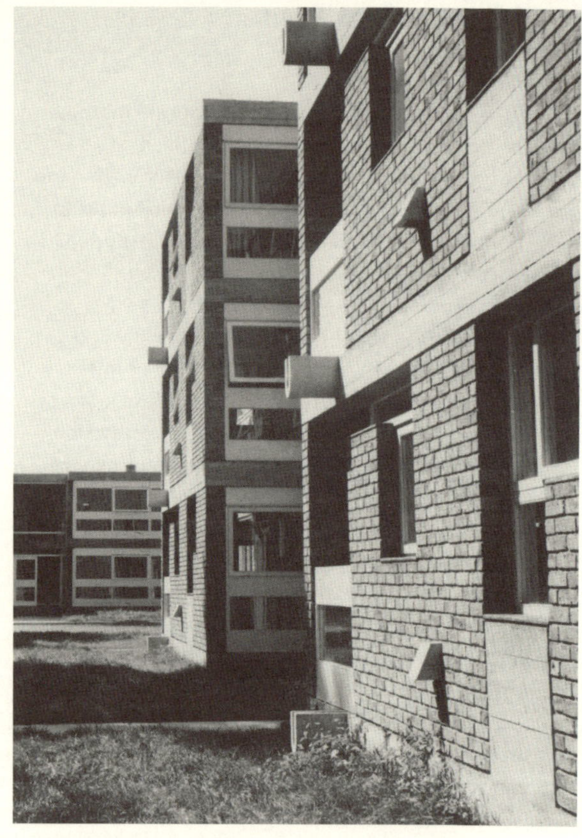

Stirling had visited the Maisons Jaoul, in an upscale Paris suburb, the year before, and had published the first English language article on the building, including his own photographs of Jaoul.[4] In the article, in which he pairs photographs of Jaoul with those of Le Corbusier's "heroic" Villa Stein at Garches from the 1920s, he struggles with Le Corbusier's "irrational" post-war building, contrasting its "deliberately crude" language with the pure machine aesthetic of the Villa Stein. Writing in a notebook that he kept at this time, Stirling described his disappointment with Le Corbusier's latest work, and of wishing the finish of the bricks had been "harder" with "definite joints" between the brick wall and the reinforced concrete floor slabs. This would have, he wrote, made the appearance "more mechanistic and I think better."[5] He finds the Jaoul houses "against the machine" and calls for a return to the principles of the "revolutionary" architecture of the 1920s.[6]

Stirling's own project at Ham Common is just that: a "more mechanistic" version of Jaoul. As a devout modernist fed a steady diet of pre-war Le Corbusier through his training with Rowe and others at Liverpool, Stirling found Le Corbusier's new work verging on sacrilege, even as its raw and sculptural forms held an undeniable allure.[7] As an antidote, Stirling rationalizes Jaoul, making it more in line with the "modern principles" he found lacking at Jaoul. For example, he inserts reveals or "definite joints" (the very same ones he found lacking at Jaoul) between the brick and concrete floor slabs. The messy brickwork at Jaoul is regularized, and he introduces a running bond pattern of London stock brick. The pointing is recessed, creating an "oblique shadow" around each brick. Even the *beton brut* is rationalized; instead of the handmade, artisanal finish at Jaoul, Stirling creates a regularized, horizontal banding across the concrete surface, aligning with the adjoining bricks.

Reyner Banham referred to Ham Common as a "tidying up" of the "casual and untidy" Jaoul.[8] True enough. But my argument here is that it's much more than a neatening of precedent. As a revision, Ham Common enacts a corrective, a "swerve" to use Harold Bloom's terminology, in which the precursor—in this case, Le Corbusier—while generally on the right track, is seen to have not gone quite far enough. The later poet or architect, in our case, finds that the precursor "should have swerved, precisely in the direction that the new poem moves."[9] For Stirling at Ham Common, that direction is more rational and mechanistic. Stirling returns us to the principles of pre-war Le Corbusier in the language of post-war Le Corbusier.[10] Perhaps, as Vincent Scully suggested vis-à-vis Robert Venturi, Stirling had a "keener sense for the precursor's jugular."[11]

Completing

Like Ham Common just a few years before it, the Leicester Engineering Building of 1963, also completed by Stirling in partnership with James Gowan, begs for source hunting, albeit across a wider geographic and historical distance. [Img.2]

Anglais," in *James Stirling: Early Unpublished Writings on Architecture*, ed. Mark Crinson (New York: Routledge, 2010), 124.

5. Stirling, *Early Unpublished Writings*, 83. A closer look at the original notebook reveals a question mark, in parentheses, immediately following this comment, and a short phrase—"not certain"—indicating Stirling's equivocation.

6. "The principles from the 20s revolution have in no way been superseded and until we create our own theories or more of a new philosophy, it is better to understand our heritage than to try to produce in a void-without direction." Ibid. Stirling would restate this notion as a conclusion to his "Garches to Jaoul" article, singling out Garches as "A monument, not to an age which is dead, but to a way of life which has not generally arrived, and a continuous reminder of the quality to which all architects must aspire if modern architecture is to retain its vitality."

Stirling, "Garches to Jaoul," in *Early Unpublished Writings*, 151.

7. "Definite art work" are the first words of his note-book description.

8. Reyner Banham, *New Brutalism: Ethic or Aesthetic?* (New York: Reinhold, 1966), 88.

9. Harold Bloom, *The Anxiety of Influence: A Theory of Poetry* (London: Oxford University Press, 1973), 14.

Image 2: Leicester Engineering Building, James Stirling. Image courtesy of the CCA. Photo by Futagawa, Yukio.

10. In Bloom's terms, the younger version of the precursor is often easier to deal with since it is less formed, less perfect. Although Jaoul was a "late" project of Le Corbusier's, it was in fact the beginning of a new system not yet fully formed. Stirling, then, can convince us that Jaoul was, at least in some respects, a less mature, or certainly a less "rational," version of his own work.

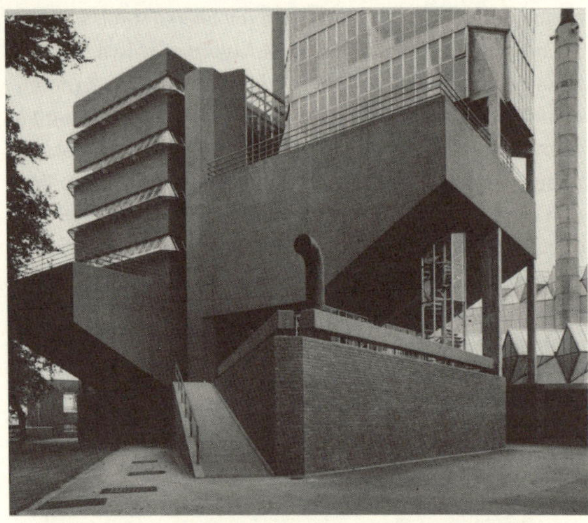

Nearly every architectural critic commenting on the building (particularly when it was first completed) couldn't escape speculating on various antecedents and alleged influences. Kenneth Frampton found connections to Frank Lloyd Wright, Joseph Paxton, Antonio Sant'Elia, and Hans Poelzig;[12] Colin Rowe included Viollet le-Duc, William Butterfield, and Frank Furness as among the influences.[13] But the "quotation" referred to again and again—though, tellingly, never by Stirling himself—is Konstantin Melnikov's Rusakov Worker's Club of 1929, and, in particular, its striking triad of lecture halls that jut out from the building's perimeter. [Img.3] The visual resemblance is unquestionable; in both Rusakov and Leicester, the trapezoidal shapes aggressively protrude from the overall building form and their shapes and proportion—though not material—are nearly identical.[14] This inescapable visual verisimilitude frees us from having to legitimize or "discover" the source, and instead allows us to consider the specific means through which Stirling's lecture halls at Leicester allow us to 'see again' Melnikov's 'original.' Here, their differences are instructive. The most significant variation between the lecture halls at Leicester and their Melnikovian predecessors is the degree of visual and structural independence they have within the overall scheme. At Rusakov, only the upper portions emerge from the building envelope; the bulk of three lecture hall volumes remains buried within the overall building form. At Leices-

     Amanda Reeser Lawrence

ter, by contrast, the volumes are revealed in their entirety. Each of the two lecture halls is suspended between a brick base below and a tower above, skewered by the concrete columns that support the towers but seemingly untethered from the other building elements. The lecture hall volumes appear as autonomous objects floating within the collection of volumetric pieces that make up the overall scheme, each with its own formal and programmatic logic.[15]

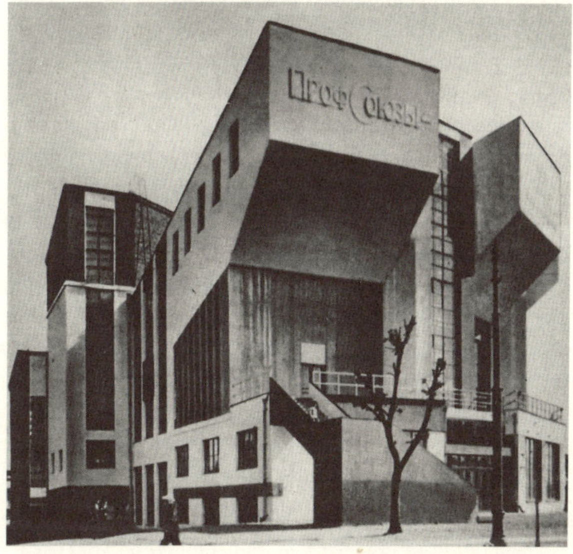

If Ham Common, as a revision, suggests that Le Corbusier's Maisons Jaoul didn't quite go far enough and offers a "swerve" in a more mechanistic and rational direction, Leicester can be seen instead as a kind of completion of Rusakov. Here Stirling's revision challenges the original for not going far enough, taking it to a greater, and perhaps, more profound extreme. When paired with Stirling's unconstrained, formally dynamic, and forceful volumes, Melnikov's lecture halls appear a weaker, more timid version. They seemed trapped within the building, incompletely expressed. Although the Melnikov buildings were the 'first' of the two, Leicester becomes, arguably, not only the stronger version of the idea, but the more original one.[16] Leicester informs Rusakov as much as Rusakov informs Leicester: through Stirling's revision at Leicester we re-see Rusakov, redeemed but also reoriented.

11. Vincent Scully cleverly illustrates this notion in his comparison of Richard Meier with Robert Venturi and their respective revisionings of Le Corbusier; by choosing Le Corbusier's later more "complete" work as his model, Scully writes, Meier never convinces us that his work is advancing the original, whereas Venturi, in choosing Le Corbusier's early work as his precedent— the Schwob Villa and the theater in La Chaux-de-Fonds, both of 1916—achieves more successful revisions. Vincent Scully, *The Shingle Style Today; or, the Historian's Revenge* (New York: Braziller, 1974).

Image 3: Rusakov Worker's Club, Konstantin Melnikov

12. Kenneth Frampton, "Leicester University Engineering Laboratory," *Architectural Design* 32 (February 1964): 61. Kenneth Frampton, "Transformations in Style: The Work of James Stirling," *A+U* 50 (1975): 135.

13. Colin Rowe, "James Stirling: A Highly Personal

and Very Disjointed
Memoir," introduc-
tion to *James
Stirling: Buildings
and Projects,* eds.
Peter Arnell and
Ted Bickford (New
York: Rizzoli, 1984),
26. "Transforma-
tions in Style: The
Work of James
Stirling," *A+U* 50
(1975): 135.

14. This was a
second-order revi-
sion for Stirling,
who had already
employed the dis-
tinctive lecture hall
silhouette taken
from Rusakov in
his competition
entry for the Arts
and Administration
Block at the Uni-
versity of Sheffield
scheme, designed
with Alan Cord-
ingly in 1953. In
this earlier projects
the lecture halls
are stacked along
the façade, flipped
from nose to tail,
and set in a kind
of exaggerated
bas-relief that at-
tempt to organize
and rationalize
Melnikov's original
rather than extend
or "complete" it.

15. For an exten-
sive discussion
of this "elementa-
rist" tendency in
Stirling's work, and
its connections to
the work of Le Cor-
busier, see Chapter
3 of *James Stirling
Revisionary Mod-
ernist.*

Returning

Nearly twenty years after Ham Common was completed,
now practicing without a partner and in the midst of a professional lull, Stirling was asked, along with twelve other international architectural teams, to "redesign" a portion of Giambat-
tista Nolli's 1748 plan of Rome.[17] [Img.4] Each was given one of
the twelve sectors of the map, with the stated goal of providing a "critical examination of the process of change in the urban fabric," and creating "a vehicle for curing the ills of the city
and its historical center."[18] In his introduction to the accompanying exhibition catalog, Carlo Argan more modestly and accu-
rately described the outcome of the exhibition and its entries,
"comprised not of proposals for urban planning, naturally, but
of a series of gymnastic exercises for the imagination."[19]

Rather than the speculative proposals offered by his most
of his colleagues, Stirling's entry is unique in that is offers
nothing new. Instead, he inserts thirty projects from throughout his career—both built and unbuilt—into his Nolli sector.
Each project is situated on the map according to what Stirling
termed a "contextural-associational" method, whereby each
project "confirms" and "complements" that which exists (or,
to be more precise, that which existed in the 18th century city
of Rome as mapped by Nolli.)[20] Projects are placed in relation
to one another (university buildings in a kind of "campus"
along the Tiber; housing projects in the more rural western
edge of the sector) as well as in relation to existing buildings
(as an extension to the Villa Farnesina, or enclosing a forecourt
in front of Villa Lante.)

In choosing his *own* works as precedents, Stirling seems to
break the rules of reference or at least call attention to certain
assumptions as to what those rules are.[21] Is it OK to quote
yourself? What does it mean to quote yourself if the project
you're quoting is itself already a revision of another project? In
Stirling's Roma Interrotta entry, the 'language' at play is Stirling's own, with each project redeployed as both a stable and
singular referent, and as the accumulation of a set of revisions.

Through this "return of the dead," Stirling rewrites his own
projects in a new (old) context, at the same time as he rewrites
Nolli's seventeenth-century Rome.[22] In using his own work as
precedent, Stirling lays bare the pretense of quotation and
unlocks seemingly endless recombinatory possibilities. The act
of revisioning takes precedence, and ultimately supersedes the

                    Amanda Reeser Lawrence

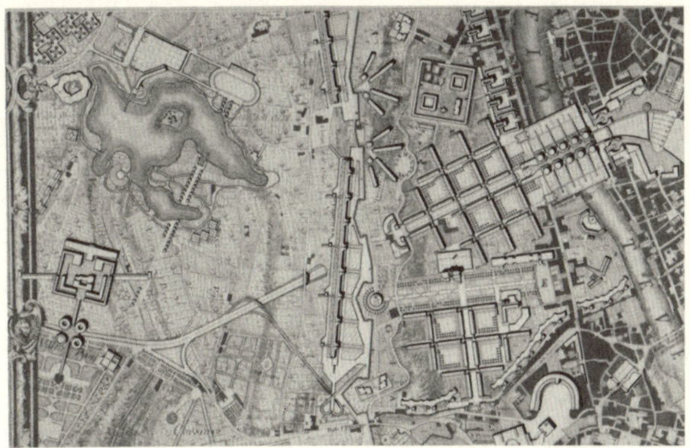

anxiety over the choice of the source. Once the distinction between quoting himself and quoting others is rendered meaningless, once all of history, both his own and others, is understood as a repository of previous forms and influences, then all of history can be "seen again."

16. In Bloom's terminology, a "tessera" is a scenario in which the later poet "provides what his imagination tells him would complete the otherwise "truncated" precursor poem." Harold Bloom, *The Anxiety of Influence."* 66.

17. The competition was the brainchild of Piero Sartugo and Michael Graves (both of whom would participate in the exhibition), among others, and was sponsored by the mayor of Rome, art historian Carlo Argan. In addition to Stirling, Graves, and Sartugo, the invited architects were Constantino Dardi; Antoine Grumbach, Paolo Portoghesi, and Vittorio Gigliotti; Romaldo Giurgola; Robert Venturi and John Rauch; Colin Rowe; Rob Krier; Aldo Rossi; and Leon Krier.

18. Grazi Graziella Lonardi, "preface," to *Roma Interrotta*, ed. and trans. Jennifer Franchina, (Rome: Officina, 1978).

19. Giulio Carlo Argan, "Introduction," Franchina, *Roma Interrotta*, 12.

20. Stirling, *Roma Interrotta*, 84.

21. For a more extensive discussion of this project as a vehicle for self-revision see my article in *LOG 22:* The Absurd, Spring/Summer (2011): 22-31.

22. For Bloom, the "return of the dead" as a revisionary ration is marked a precursor who haunts a later poet, so such an extent that the later poet appears to embody the later poet, to both completely inhabit but also supercede him. "The new poet's achievement makes it seem to us, not as though the precursor were writing it, but as though the later poet himself had written the precursor's characteristic work." Bloom, *Anxiety of Influence*, 16.

Thing Rights
Ines Weizman

THING RIGHTS:
THE SECOND AFTER-LIFE OF ARCHITECTURE

The emergence of modern architecture strangely coincides with the development of copyright law. In fact, one could argue that the development of modern architecture—its production, seriality and export across seas —and that of copyright laws are necessarily entangled. These days, the question of copyright is challenged by new modes of architectural production. Both computer-generated and parametric work, as well as ever-larger networks of production, put pressure on the notion of authorship and ownership. Paradoxically, the more net-worked and diffused architectural production becomes, the more the concept of the 'star-chitect' emphasizes the absolute nature of authorship. These paradoxes must be challenged by a proposition for a new mode of archi-tecture: 'copy-right' and 'copy-left' and modes of critical appropriation to be debated by architects, lawyers and in-tellectual property activists. Partly in response to such de-bates, and partly as a catalyst, we can currently observe a fascinating variety of appropriations, copying practices, and architectural doppelgängers that challenge the legal confines of the profession. Architectural doppelgängers appear to be produced in a kind of shadow economy without exact records, statistics, central planning agency, archive, or lawyers. Architectural copies can be easily ig-nored, dismissed as low art, or appear irrelevant for truly disturbing the nature and esteem of the 'original.' But of course the difference between production, copying, and faking lies in the position the object has in relation to the law. Although architecture features in many types of legal processes: as crime scene, as a cause for damages (in property law), as criminal evidence, or even as war-crime. At the center of this investigation is copyright law itself, and the way it is applied to architecture.

Copyright is generally understood as the conse-quence of a conferring of a maker's identity on an object, a thing, a structured assemblage, or a building. It is the right to copy, replicate, duplicate and receive the financial benefits of this act. As such, new copyright regulations appear exactly at the moment when new practices and new architectural works are reacting to and advancing the condition of modernity. Perhaps one could argue that it was in fact copyright law that "allowed" architecture to be copied, replicated, mass produced, and exported across the world. What makes the copy, and in particular the architectural copy, so interesting is that it is a phenomenon of modernity. Just like the print, the photograph, the film, or the digital file, it is both a product of the media and a media form in itself that, in every situation and period, reflects on the existing means of production and reproduction, part of an endless series of 'aura-less' multiplications.[1]

1. Ines Weizman "Architectural Doppelgängers," in *AA Files* 65, ed. Thomas Weaver, (London: Architectural Association, 2012), 19-24

The state defines the right of authors both during their lifetimes and even beyond death. In international law, copyright is applied in accordance with the country in which the author is a citizen, but not outside of its borders unless the country is a signatory of an international convention. *The Bern Convention for the Protection of Literary and Artistic Works* defines a minimum duration for the legal copyright protection that is calculated as fifty years after the death of an author, but many countries have raised this figure to up to 75 years. This rule aligns the life of a copyright protection to the average lifetime of a person. Perhaps we could think of this protected term of a creative work of art as its second life. As soon as its copyright protection expires, the work falls into the public domain; that is, the work effectively becomes public property and may be used freely. At that point, the work enters its third life, which should, in principle, be infinite.

Interestingly, in the 2000s, we are entering an era of 'modernism's third life', the period past the 75 year long second life of those authors who died in the period of pre-Word War Two and whose works are now entering their third life. Seen that way, this new era in which we live might be an opportunity to give modernism a second chance. We have finally arrived at Modernism, in which the person has been completely abstracted and his or her work made public. Perhaps this moment can help us revisit modernism with renewed, 'dis-interested' (literally, without any financial interest) judgments, and potentially rehabilitate Modernism's apparent failures.

In no other field is this question more important than in the case of Modern architecture, which sought to distance the author from authorship, the building from uniqueness, and the individual from mass production. These are of course shorthands, but still allow us to make the point. Finally, 75 years after the first generation of modern architects died their second death, Modernism has been fulfilled in the dissociation of the work from their persons. We could even say that only in its third life can the work become truly modern! Now as we have for the first time freely reproducible architecture, and we enter the first life of architecture to give it its third life, modernism can finally be fulfilled.

In this third life, we might see architecture turn into *things*. In *thing-world*, copying is the means of reproduction, and copy-rights are thus the most fundamental and inalienable of *thing-rights*, potentially beyond and in spite of those of their makers. 'Copy-rights' must be for things what human-rights are for humans, because things are also haunted by their potential or actual doubles, replicas, simulacra, reproductions, and fakes. Architecture evolves in the physical and digital domain as sequences of copies. Gradual differentiations, variations, distortions, and mutations occur as things reproduce themselves. This process is not beyond the human. For things to reproduce themselves, they need humans, just like humans need their physical or technical prostheses: computers, cell-phones, pacemakers, and walking sticks...

In 2008, 75 years after the death of the Viennese architect Adolf Loos, one of the famous modernists of the first generation, I attempted to set foot on this new terrain of the third life of modernism. I proposed to celebrate the making public of the copyrights of Loos' oeuvre by building a facsimile of House Baker, the house Loos designed in 1928, but never realized for the legendary singer Josephine Baker in Paris.

This architectural re-enactment was a response to the generous invitation to participate in the by-now infamous master plan of Ordos 100. In the early 2000s, the city of Ordos in Inner Mongolia (China) was prophesied to become a megacity by 2020. Reflecting the urgency to provide housing for the new inhabitants, a new city district for 200,000 people was being planned. A portion of it was reserved for a private initiative to build an exclusive settlement for wealthier dwellers. The master

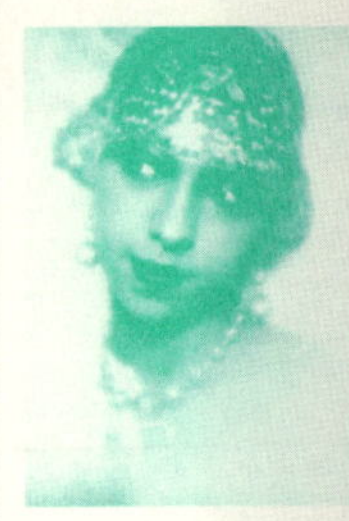

Reference: Josephine Baker (http://lascasartoris.tumblr.com/post/23992257618/josephine-baker-by-madame-dora-c-1928-source)

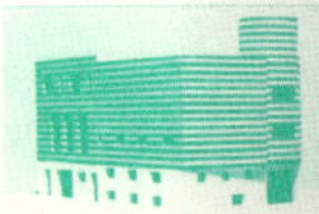

Reference: Josephine Baker House, Adolf Loos, unbuilt. (http://cargocollective.com/adolfloos/Josephine-Baker-House-Unbuilt)

Image: An architectural re-enactment of the House for Josephine Baker by Adolf Loos, proposed for Ordos (China), 2008, Ines Weizman & Andreas Thiele (http://pr2012.aaschool.ac.uk/students/Architectural_Dopplegangers)

The façade of the re-enactment is produced by a projection of the photograph onto the entire extent of the façade, faithfully recreating the photographic

plan for 100 luxurious villas, a museum, a clubhouse, and artists' residences was developed and curated by the artist Ai Weiwei's FAKE studio in Beijing and the practice of Herzog & de Meuron in Basel. It was Ai Weiwei's idea to invite 100 international architects to design 100 villas in the middle of the desert where the young architects could enjoy their architectural fantasies of design for an enormous residence of 1000 square meters. There were only a few conditions: it had to have a swimming pool (to help create a certain humidity in the desert air) and parking facilities for two cars. Loos' House Baker seemed perfectly suited for the brief and somehow, without initially noticing, this architectural doppelgänger began its own, now third life. Although, of course, being awkwardly placed in time and loci, seemingly unaware of its new geopolitical and cultural context, it was now the building itself that began to enjoy its freedom.

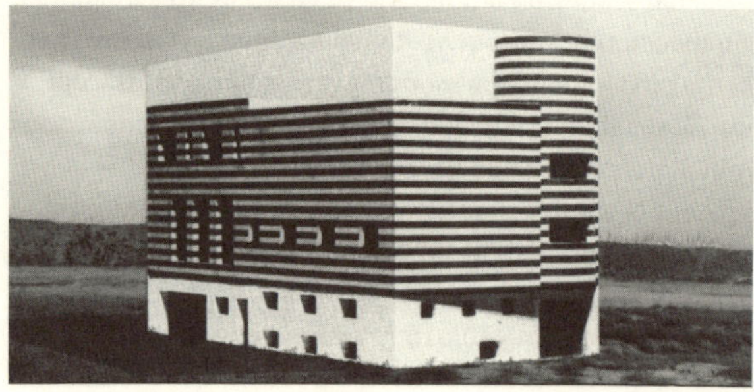

First of all, it asked itself about the architectural features of its re-enactment. To answer this question, drawings and documents had to be found related to Adolf Loos' ideas and design instructions for House Baker. The Albertina in Vienna, one of the largest and most important art collections of Austria, holds the almost complete Adolf Loos Archive, which also includes the model of House Baker. The model is occasionally taken out of storage to be presented in exhibitions, but the image that made it famous is the 1930 photograph of it by Martin Gerlach Jr., a young Viennese photographer commissioned by friends of Adolf Loos to capture the architect's life work for an exhibition and a monograph in honor of his 60th birthday in December 1930.[2] The photograph of the model was published a year after the birthday, first in a smaller

French monograph published by Franz Glück, and then in a much larger monograph by one of Loos' closest collaborators and friends, Heinrich Kulka.[3]

There are different scholarly attempts to explain why Loos decided to clad the Josephine Baker house with horizontal stripes of black and white marble. Some refer it to his interests in tattoos, while others see in it a reflection of the black American star succeeding in a mainly white environment in Paris. However, if we look at Baker's stowaway comedy in *La Sirènes des Tropiques* of 1927, which Loos most certainly had seen when he was in Paris, and in which the wet actress falls once into coal and once into flour, we find yet another possible explanation. I will never be able to defend why the 1:100 model, which my collaborator Andreas Thiele and I took to Ordos, lacked the stripes. Obsessed with its interior we were content with its sterile whiteness, which might also explain why it was not recognized among the 100 models presented in the hotel lobby (later to be deposited in the museum that had turned into a showroom for real estate agents). But of course, at this stage we still had to become acquainted with a project that had itself been inspired by a very short encounter, a party chat between Loos and Josephine Baker, probably also in 1927. Loos' third wife Claire Beck tells about it in her memoirs, which she published in 1936 in the hope of being able to raise funds for a tombstone on Loos' grave. It was the evening of their engagement and she remembered very clearly how Loos had been offended when he learned that Baker did not know that he was an architect, or as he told her at the occasion, that he was the 'most famous architect in the world'.[4] Baker, who on earlier occasion had taught Loos how to dance the Charleston, probably talked to many guests of the cabaret that night, while Loos, in a mixture of anger, pride, and admiration directed towards the Black Venus of Paris conceived of a love letter in architectural form.

With similar affection, we searched through the few drawings and documents about House Baker, trying to translate them into workable plans and volumes. Together with my collaborator (who was fortunately up for full-heartedly debating Loos-details), we prepared an enormous set of plans of over 120 pages in A0 format,

representation including its grain and distortions by a pixelated mosaic.

2. In fact, the glass plate was never used after the first paper print was developed from it, which is until today used as the 'original' by the Adolf Loos Image Archive at the Albertina in Vienna.

3. Adolf Loos and Heinrich Kulka, *Adolf Loos: Das Werk des Architekten*, (Anton Schroll & Co, Neues Bauen in der Welt, IV, 1931).

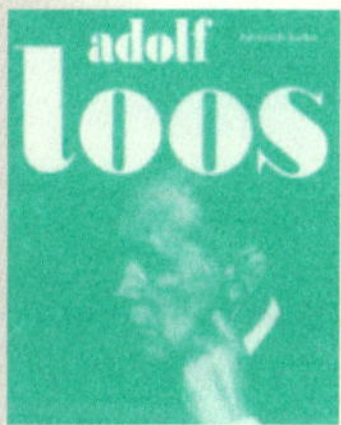

Reference: Cover of Heinrich Kulka's book on Adolf Loos. (Image from http://www.yama-semi.com/)

4. Claire Loos, *Adolf Loos Privat* (Vienna: Czernin Verlag, 2007), 8-10.

containing the details of how we visualized the project and specifying materials and details closely referring to the works of Adolf Loos.

But the project seemed to endlessly stimulate new questions and retrospectives, and the larger the convolute of documents grew, the more it needed insights from experts, lawyers, historians, architects, collectors and self-acclaimed heirs of the Loos estate to realize a copy of a project that in fact had no original. Designing the copy appeared impossible without consulting and considering their claims.

Apart from the model, the Albertina only holds two sets of inked plans. These were probably drawn in 1931 by Kurt Unger, Loos's closest assistant in those last years in which he was still searching for his dream commission. Loos likely asked to have the drawings for House Baker redrawn and slightly corrected in ink, so that they could be published in Kulka's monograph. But Unger did not complete them before Kulka's deadline had passed, and so the first time they were reproduced was in 1964, when the long-awaited monograph *Adolf Loos: Pioneer of Modern Architecture*, completed by Gustav Künstler after Ludwig Münz' death, was published.[5] When the book appeared internationally, and presumably in a bookshop in Buenos Aires, a lady in her mid-sixties decided to write a series of letters to Vienna. The lady was Elsie Altmann, Loos' second wife to whom he had entrusted all his belongings to in a will from 1922. In 1933, Altmann was at the height of her career as Vienna's last grand operetta star. Shortly after Loos' death, she was invited to a short-term theatre engagement in Buenos Aires. She assumed that her absence from Vienna would only last for two months, and that she would complete the remaining paperwork for the inheritance upon her return. But the increasing anti-Semitic sentiments and eventually the Anschluss of Austria to Hitler's Germany in 1938 made her return impossible.

Of course, Altmann was surprised and disappointed when to learn of the 1964 publication because she had not been credited or received a copy of it.[6] She understood her exclusion from the credit lines of the Loos estate, and started a legal dispute with the Albertina. Despite her claims, under the leadership of its director, Koschatzky decided to buy the Loos documents and drawings in possession of the heirs of Ludwig Münz, who for years had worked on the

5. Ludwig Münz and Gustav Künstler, *Der Architekt Adolf Loos: Darstellung seines Schaffens nach Werkgruppen: chronologisches Werkverzeichnis* (Vienna: Anton Schroll & Co, 1964).

6. Elsie Altmann-Loos, "Letter to the director of the Graphische Sammlung Albertina, Vienna, Buenos Aires, 21. March 1966," in *Mein Leben mit Adolf Loos*, ed. Adolf Opel (Berlin: Ullstein, 1986) 284-89, 313.

monograph for Loos, but had died before its completion

In the last years before her death in 1984, Elsie Altmann met Adolf Opel, a Viennese filmmaker, novelist, and dandy who by chance was a guest in the hotel in Buenos Aires where Altmann earned her living as a receptionist. Charmed by his courtesy, the old lady decided to confer Opel her rights over the Loos assets. This was controversial, of course, with Altmann's daughter Esther Gonzales-Varona, who contested this fact until the 1990s, but all her claims failed in front of the court in Austria.

Meanwhile, Adolf Opel began collecting, editing, and publishing the writings of Loos claiming to be the righteous owner of the 'Adolf Loos archive'. When the Herold Publishing House refused to accept Opel as the rightful heir to royalties paid to Altmann, Opel began to construct his own collection of Loos' writings, reproducing what had been published in earlier collections (*Ins Leere gesprochen,* 1921; *Trotzdem,* 1931). Most of Loos's writing has been published by Adolf Opel. But Opel also claimed rights to the documents and drawings. In an interview I conducted with him in 2012, he stated that he owned all of Adolf Loos' copyrights and that all reproductions of Loos' works needed to have his permission. He seemed oblivious to the fact that in 2008, quietly and without fanfare, 75 years after the death of Loos', the work has slipped into its third life.

Image: Mapping of Adolf Loos ownership trails

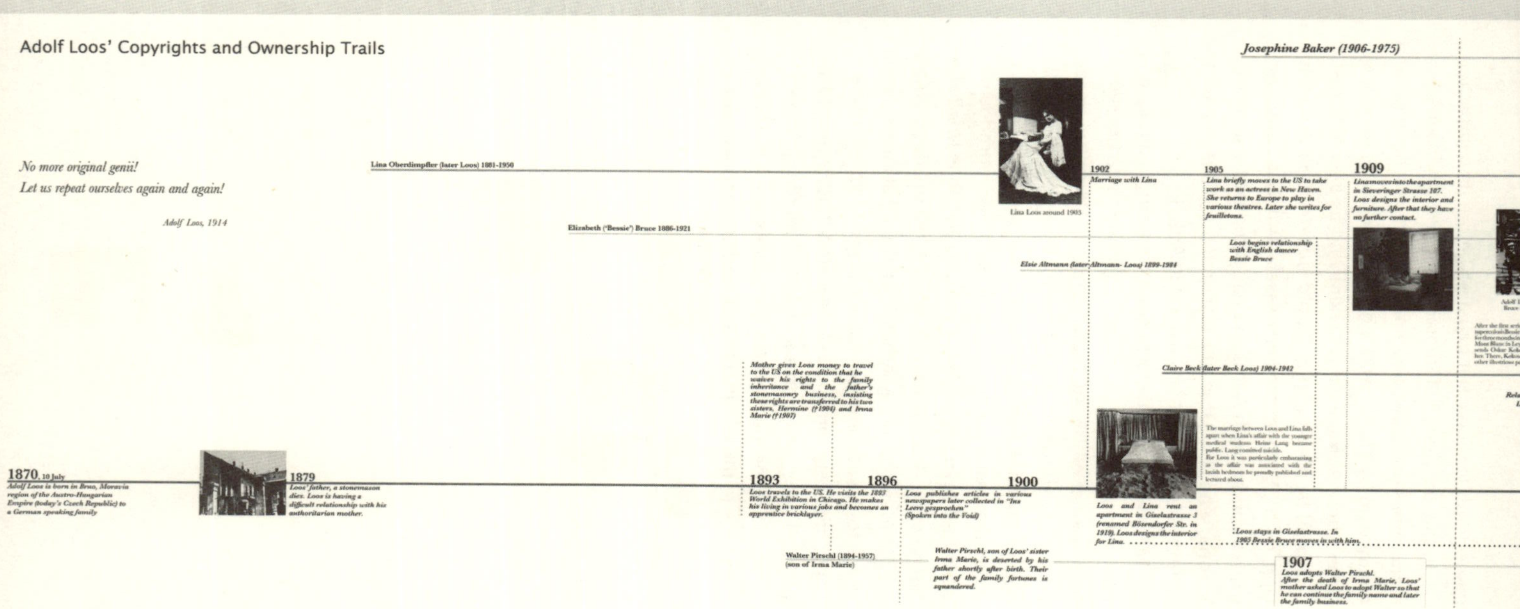

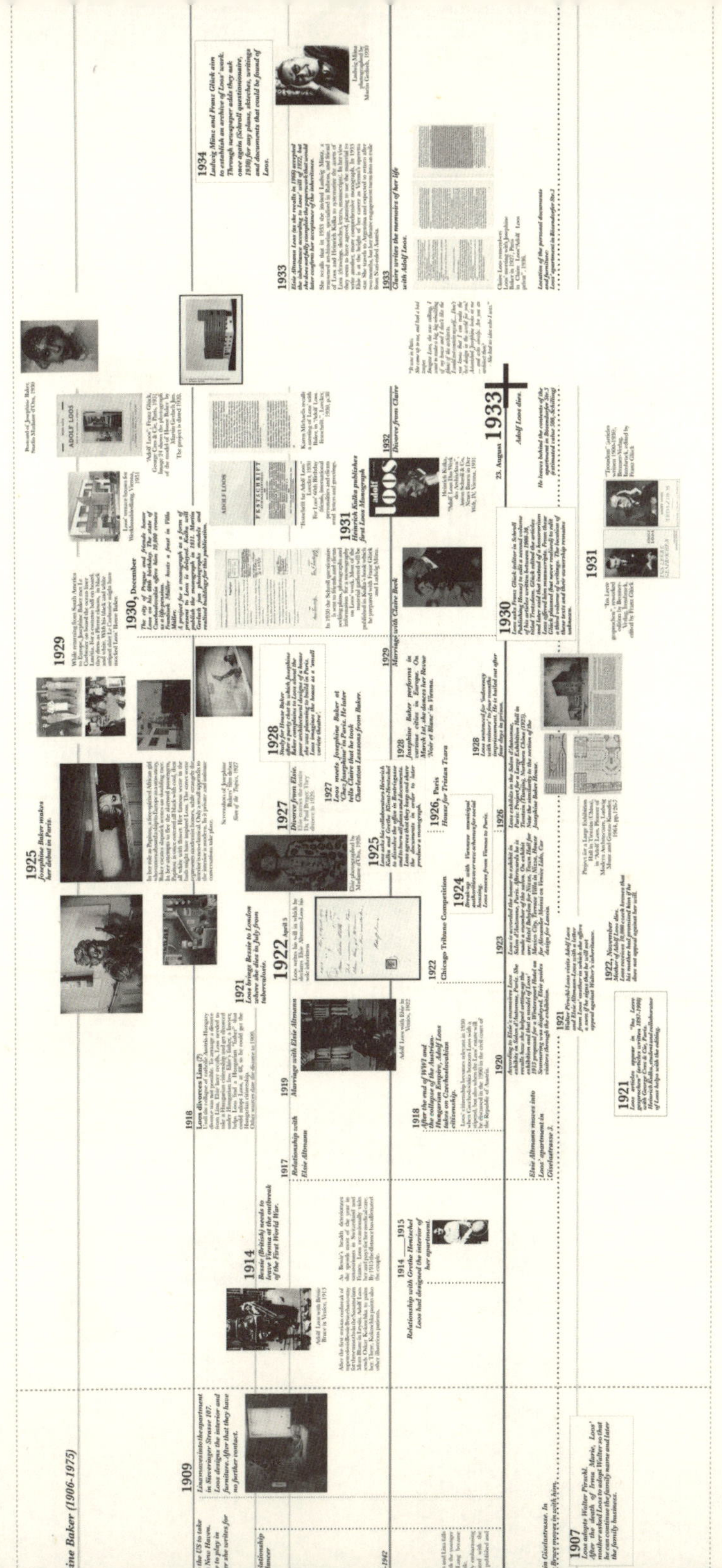

1938, *March*
Anschluss of Austria to Hitler Germany. Jews are banned from the civil service and required to register the assets of their business enterprises.

1938
Heinrich Kulka flees first to Czechoslovakia, then in 1939 to England and in 1940 to New Zealand. Kurt Unger, another collaborator of Loos goes to Palestine. Before they leave Vienna they give all documents relating to Loos to Glück and Münz. They seem to have divided the material into: texts and manuscripts (Glück) and architectural plans and documents (Münz).

Ludwig Münz flees to London, taking the "Loos Archive" with him. Elsie later claims that Münz took Loos' documents from the apartment in Bösendorfer Str.3 without her permission.

1940
Münz hands over the "archive" to Edward J 'Bobby' Carter (1902 - 1982), Librarian of the RIBA in London.

1942
In 1941 Claire Beck Loos and her mother Olga Feigl Beck are deported to Theresienstadt. They die in a concentration camp in Riga, Latvia.

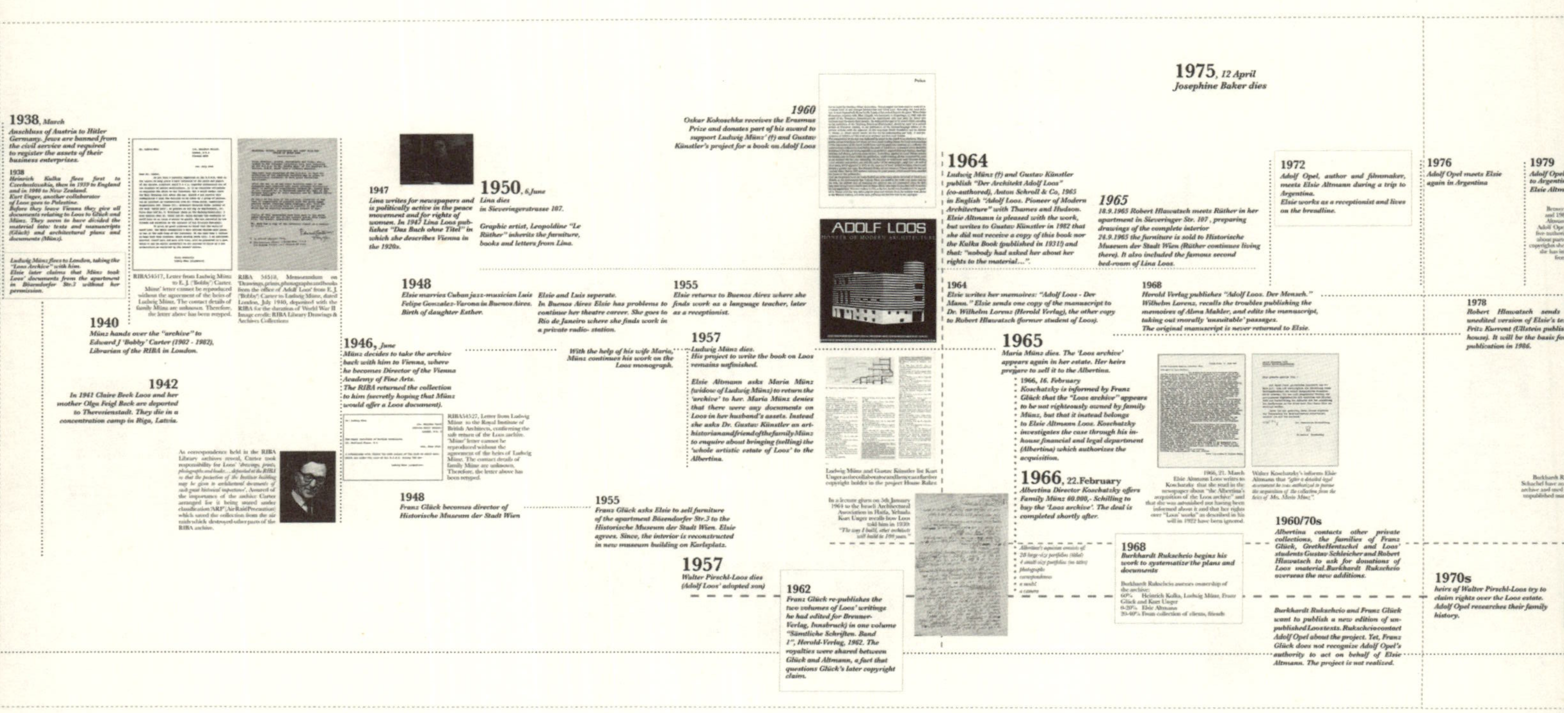

RIBA54517, Letter from Ludwig Münz to E. J. ('Bobby') Carter. Münz' letter cannot be reproduced without the agreement of the heirs of Ludwig Münz. The contact details of family Münz are unknown. Therefore, the letter above has been retyped.

RIBA 54510, Memorandum on 'Drawings, prints, photographs and books from the office of Adolf Loos' from E. J. ('Bobby') Carter to Ludwig Münz, dated London, July 1940, deposited with the RIBA for the duration of World War II. Image credit: RIBA Library Drawings & Archives Collections

As correspondence held in the RIBA Library archives reveal, Carter took responsibility for Loos' *'drawings, prints, photographs and books… deposited at the RIBA so that the protection of the Institute building may be given to architectural documents of such great historical importance'*. Assured of the importance of the archive Carter arranged for it being stored under classification 'ARP' (Air Raid Precaution) which saved the collection from the air raids which destroyed other parts of the RIBA archive.

1947
Lina writes for newspapers and is politically active in the peace movement and for rights of women. In 1947 Lina Loos publishes "Das Buch ohne Titel" in which she describes Vienna in the 1920s.

1950, *6 June*
Lina dies in Sieveringerstrasse 107.

Graphic artist, Leopoldine "Le Rüther" inherits the furniture, books and letters from Lina.

1946, *June*
Münz decides to take the archive back with him to Vienna, where he becomes Director of the Vienna Academy of Fine Arts. The RIBA returned the collection to him (secretly hoping that Münz would offer a Loos document).

1948
Elsie marries Cuban jazz-musician Luis Felipe Gonzalez-Varona in Buenos Aires. Birth of daughter Esther.

1948
Franz Glück becomes director of Historische Museum der Stadt Wien

RIBA54527, Letter from Ludwig Münz to the Royal Institute of British Architects, confirming the safe return of the Loos archive. 'Münz' letter cannot be reproduced without the agreement of family Münz. The contact details of family Münz are unknown. Therefore, the letter above has been retyped.

1955
Elsie and Luis seperate. In Buenos Aires Elsie has problems to continue her theatre career. She goes to Rio de Janeiro where she finds work in a private radio- station.

1955
Elsie returns to Buenos Aires where she finds work as a language teacher, later as a receptionist.

With the help of his wife Maria, Münz continues his work on the Loos monograph.

1957
Ludwig Münz dies. His project to write the book on Loos remains unfinished.

Elsie Altmann asks Maria Münz (widow of Ludwig Münz) to return the 'archive' to her. Maria Münz denies that there were any documents on Loos in her husband's assets. Instead she asks Dr. Gustav Künstler an art-historian and friend of the family Münz to enquire about bringing (selling) the 'whole artistic estate of Loos' to the Albertina.

1955
Franz Glück asks Elsie to sell furniture of the apartment Bösendorfer Str.3 to the Historische Museum der Stadt Wien. Elsie agrees. Since, the interior is reconstructed in new museum building on Karlsplatz.

1957
Walter Pirschl-Loos dies (Adolf Loos' adopted son)

1962
Franz Glück re-publishes the two volumes of Loos' writings he had edited for Brenner-Verlag, Innsbruck) in one volume "Sämtliche Schriften. Band 1", Herold-Verlag, 1962. The royalties were shared between Glück and Altmann, a fact that questions Glück's later copyright claim.

1975, *12 April*
Josephine Baker dies

1960
Oskar Kokoschka receives the Erasmus Prize and donates part of his award to support Ludwig Münz' (f) and Gustav Künstler's project for a book on Adolf Loos

1964
Ludwig Münz (f) and Gustav Künstler publish "Der Architekt Adolf Loos" (co-authored), Anton Schroll & Co, 1965 in English "Adolf Loos. Pioneer of Modern Architecture" with Thames and Hudson. Elsie Altmann is pleased with the work, but writes to Gustav Künstler in 1982 that she did not receive a copy of this book nor the Kulka Book (published in 1931) and that: "nobody had asked her about her rights to the material…".

1964
Elsie writes her memoires: "Adolf Loos - Der Mann." Elsie sends one copy of the manuscript to Dr. Wilhelm Lorenz (Herold Verlag), the other copy to Robert Hlawatsch (former student of Loos).

1968
Herold Verlag publishes "Adolf Loos. Der Mensch." Wilhelm Lorenz, recalls the troubles publishing the memoires of Alma Mahler, and edits the manuscript, taking out morally 'unsuitable' passages. The original manuscript is never returned to Elsie.

1965
18.9.1965 Robert Hlawatsch meets Rüther in her apartment in Sieveringer Str. 107, preparing drawings of the complete interior 24.9.1965 the furniture is sold to Historische Museum der Stadt Wien (Rüther continues living there). It also included the famous second bed-room of Lina Loos.

1965
Maria Münz dies. The 'Loos archive' appears again in her estate. Her heirs prepare to sell it to the Albertina.

1966, 16. February Koschatzky is informed by Franz Glück that the "Loos archive" appears to be not righteously owned by family Münz, but that it instead belongs to Elsie Altmann Loos. Koschatzky investigates the case through his in-house financial and legal department (Albertina) which authorizes the acquisition.

1966, *22. February*
Albertina Director Koschatzky offers Family Münz 60.000,- Schilling to buy the 'Loos archive'. The deal is completed shortly after.

Ludwig Münz and Gustav Künstler list Kurt Unger as the collaborator and therefore as further copyright holder in the project House Rufer.

In a lecture given on 5th January 1964 to the Israeli Architectural Association in Haifa, Yehuda Kurt Unger recalls how Loos told him in 1939: "The way I build, other architects will build in 100 years."

Albertina's aquisition consists of:
28 large-size portfolios (titled)
4 small-size portfolios (no titles)
photographs
correspondence
1 model
1 camera

1968
Burkhardt Rukschcio begins his work to systematize the plans and documents

Burkhardt Rukschcio assesses ownership of the archive:
60%: Heinrich Kulka, Ludwig Münz, Franz Glück and Kurt Unger
6-20%: Elsie Altmann
20-40%: From collection of clients, friends

1966, 21. March. Elsie Altmann Loos writes to Koschatzky that the trust in the newspaper about "the Albertina's acquisition of the Loos archive" and that she was undeceived not having been informed about it and that her rights over "Loos' works" as described in her will in 1922 have been ignored.

Walter Koschatzky informs Elsie Altmann that "after a detailed legal assessment he was authorized to pursue the acquisition of the collection from the heirs of Mrs. Maria Münz."

1972
Adolf Opel, author and filmmaker, meets Elsie Altmann during a trip to Argentina. Elsie works as a receptionist and lives on the breadline.

1976
Adolf Opel meets Elsie again in Argentina

1979
Adolf Opel c… to Argentina… Elsie Altma…

1978
Robert Hlawatsch sends t… unedited version of Elsie's text Fritz Kurvent (Ullstein publishi… house). It will be the basis for… publication in 1986.

1960/70s
Albertina contacts other private collections, the families of Franz Glück, GretheHentschel and Loos' students Gustav Schleicher and Robert Hlawatsch to ask for donations of Loos material. Burkhardt Rukschcio overseas the new additions.

Burkhardt Rukschcio and Franz Glück want to publish a new edition of un-published Loos texts. Rukschcio contact Adolf Opel about the project. Yet, Franz Glück does not recognize Adolf Opel's authority to act on behalf of Elsie Altmann. The project is not realized.

1970s
heirs of Walter Pirschl-Loos try to claim rights over the Loos estate. Adolf Opel researches their family history.

*Dass ich auch hier kopiert werde, kränkt mich nicht -
im Gegenteil: das ist ja das Ziel meines Lebenswerkes!
Auch um das Finanzielle kümmere ich mich wenig:
die Anderen schaffen Geld - ich schaffe Architektur.*

Adolf Loos, 1931

1976
Adolf Opel meets Elsie again in Argentina

1979
Adolf Opel comes with a film team to Argentina to produce a film about Elsie Altmann

Between 1979 and 1981 Elsie Altmann gives Adolf Opel about five authorisations about parts of the copyrights she claims she has inherited from Loos.

1981
Adolf Opel visits Buenos Aires to open a Loos exhibition and to present the film on Elsie Altmann

17.11.1981 Elsie Altmann sells Adolf Opel all rights to the work of Adolf Loos. They agree that after her death all copyrights will be transferred to Adolf Opel. Opel commits himself to share royalties and earnings with Elsie Altmann (50%) until the end of her life.

1978
Robert Hlawatsch sends the unedited version of Elsie's text to Fritz Kurrent (Ullstein publishing house). It will be the basis for the publication in 1986.

1981
Elsie Altmann asks Herold Verlag for the remaining documents which Glück had planned for a third volume of writings, but did not receive a response.

23.4. 1981 Franz Glück dies.
Elsie Altmann's manuscript is found in the assets of Glück.
Together with Elsie Altmann, Adolf Opel reconstructs the manuscripts and extends the text with new chapters and details added by Elsie.

1984, 19. May
Elsie-Altmann dies
daughter,
Esther Gonzalez-Varona claims to be the sole heiress of Adolf Loos's assets. She appeals (unsuccessfully) against the contracts Elsie made with Adolf Opel.

1986
Publication:
Elsie Altmann-Loos, Mein Leben mit Adolf Loos, ed. Adolf Opel, Ullstein

*"The way I build, other architects
will build in 100 years."*

Burkhardt Rukschcio and Schachel have access to Glück archive and used fragments of unpublished manuscripts and typescripts.

1982
Burkhart Rukschcio and Roland Schachel publish a comprehensive monograph. "Adolf Loos: Leben und Werk", Salzburg, 1982

1982
Adolf Opel publishes "Trotzdem", reproducing them from newspapers, and primary publications as Herold Verlag and heirs of Glück don't want to pass on the manuscripts to Opel.

1970s
heirs of Walter Pirschl-Loos try to claim rights over the Loos estate. Adolf Opel researches their family history.

1981
Adolf Opel publishes "Ins Leere gesprochen", reproducing its 1921 edition. (Franz Glück had based his second edition on the 1931 edition.)

1983
Adolf Opel publishes "Die Potemkin'sche Stadt", reproducing articles in laborious library research from newspapers and primary publications.

1989
Yehuda Kurt Unger dies in Haifa

Yehuda Kurt Unger in conversation with Adolf Loos in 1930

Yehuda Kurt Unger's letter to the editors of Architectural Review, April 1968, p.308 in which he responds to an article of Thomas Stevenson in the AR, February 1968, p. 98.
Ungers explains his work on House Baker.

Page 3 of Yehuda Kurt Unger's article "Meine Lehre bei Adolf Loos", Bauwelt, Nr 17, 6. November 1981, 77 Jrg., pp.1682-1692. In the article Unger states that Münz and Künstler wrongly assign him the position of a collaborator in the project for House Baker. He writes that he was asked to "merely redraw" the existing plans, that is to prepare accurate but not highly detailed plans for publication. In order to be more accurate he had to correct a few mistakes such as add missing columns and support for the swimming pool on first floor.

1997
*Adolf Opel brought a civil action against the Republic of Austria and the Albertina in the hope of forcing the publication of the contents of the Adolf Loos Archive in the possession of the Albertina. To hinder publication, the Albertina placed a preservation order on the Archive.
The Viennese Landgericht found in favour of Esther Maria Gonzalez, decreeing that the Albertina should publish the parts of the Archive purchased from Maria Münz in 1966. The Republic of Austria appealed against the decision and won. The reason was that a letter from Esther did not arrive in time.*

2008
*75th years after the death of Adolf Loos international copyright protection term ends.
In this year a proposal for an Architectural Re-enactment of House Baker by Adolf Loos (1928) is made for a residential neighbourhood in Ordos, Inner Mongolia, China.*

2009
The project architects of the Ordos 100 project in China prepare a rendering of the rear fassade.

Bibliography

Elsie Altmann-Loos, Mein Leben mit Adolf Loos, ed. Adolf Opel, Ullstein, 1986

Beatriz Colomina, Privacy and Publicity: Modern Architecture as Mass Media, Cambridge MA: MIT Press

Janet Stewart, Fashioning Vienna. Adolf Loos's Cultural Criticism, Routledge, 2000

Thomas Weingraber, "Wem gehört Adolf Loos? oder Das Verbrechen wider den Heiligen Geist." Parnass 2/ 1982, pp.6-11

Discussion 02
Moderator: Ana Miljački

**PARTICIPANTS:
CRISTINA GOBERNA,
URTZI GRAU,
SAM JACOB,
AMANDA REESER LAWRENCE,
INES WEIZMAN**

0:00 Ana Miljački: All the participants in this session have been involved in writing about and working though questions of architectural copying. Consequently the ideological gaps between them may appear smaller than in our first panel. So because the key questions of this symposium restate, perhaps borrow, or maybe even copy the very interest in the architectural copy demonstrated by the participants in this panel, we may have to dig more deeply and more intricately through their material to highlight the specific differences between the positions and work presented by FKAA [Cristina Goberna and Urtzi Grau], Sam Jacob, Amanda Reeser Lawrence, and Ines Weizman. Although the ideological divide may be narrower in this panel than the last, we have definitely traversed different territories across the papers, from methods of conceiving architecture to literally making it, from the politics surrounding it to the politics—and even rights—intrinsic to it. The fact that we are, at no point, really talking about originality may be the key connective thread among the presentations. We discussed ingenuity, or displaced originality, leading to the creation of something that is more promiscuous, richer, and still very specific. In all cases, ingenuity is found in the act of revision, copying, reenacting, or the agonistic reply.

In displacing originality or novelty for something else, we enter a realm of politics and possibly history, or a space of writing history that is different than the one we are used to.

2:26 Amanda Reeser Lawrence: I will stop on the question of ingenuity for a minute. When you say ingenuity, are you suggesting another vehicle through which one arrives at a kind of originality? Yes, we're focusing on appropriation, but in the end it is still generating novelty in some way. Even a replica is an ingenious and novel response.

3:10 Miljački: I think your point certainly applies to your own presentation and reading of James Stirling. The three other presentations were more adamant about pushing originality aside.

3:30 Lawrence: Right, yes.

3:32 Miljački: Originality was sidestepped for very specific ends by Sam Jacob, for example, who proposed that once we stop focusing on originality, we may be able to see the act of copying and reproducing as important and rich in its own right, producing a world of its own. Though his key point about the Rotunda for the Venice Biennale focused on questions arising from the very literal tasks of making it, the series of critical categories that Sam and Ines Weizman produced in their research highlighted different operative functions of doppelgangers: diplomatic, historical, communicative, etc. Similarly, placing originality on hold allowed Cristina Goberna and Urtzi Grau to propose that another form of new knowledge can emerge as a result of reproducing. So the novelty pursued here is not necessarily formal, but it takes the form of architectural and cultural knowledge specific to a given project.

4:47 Sam Jacob: It is telling that there are enough people who are interested in this kind of subject to fill a room. Opposed to these issues is this tyranny of novelty that's sat on us like some kind of depressing weight over the last fifty years: the endless production of novelty, which has become increasingly similar, boring, and ineffective. One of the projects that launched my interest in replication was a kind of reenactment by artist Jeremy Deller. It was a type of Civil War reenactment, where people dress up and act out particular historical battles. He reenacted a battle between some striking minors—in Thatcher's Britain of the 1980s—and the police in the same place that the original events had taken place and with the same community. Sometimes people were playing themselves, sometimes they were playing the police. Of course, in some sense, his reenactments were a way of reanimating a certain kind of political and social history. In another sense, his performance was able to rewrite that history, or certainly the perception of the events, as they were understood through the original media. His project emphasized the possibilities present in something as

seemingly banal as reenactment. For me, that seemed to
offer an incredibly different way of working than producing something that was formally novel in of itself. The key
question then for me became, how could similar tactics
operate within architecture?

7:08 Cristina Goberna: To answer Ana's provocation, I would say that we at FKAA are not interested
in processes that rely on copies in order to get to new
knowledge. We're more interested in the raw agency of
the copies and especially in the external reaction to our
work.

7:41 Miljački: The invocation of 'new knowledge'
was a quote of a line in your own talk, so, in disowning it
now, you've made me more curious about it.

7:48 Urtzi Grau: Yes, let me ask my own partner,
because we always disagree… These discussions are
great, but they also lack precision. Terms like 'originality,'
'authorship,' 'novelty' are more or less used the same
way, but I think mean different things here. There is one
important clarification that might help us be more precise. In architecture, the above terms—especially when
lumped together—invoke a kind of anachronism, which
they don't necessarily do in other creative fields. We like
to defend copying. In music or any kind of art, no one
gets into impassioned discussions about what it might
mean to take a picture of an existing picture. Remakes
have been produced for ages in art and music and in
these fields, there is nothing contentious about the fact
that there is an author, novelty, and originality in the operation. That being said, we were really interested in the
fact that architecture has a troubled relationship with this
kind of operation. Copying is one of the biggest taboos
in architecture schools, in competitions, with clients,
and within discourse. Beyond the acts and operation of
copying, what interests us is the effect produced though
these operations. Sometimes we call it 'new knowledge,'
sometimes we call it an 'agonistic response.' Awareness
about copying is important. It opens up opportunities
for architects. If you are engaged and aware you recognize that thing is actually real and tangible and amazing
because you're copying…

12:26 Miljački: The point of this event is not to say:
"copies are great." The point is to discuss exactly how we

look at the discipline of architecture, what we draw from it, what the techniques are by which we converse with its history and future, and how we tell stories about the ways in which reproduction or appropriation take place. The point is also not to kill originality or novelty. What I'm interested in, especially with this panel, is the way in which the questions of originality and novelty are held aside for long enough that other things become central to the discussion of the project. Design produces something we can still discuss in terms of novelty or originality, but it simultaneously succeeds at a number of other goals. Since the aim of the whole event is to complicate and perhaps draw out the nuances and taboos of influence, I want to make sure that we don't kill originality completely and end with too simplistic a proclamation like "copying is super."

13:48 Lawrence: I think it is also worth stating that, within the work presented here, formal originality may not be the end goal, but rather originality within the realm of the techniques of appropriation. Novelty emerges in the techniques, and I think that still maintains a kind of discursive function.

I think it's also important to lay out the disjunction between influence—which shares etymological roots with influenza, something that descends like the vapors (maybe Eric Höweler will talk about this in the next round) versus appropriation. There is clear agency in appropriation. I think that all of the projects presented in this panel rely on a kind of agency and, maybe as the historian here, I feel a little out of place.

Contemplating especially Ines Weizman's Ordos project, I am struck with the question of how one operates differently as a historian than as a designer. The legitimacy of, and thus the possibility for, copying Loos' design when you were operating as a historian seemed unproblematic, but when you presented yourself as a designer, copying induced a kind of anxiety for the archivists. That is fascinating. You were in a unique position, Ines, to put on both hats and negotiate the positions and respective anxieties they might invoke.

15:12 Ines Weizman: Yes, I almost needed two advisors: a legal advisor and a historian. As a designer, I was afraid of both of them. In design, you are always restricted, but also free at the same time. However in my Ordos house project, I thought freedom could be inverted. Rather than exercising freedom in the desert, it was an exercise of gathering more knowledge at 'home'. Rather than exploring the fantasy and possibilities of form, I found the restrictions and guidelines for design decisions within the work of Adolf Loos.

15:58 Enrique Walker [from the audience]: Is the key issue at stake here whether copying is acceptable within the field or not (the transgression is implied in all the presentations) or is it about the argument advanced through a certain condition of copying? For instance, when it came to [Han] van Meegeren's copies of Vermeer, the act of copying was indeed novel because he aimed to persuade a number of art historians that his copy was an actual Vermeer. He painted for a specific fantasy of an earlier phase of Vermeer, for which art historians didn't have enough evidence. In so doing, he both copied and invented something, while copying for a certain set of goals. The question then might be, what are the arguments that are being produced through the action of copying, rather than is copy, per say, the issue?

17:28 Grau: In our presentation, we laid out four different instances in which copying opens up a kind of intellectual space. They were stated as hypotheses on purpose because this is ongoing research. Cristina and I could describe in greater detail the pedagogical experiments we have conducted so far in trying to resist falling into the Beaux Arts model of copying, while retaining a direct relation between the masterpieces and what the students are learning as they examine objects very closely. We have also been expanding the goals of our practice, from looking at disciplinary discussions, to using copies within the public space, to animating our relationship with the client, to even rethinking the contract structure.

1:45 Alexander D'Hooghe [from the audience] We generally judge the copy of the Austrian village reproduced in China, presented by Sam Jacob, as very vulgar. The project Ines Weizman presented, again an Austrian design reproduced in China, could certainly be equivalent, but we don't judge it as vulgar. It seems to me that adding the projected sky as a big massive block on top of Weizman's House Baker project was a critical maneuver in evading the accusation of vulgarity. Could you talk about these types of design decisions?

2:46 Weizman: I was well aware that to really copy House Baker would risk destroying the original. I intended my project, like Loos did, as a love letter in built form. I went to Ordos and proposed building it. It was already a vulgar act. It also seemed cruel to build something that Loos left safely behind, unbuilt.

The whole issue of where the House Baker plans came from was another adventure. I resisted participating in the masterplan for Ordos, and this resistance in a way shaped the whole project. My instinct was to refuse the invitation, so I contemplated a way to not do it and still take part in the project. I was always hoping that Ordos 100 would never be realized, and so far I have been lucky.

The House Baker is obviously a fantasy. I learned about it in architectural school, and I teach this building now. Everything anyone knows about this building, all of our visual memory, is based on one photograph that was taken in 1930. Josephine Baker's house is this image. So it seemed appropriate to turn that photograph into the actual façade. I was really keen about that image and projecting it as a photograph…and it wasn't only the black and white slates (which we all remember from the photograph), but also included the sky, as well.

5:40 Mario Carpo [from the audience]: In the case of Medellín, you sold the local government a script to replicate roofs similar to those designed by you. Like mushrooms, which are all different but of the same family, these roofs are all different. In this case, you offered the city [the opportunity] to use your script to make more roofs, different from the ones you made, but still showing that it belongs to the family. Do you have a legal way to control similarity? The case of the house of Josephine Baker proves that, with the blueprint, you can control identical replication. This is the modern, mechanical way of being in control, with one blueprint to make multiple copies. How do we control, not identical copies, but the similarities that your design intention is meant to generate?

7:27 Goberna: In terms of music or literature, whenever you use a certain amount of material that's copyrighted, you could be sued. In architecture, the legal

          Moderator: Ana Miljački

boundaries are still vague. So we hired a lawyer (an expert in copyright) to help us define the protocols that would govern similarity to and difference from our project. We have different options, of course. The first option would allow everybody to copy while following certain rules, and the second would allow everyone to copy our work without any control whatsoever. The second may be more interesting…

8:04 Grau: It's basically a legal definition. We are trying to find an equivalent of creative commons, and its repercussions, at the scale of architecture. That's becoming a project in itself for us. Here, the legal procedure validates replication, while providing some security for the authors. What happens currently, at least in Colombia, is you sign the contract and the owner can build [the design] again as many times as they want. The owner can build two or three of the same buildings without involving the architect again. That actually happened to our partner there, and is one of the reasons we were interested in the legal dimension of the project.

9:39 Carpo [from the audience]: We have a legal framework to control identical copies, but we do not yet have any legal tool to control variability and similarities.

10:13 Lawrence: Mario, you've presented this as a conundrum to which you had no answer: our desire to maintain authorship in direct opposition to this obsession with the indeterminate. It strikes me that a lot of these operations are precisely negotiating that contentious ground. This comes to Enrique's point about technique: what is the aim of the technique? Maybe, on some level, this technique enables a kind of control and authorship, which, at the same time, introduces an indeterminacy in the process that is legitimized by the copying itself. It seems to allow for a space in between those walls.

11:08 Ana María León [from the audience]: I have to preface by saying it causes me great anxiety and agony to ask this question. Since you brought these terms up, hopefully it can be productive. There's a tradition in Latin American colonial architecture and painting of reproducing Spanish architecture and painting. So when I first saw the renderings and the explanation of your project, it was presented to me as a Spanish project in Latin America—a Spanish design populating the public spaces of Medellín. Maybe this was deliberate or can be made productive. Was this discussed during the design?

13:02 Goberna: But ours is not Spanish architecture in Medellín. We have a partner that is one of the biggest practitioners in Colombia, so I would never call it Spanish architecture in Colombia.

13:37 Grau: We should have brought this up earlier and we haven't. The project is co-authored by a group of people from Colombia. The structure is from a French engineer and the technology to build it is half from the Netherlands, and half from Mexico.

15:11 Miljački: I want to pose a question about the kind of writing of history that focuses on following of the ghosts of appropriation. I think we encountered versions of that type of historical work both in Ines's and Amanda's case, but differently. It took the forms of sniffing out of the trail of ownership across a more than 50 year-long timeline in one case, and, in the other, it seemed to require looking through notebooks to find the architect's direct and intimate pronouncements of interest. I am curious if you can help us discuss how the question of appropriation, copyright or influence changes the production of history.

16:03 Lawrence: I think that is an important question. For me, the Stirling project has to do, as you are suggesting, with moving away from the identification of the source and any desire to find the true intent of the architect and locating the interest in the act of the revision and the appropriation itself, precisely disassociated from any kind of proclaimed intent either by the historian or the architect. The project becomes one of understanding the operations that are being performed to move from one to another.

16:49 Weizman: I started to draw the ownership trail in response to the questions posed by the copyright lawyer. I had to explain to him what really happened to the material. The most interesting challenge was to present architecture, or the history of architecture, in such a way that a judge could follow the story, as well. Making a drawing of the ownership trail was also a way to bring architects into the conversation about legal rights.

Besides the story about the ownership of rights to his

drawings, deeply embedded in this Loos project is also perhaps another story about late Socialist architecture. In that late Socialist context, copyright could have perhaps saved some objects from demolition because the law, or better, the copyright holders (the architects) demanded it—not as an interpretive architectural historical reading by the new regime, but as a kind of legal instance. In this context, the law was more powerful than interpretation of heritage in shaping and limiting interventions, to the built environment. What really interests me is this engagement with history through the lens of law, in order to find possibilities outside of our internal disciplinary discourse conducted among architectural theorists and historians.

0:00

This presentation is in two parts. The first, 'Color,' has a relatively simple ambition: to look at color as an analog medium in relationship to the idea of digital sampling in music. The second part, 'Sample,' looks, in turn, at digital sampling in music as a way to re-understand color, and then applies this 'color sample' idea back into architecture. So, in starting analog (or with an analogy), then moving to the digital, and back to analog (that is, architecture), it is, in its way, a sampling of a much larger (and complete) argument.

The presentation originally had another title, "...with apologies to Sylvia Lavin and Pierre Menard," reflecting perhaps more overtly the original conception of the argument. Pierre Menard is the author of *Don Quixote*, according to Borges' "Pierre Menard, Author of Don Quixote", not in its original iteration, but of a verbatim reconstruction of the original text; and architectural theorist Sylvia Lavin is the author of the text "What Color is Now?" Initially, I was preparing to simply re-present Sylvia Lavin's text, as a way of invoking both color and sample, but that seemed too high-concept. Instead, I make use of Lavin's ideas, and, in so doing, re-discover them on my own. In her essay, Lavin argues for a manifestation of contemporaneity within design, and as example offers the case of "cathode-ray blue" (as in a computer screen) and how its coloration becomes apparent within a wide range of projects as the hue of choice, at the same moment that the designs are starting to be envisioned on the screen rather than paper.

The book *Understanding Color: A Designer's Guide* presents (among other things) a series of palettes that describe the affective dimension of color: The Dreamy Palette, The Breezy Palette, The Arcadian Palette, The Luxurious Palette, and The Dynamic Palette. So on one hand, color has this association with bringing forth an emotive response. At the grocery store, we see another signification of color, a notational association. Yellow products have connotations of the tropical or citrus; that green products have to do with vegetal or health; black products bring forth notions of density or luxury. We can understand color in this notational sense operating as a kind of language. These distinctions are manifest in the spectrum of corporate identities that take advantage of those associated values to make distinctions of one brand from the next.

3:30

Turning our attention to music, we can take, for example, "What's It All About" by Girl Talk, a musician who operates only through sampling. If you've ever heard it, you know that it's technically intricate, composed purely of mere snippets of music, but is also highly danceable. The snippets are not just blank registrations, but signifiers that build on each other and, in their multiplicity, induce a pleasure. Here is where color is a helpful parallel. Color can help us understand what's actually going on within music. From these musical samples, there's an affective dimension: the rate, the beat, the rhythm, the music that one feels and one moves to. But also, over the course of listening to it, you're getting the notation, the references to these specific samples. Part of the joy of the music is the synthesis of these notational and affective dimensions; which give one both the pleasure of knowing and the pleasure of doing. It's a useful model for understanding the kind of theory of reception that's going on in sampling as a form of appropriation.

4:54

The manipulations of digital music and the idea of sampling seem entirely a product of recent technology. The analog musical source, once acquired, is digitized. That digitization renders it into computer code, which is what allows it to be so easily manipulated, as in the example of Girl Talk. But, of course we know that this is not purely a manifestation of computer technology. It has a pre-history in the DJ turntable setup found in the Bronx of the 1970s, at the beginning of scratch and hip-hop culture. So already, without digital, there is a pre-history of appropriation of music. It goes back even further in the history of music, as seen in the example of the Hungarian composer Béla Bartók's notations from his travels around the Hungarian countryside, collecting examples of folk music that he would then re-deploy into his own compositions. So within the project of music itself, we have these three

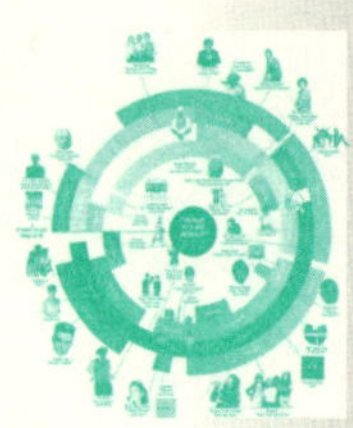

     John McMorrough

components that are part of the logic of the sample: the signal, the mixture, and a notion of the cultural milieu in which it operates—its context.

9:15

Architect Peter Eisenman has stated his preference to have photographs of his buildings be in black and white, because the color distracts from the form. This mentality is not only a matter of individual preference, but also indicative of a disciplinary prejudice: a longer trajectory of an emphasis on form and a subtraction of color from architecture. This goes back to the exterior of the Villa Savoye, and further, to Johann Joachim Winckelmann, which reflects an ongoing fascination with the idealization of a white-on-white vision of the classical, understanding the monuments of antiquity as being white marble in the Mediterranean sun.

Of course we know, and have known for a long time, that things were not that way that those sculptures and buildings of the classical past were not white. Color was applied onto these monuments and they existed, in their own time, in a much richer, polychromatic mode. Instead of taking a white stone bust as a starting point, we could actually articulate by its absence, and a genealogy of its hidden presence, a more interesting concept about color sample as it operates in architecture. Using the model of the sample, we arrive at a possible new history or trajectory to consider. In that way we actually have a non-textual model for understanding the logic of appropriation and influence. I'll do that by offering a few examples, most of which are historical, but retain a contemporary relevance in their potency vis-à-vis the idea of the 'color sample.'

10:00

The first example is Johann Wolfgang von Goethe's house in Weimar. Goethe, of course, the author of *Faust*, among other literary efforts, and also a natural philosopher, whose *Color Theory* responded to Isaac Newton's diagrammatic conception of color, providing his own observational, experimental sense of the way color operates through a prism (natural refraction). However in a more poetic and affective sense, he describes colors as he understands them; in terms of their emotive potential, taking those potentials and applying them to his home. These colors were used in a programmatic sense. For

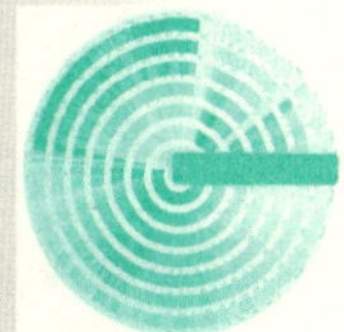

Reference: Color wheel (http://www.studyblue.com/notes/note/n/color-theory-midterm/deck/5444897)

Goethe, yellow was cheerful, lively, and stimulating, and he made a whole room of it, [which he called] the Yellow Room. The Ceiling Room is rose pink, which he describes as the color of beauty. The living room was blue, which he characterized as a 'mean' color. (To have 'mean' associated with living is a bit strange.) Nonetheless, we see schematic analysis of the way Goethe used color throughout his architecture as the primary means of creating this simultaneously notational and affective dimension.

12:30

Another example I would add to the color sample list is Le Corbusier's Villa La Roche. Doctor La Roche commissioned Le Corbusier to do his house and also this project, the painting gallery. La Roche was a collector of Le Corbusier's Purist paintings, which evolved as a post-Cubist style. The initial version of the painting gallery was shown as being full of paintings, the walls treated in a rather nondescript fashion. After seeing the exhibit of the de Stijl show in Paris, Le Corbusier made a sort of translation of this project into the way we now know it, basically the palette of the Purist painting reapplied it to architecture, employing a structural notion of color. The color affiliates to different spatial planes, and articulates and disarticulates the space along those lines. Further, we can see that this is part of a whole interest in color by Corbu, to the point where he was commissioned by a Swiss paint company to create a catalog of paints. His well-known Color Keyboard makes a kind of formula of selection, and a machine of sampling. As you move the guide across the color swatches (color samples), it makes the palette for you. You could almost understand it as a modulor of color, making bad color combinations impossible.

14:25

As we get into the present moment today, how could we start to think about this notion of color sample within architecture? We could look at the Pharmacological Research Laboratories in Biberach by Sauerbruch and Hutton, which uses color in the glass and the panel work, as a sampling of the graphic diagrams or outputs of viral material being worked on inside the building. The material is then sampled and re-deployed as a facade strategy. We could also look to a book published a number of years ago, *30 Colors* by Rem Koolhaas and OMA, featuring a palette created for a paint manufacturer. In the book, the pages are interspersed with color samples and photographs of people in the office. Each person is referenced by a color. For example, the color for Dan Wood is called 'It's the Color of my Car' and is a sports car red. So we have color as not only as sample, affect, and notation, but also as biography as a form of context. If geometry was the abstract description of an architecture that became form, then color and color sampling might be understood as a model for a possible architecture of ambience.

Side Effects
Mariana Ibañez
& Simon Kim

0:00 Mariana Ibañez

We took on the provocation of Under the Influence, and we are going to show projects and present a few arguments about how influence operates in our work. We're actually very explicit about it in our work, grouping ideas, and identifying domains that have influenced each new project. As with any research, when beginning our projects, we map out what has been done before, what audience we are addressing, and what our original contributions can be to the field of discourse and production.

1:13 Simon Kim

There was an interesting debate last night on the specific site of authorship as a function of trends, close proximity among designers over time, and the choice of design medium. The discussion led us to talking about affinities that were perhaps too superficial, based on similarity of representation. In our view, the Greg Lynn Embryological House for example, is not the antecedent to Lars Spuybroek's Off the Road 5-Speed community simply because both works rely on animation software. Or, to repeat with an example from the previous generation, the works of Steven Holl, John Hejduk, and Aldo Rossi are not necessarily the same because they all used watercolor.

We thought it would be interesting to note the role of copying or reenactment from the outset, as well. It is perhaps too easy to blame China for all things duplicated, just as it is easy to be scandalized by Le Corbusier's Ronchamp cathedral replicated on a different site and at a different scale, but there's also an unusual side effect associated with posthumous work such as Le Corbusier's church in Ferminy. What does it mean to have one's work literally produced by others in a fundamentally different context from the one that allowed for the conception of that same work? Along these lines, there were admittedly a few moments in the exhibition that positioned us in a broader discussion, which we are perhaps not prepared to have...yet. The ease with which tectonic forms—hard-fought empirical knowledge from failure—have become clean mathematical procedures suggests to us that all

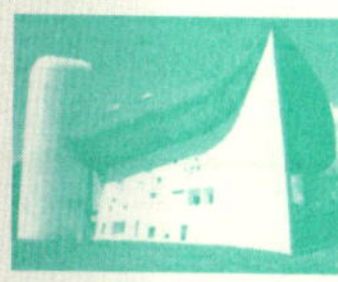

Reference: The Chapel of Notre Dame de Haut, copy, Shanghai, China. (http://farm1.staticflickr.com/36/86737659_b9ee84ae15_o.jpg)

form is simply choice from a catalog. Unlike the catalogs of Durand or Quincy, where decisions are made from the preservation and expansion of building type, advanced fabrication techniques produce these forms with little risk or danger in their outcome.

3:00 Ibañez

Going back to our own work and the way we use references; for each project, we create what we call, "The Map of the World."

These are diagrams in which we chart out territories or ideas we consider as part of our architectural discipline. We use these maps to deliberately collect influences and expose our affinities to other traditions. Including the advances and discoveries that directly influenced what we do helps us remember that we are not alone in a special bubble and often reveals the limits of our own methodologies. Our Maps of the World help us resist a particular type of tunnel vision. Of course, we cannot address the entirety of the world in every work, and these maps become smaller in scope and range over time, but the connections among nodes often lead to new understandings. In this manner, our maps are not simply documentation, but also acts of design.

In order to create a Map of the World for a project, we already have to be aware of the framework for our exploration. We place our initial idea among a set of preliminary references. This is to always remind ourselves that our work is not *sui generis*; it is part of a tradition of discipline that establishes discourse, even if it is not always architectural in origin. This does not preclude newness or unexpected discoveries from occurring, what we define side effects.

3:43 Kim

Before we present any of our own work, we offer you three projects to contemplate. All of them are interesting to us because they fall somewhat outside of the architectural canon. Here is Cedric Price, who designed this very flexible Fun Palace, and as Alexander [D'Hooghe] described this morning, perhaps a predecessor to the big box typology. However, there is also another key figure in this project, Gordon Pask, a cyberneticist who was charged by Price with generating the idea of *equal agency*. Price and Pask were not interested in a hierarchical building that would deliver on the expectations of a user-group, but a reciprocal agency between the building and its occupants. Under this scenario, even unpredictability and boredom from the architectural machine was possible, as proposed in Pask's *Conversation Theory*. For Pask, a dynamic learning between humans and non-human machines, or 'teachbacks', was required for full realization of a shared awareness.

This project was ongoing as Price and Pask tried many years to find different sites for it. You can see now how evocative the original drawings were became. They tried again and again to find a site around East London to realize this revolutionary building. It was finally realized, but not by them, and not in England. The fun palace was ultimately embodied in The Centre Pompidou by Rogers and Piano in the Beaubourg area of Paris.

Another group which is fascinating to us and has been at the core of many of our discussions is E.A.T. Their event, 9 Evenings was held in the 1960s and organized by Robert Rauschenberg, John Cage, and several of their colleagues force-paired with—or perhaps they elicited the responses from—Bell Lab technicians and engineers. 9 Evenings had immediate and far-flung repercussions, one of which was a project that was so aberrant and unusual that I don't think I've yet seen the corresponding lineage. This was the Pepsi Pavilion in 1970s Osaka, where every possible derivation of responsiveness and interactivity was forced into one location. The effects of this jamming were dizzying, and the resultant euphoria, powerful.

And finally, the third project we want to bring to the table, so to speak, is quite well known. The Philips Pavilion is an outlier of the extended works of Le Corbusier. It was designed by his employee Iannis Xenakis. Working with scores and new musical compositions, Xenakis designed an envelope made of mathematically-driven, hyperbolic paraboloid shells. Xenakis is an interesting polymathic figure, prescient in architecture, composition, and electronic music, who found himself locked out of Le Corbusier's office. He employed innovative tape systems to move sound around hundreds of speakers, integrated lights and projections, and the non-planar geometry of the shells to immerse visitors for a sound and light performance showcasing the development of human civilization.

6:33 Ibañez

So the notion of side effects supports a central position
in which architecture carries and produces manifold meanings. But the explicit interest in side effects also promotes
an unexpected peripheral zone from which unwelcome
or aberrant scenarios may emerge, including vertigo,
imbalance, amnesia, but also wonder, or the sublime. Our
practice and our larger project aims to establish a *terrain
vague* that is wholly part of architectural tradition, our
discipline, but extends what has been termed experimental
and radical. These classifications were meant to marginal-
ize or obscure work that is not normative or easily understood, but as witnessed by the aftermath of many MoMA
shows—including the *Deconstructivist Architecture* exhibition, where the paintings of the Peak and others projects
by Zaha Hadid did more to influence early architectural
representation in computer graphics than the other six architects in the show—the outsiders repeatedly become the
center. We prefer to continually augment and enlarge the
field with extended techniques and meanings that become
entrenched and inseparable from what is considered core.

7:20 Kim

The Philadelphia Masque project was self-initiated. Its
aim was to expose and speculate upon a blight of empty
lots unique to Philadelphia. These 40,000 vacant lots are
distributed throughout the city and although many are pri-
vately owned, strict regulations impede any development.
We took this as an opportunity to work at a larger scale
and use an urban multi-agent system that could simulate
multiple scenarios and stage data to suggest a newness
for Philadelphia. It also replicated an older idea—not
developed by us—of characters in a narrative that could
reinvent Philadelphia.

We were interested in layering computer simulations
with the work of John Hejduk. The work that he produced
in Berlin for the Prisoners was also coupled with the making of these figures, so that although the relationships
among them were clearly defined as agents, they still
had some kind of underlying speculative premise. As the
agents had distinct features and sets of goals, they would
continually assess their location and the location of their
neighbors to generate connections dependent on those
dynamic conditions.

Mariana Ibañez
& Simon Kim

Image: Philadelphia Masque project

Given that unusual and perhaps forced pairing of Hejduk and multi-agents, we developed characters based on their location and on the particularities of sites' properties and values. We also used what is called fiducial markers so that cameras could track their position and rotation. Those two degrees of freedom were enough to allow outside human interaction and produce very different maps of Philadelphia sorted by real estate value, demographics, and other datasets.

Meet the first character from the project, The Fat Controller.[1] The Fat Controller is located right next to the *Philadelphia Inquirer* office building. It is an object that gathers and disseminates information through this field of antennae, guarded by a wall, with no perceptible interior.

10:27 Ibañez

It may be important to note here that our design operation was not a direct reenactment of Hejduk's Masques and characters. Through a multi-agent system, we produced a constellation of agents, loaded with certain technological and geometrical behaviors, which were self-productive in the city. The initial reference, to a certain degree, survived in the final product only as a trace and a type of humor, whose specific origin disappeared within the fabric of the new proposition.

Again, the idea of side effects approximates the relationship between the Philadelphia Masque and Hejduk's Masques. We did not have the term 'side effects' to

1. These are names that we made from Vladivostok and the work of Will Self.

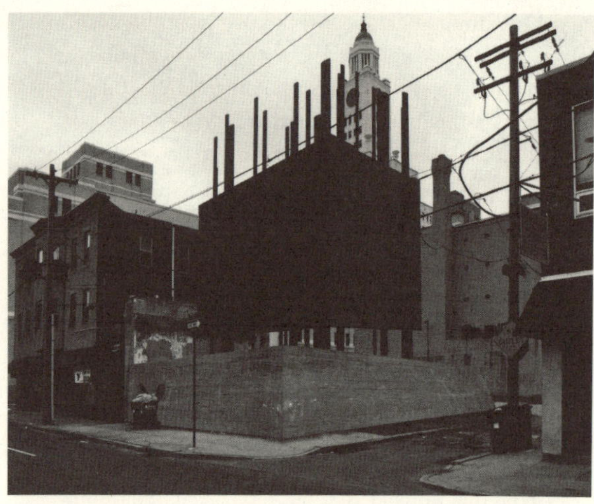

describe our work before this conference, but we will
now certainly abuse it. For us, it appropriately captures
the possibility of the uncontrolled, and which is continu-
ously engaged in indeterminacy. I would like to expand
on that definition. It refers to an internal outcome that is
wholly emergent and unplanned, but is controlled within
the framework of the original design intention. We design
the range of actions and variables. We make matrices of
historical references from architecture, explore ideas from
related disciplines, and find a cross-product between
them. If we look at what has come before us, the merits
of side effects produce a dark region that is then gainfully
measured and replicable as a disciplinary procedure.

12:00 Kim

This takes us to another type of project, a realm of
projects that deal with the body in space. We are curious
about the disciplinary domain that hovers between the
loss of body and a completely post-human scheme in
which we are no longer central. One frontier that we think
has potential in this realm, and perhaps is the scalar link
from body to space, is the wearable, computing device.
We are not the first architects to design wearables—Diller
Scofidio's Bad Press, Oskar Schlemmer's Triadic Ballet,
and World Upside Down by Williams and Tsien are hall-
mark examples in a line of inquiry.

Cloud Cloak device is part of a research project into
augmenting our physiognomy, our morphology, and our

means of communication. We can use wearable technology to not just communicate but perhaps even obscure identification as well. The wearer can suddenly become enveloped in this fog that obscures their gender, their race, and their identity, which we find to be an extremely interesting idea.

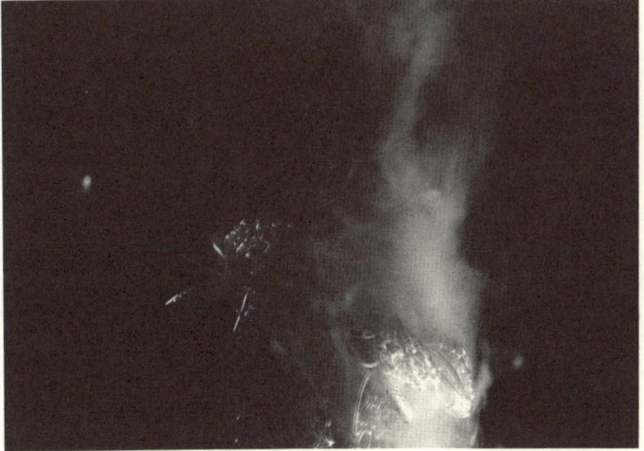

13:13 Ibañez

In showing the wearable devices, which are clearly not central to the conventional production of architecture, we still argue for their outcome as active producers of environments and spaces for inhabitation.

13:27 Kim

If we could make clothing for ourselves, we could also make clothing for other agents, as seen in this next research project. PR2 Robot needs to keep its joints clean from debris. We devised a kind of proof of concept for the wearable device, showing that we could simply make a garment for it. However, what was translated as useful from the human perspective did not work for the robot's local sensors and actuators. We then turned from the idea of a garment to a collar, for which there is a clothing tradition. An interesting property of the Dutch ruff collar is its shape and surface area. The design brief was to protect this research robot from particulates and dust in the air, which can get caught in its joints and break them down. So we found that instead of actually making a garment, as we had originally tested, what would be more interesting would be an electrically charged surface with a very large area. Therefore, we identified and made Enneper surfaces to create ruffles with more area than is possible from a planar surface. Placing these ruffles around what we call the robot's 'neck', the surfaces can become mildly electrostatically charged. Any particles will be drawn to the collar, and the robot can maintain all of its degrees of freedom.

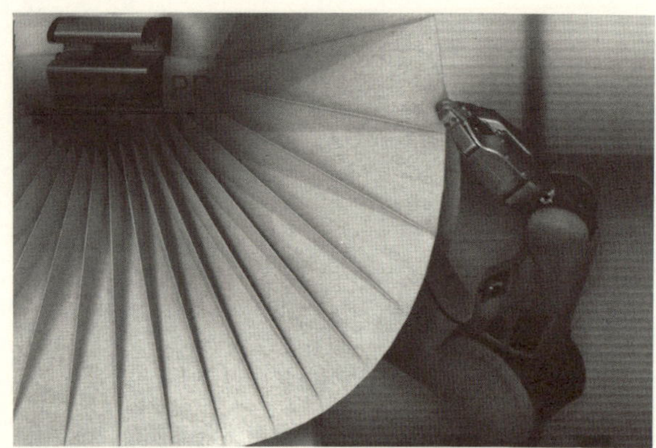

15:15 Ibañez

Taking the idea of wearables, and also seeing how they can become extended to an environment, we arrive at the Seamless show. We already think of computational couture as a modulus of space, but we make a more explicit case for it here. This Clothing-Cladding project is a dress made of a developable surface. We also have it networked and tiled together into a larger envelope. These are the different types of modular surfaces that demonstrate pliability, from the tall to the horizontal. The idea that there is a production and scale of architecture is studied through a system of tests. More importantly, we are dedicated to a production of knowledge that is consistent with architecture as a means of communication. Without a meaningful or affective outcome with cultural or visual significance, any research project becomes merely a recipe of techniques.

14:42 Kim

Therefore, we test ideas that may be peripheral to architecture in full-scale prototypes. We fabricate what we propose. We physically prototype, run serial tests, and if our tests do not produce higher meaning beyond simply working, the idea is invalid for us. For Clothing-Cladding

Mariana Ibañez
& Simon Kim

we discovered that for the tiled surface of dresses to work, one would have to carry around car batteries to power them for any sufficient length of time. That obstacle generated the exploration into wireless electricity. With a receiver coil, a transmitter coil, and some distance, electricity can flow from a building to an occupant. The more interesting invention came from spatial orientation. These two coils have to be somewhat parallel to make it work. Our first test turned the occupant into the wearer of the receiving coil. But if the coils are turned into tubes and deployed around the room, the Modernist idea of how you orient yourself in space is radically redefined. The occupant may choose an allegiance to one space over another, simply by orientation.

16:48 Ibañez

The above discovery became the premise for a house. The Tesla House project's systems of coils are deployed throughout every internal surface, and also on the body of the wearer. As one moves through the house, one experiences different levels of engagement and responsiveness based on the orientation of the body.

Again, we present this particular sequence of projects because of the way in which they transition from the device and prosthesis directly attached to the body and extend them to architectural agendas that may be transformed or reinterpreted.

17:27 Kim

ModHouse was designed with Mark Yim, a specialist in modular robots. These are robots made of pieces that aggregate. They are not designed to look humanoid and do not serve a one-function role. Modular robots can become many things: biped, quadruped, wheel-based, as required in changing conditions. For us, the first reaction to seeing Mark's work was surprise that it was not conceived as a building, or why each module could not be scaled up and be occupiable. So we tried to make a walking robot architecture that can be ridden. The motors and current are quite heavy, but there is another non-electric option to ride, or push the module up and down like a lever, starting a chain of incremental movements producing a wave gait.

The side effect of this project was the discovery of modular chains behaving as mat buildings. Linear, single program units can pack into larger spaces, describe courtyards, or fold into different aggregate assemblies as required.

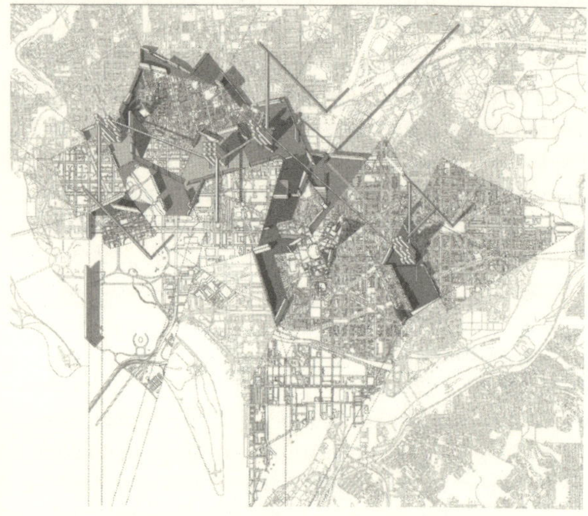

19:05 Ibañez

D.C. Loci is the last project we are going to present. It is the second urban study following the Philadelphia Masque. D.C. Loci of course is an examination of the national capital, both its original altruistic design by L'Enfant, and its present perception.

19:30 Kim

Our motivation was to explore—not in Paris, but in Washington, D.C.—the tethering of broad avenues with power. The project became premised on the agency of boulevards. They can be reconsidered and perhaps imagined as something else. We translated them into fixed formal linkages, a mechanical assembly in which the avenues can be shifted and reordered. This reordering metaphorically broke the network of privileged connections linking government buildings towards a redistribution of civilian accessibility and public space.

For this urban project we created two orders of study. One was a film introducing different characters in a story of Washington D.C. civil life, and one was a mechanical system. These loci, or spaces, are domains of city fabric carved from the network of avenues. They have different boundaries for how they connect with each other.

Mariana Ibañez
& Simon Kim

We want to spend a little more time explaining this particular project (due to something that was offered up yesterday in Mario [Carpo's] lecture within his refrain on architects and digital media described as a monolithic whole that is ahistorical and anti-tradition). This is a drawing of the computer programming for this project. We developed code for the static and the interactive parts of the project.

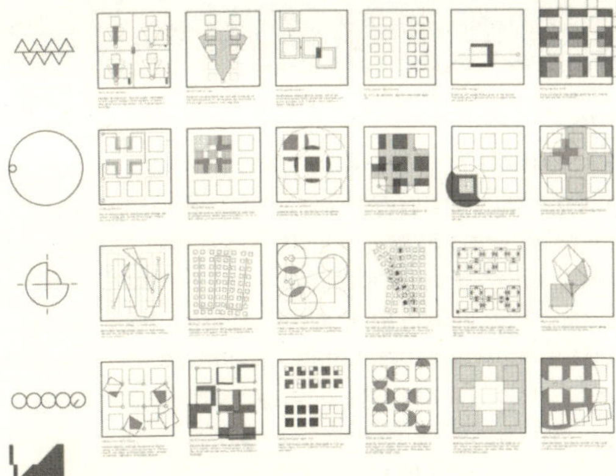

We are architects who work with computer programming and we write code, but we also communicate as architects. Like a diagram or storyboard, these drawings are a design medium within which we control the programming. One of the arguments that we put forward is that when we write code, we must still maintain design authorship; it is a design act in itself. And we express design intention via graphics and representation in the same way we would in any other architectural project.

21:26 Kim

This is a drawing of behaviors and logics. As the linkages are deployed they create domains, that produce the movement of the grand avenues. They start to shift with their own degrees of freedom as bound within a parametric relationship, and they suggest radical urban newness. The avenues-as-linkages do not rotate in a manner that we might find pictorially pleasing. Instead, they have a prescribed internal logic that they follow. Ultimately they provide opportunities for urban design and opportunities for interstitial spaces.

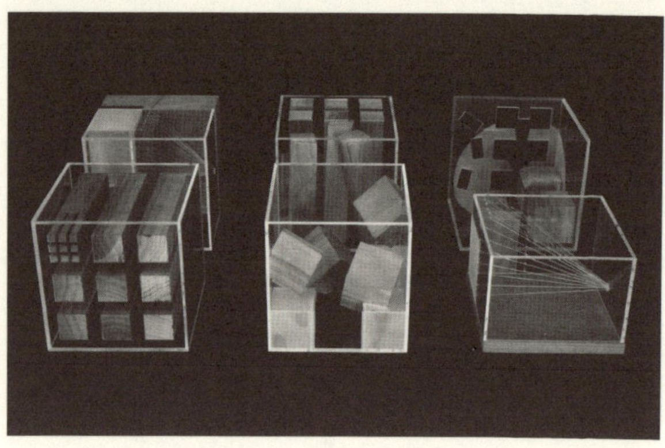

22:04 Ibañez

In conclusion, how do we validate or make evaluations about side effects? Is it vis-à-vis fidelity to source material or in terms of new effects? We prefer to think of working with the ambition for and love of side effects as a method that allows us to acknowledge disciplinary traditions from, while maintaining openness towards the unknowable ways in which those traditions may be received. For us, side effects will always constitute a dual operation, which is both internal to us and to our processes, and framed by others, who may or may not be our target audience. Social media and electronic devices have created an immediacy and overabundance of information that supersedes any levels of communication that even media-savvy architects such as Le Corbusier have managed. Side effects are a desirable outcome, for us, part of a discovery we don't feel is bounded or pressured to produce within a narrow set of principles and techniques. However, what is isolated as a side effect must always face scrutiny to provide meaningfulness beyond novelty and to become an original contribution to the field.

References play a key role in this form of practice, in which exploration, mediated by disciplinary principles, expands the boundaries of practice itself.

Mariana Ibañez
& Simon Kim

Signature
Timothy Hyde

SIGNATURE:
OR, THE DEATH AND LIFE OF ANONYMOUS

The death of the author is by now a familiar figural manifestation that carries one into that sphere of textuality in which intention, significance, meaning are diffused among the biographical fragments of a life lived; fragments disassembled and reassembled as interpretation, proposition, or possibility until the author as such has faded almost entirely from view. But we should not let the familiarity of this figurative death of the author prompt us too quickly to overlook its accompanying literal manifestation—the actual death of an author.

One such death occurred on August 17, 1969, with the author in question being the architect Ludwig Mies van der Rohe. Mies was 83 years old, 30 years on from his arrival in the United States, ten years on from the completion of the Seagram building. From his office in Chicago, with a cohort of associates that included his grandson

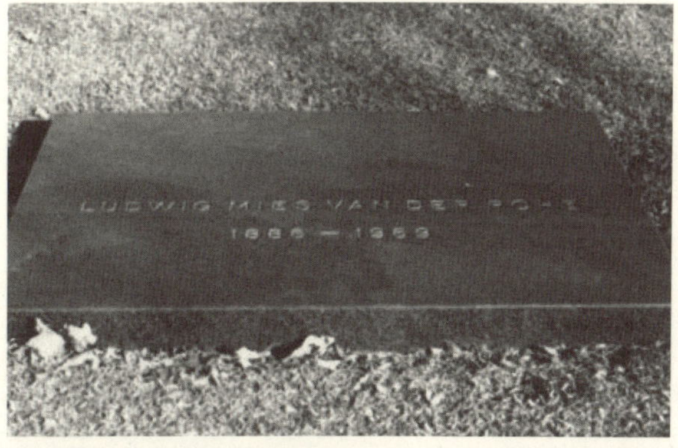

Image: Ludwig Mies van der Rohe gravestone, Scott Covert.

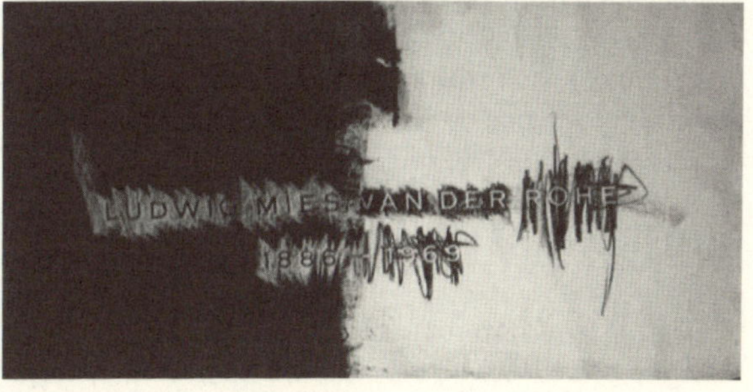

Image: Rubbing of etched lettering of Mies' gravestone, Scott Covert.

Dirk Lohan, Mies had followed the final stages of work on the Neue Nationalgalerie and the more preliminary stages of several other projects. It is one of these latter projects that occupies, alongside the persona of its architect, the central role of the story that I want to recount here.

In 1958, the property developer Peter Palumbo (now Baron Palumbo of Walbrook) set out to purchase plots of land in the City of London in the blocks near Mansion House and the Royal Exchange. Four years later, in 1962, with the intention of soon acquiring enough adjacent lots to assemble a sufficiently large parcel, he commissioned from Mies van der Rohe the design of an office tower and an open plaza. Over the next several years, and with one visit to the site, Mies and his Chicago office developed a scheme for the tower and the plaza that Palumbo presented to the City of London planning authorities in 1968. This consultation with the authorities was required for several reasons, including the atypical height of the building and the alteration of existing street and traffic configurations, as well as the nature of the site itself. Mies' tower was surrounded by the work of other well-known architectural authors—George Dance the Elder's Mansion House and Edward Lutyen's Midland Bank would form two sides of the proposed plaza—and a number of less-regarded though still authored Victorian buildings would have to be demolished to clear space for the tower.

The city authorities viewed the proposal favorably, but because Palumbo owned only some of the properties that were to be demolished permission was withheld with an instruction that he must first attain sufficient control over the relevant properties to ensure that the project would not be subject to endless delay during construction. Over the next fourteen years, Palumbo followed this instruction, buying up a dozen freeholds and hundreds of separate leaseholds. In the meanwhile, additional refinements were being made to the design in Mies's office and a set of working drawings was prepared and ready for presentation in 1982, the year that Palumbo returned to the Common Council of the Corporation of the City of London with almost all of the required property under his control.

By this time, now more than twenty years after Palumbo had conceived the project, a number of relevant

circumstances had changed. With the rapidity of postwar
reconstruction evolving easily into the rapidity of the development of the finance economy, new towers had appeared on the City of London skyline, but partially in consequence a strong trend of preservation had emerged,
so that the demolition of older buildings, even those
of minor distinction, was now approached with more
hesitation. Conservation areas had been defined within
the City, one of which contained parts of the proposed
development, and some of the affected existing buildings
had been listed—given various degrees of legal protection as historic structures either individually or as groups.
More generally, a significant revaluation of architectural
style had, in Britain as elsewhere, catalyzed a concentrat-
ed hostility toward modernist architecture paralleled by
an increased veneration of English Victorian architecture
(and of historicist architecture more broadly). At this point
in time, the architecture of Mies van der Rohe would no
longer be presumptively contemporary, nor would the
Victorian commercial buildings on the existing site be
readily designated as insignificant or obsolescent.

Palumbo's renewed application now faced strong
criticism, and was summarily rejected by the Common
Council. Palumbo elected to appeal the decision, prompt-
ing a review of the case by an appointed inspector with
authority to gather information and opinions and then to
convey a recommendation to the Secretary of State for
the Environment. To carry out this process, and aware of
the now considerable attention focused upon the proposal by media and by professional groups, the Inspector
Stephen Marks convened a public inquiry held over ten
weeks in 1984.[1] This inquiry, while not actually a judicial
proceeding, was nevertheless organized as one, with
evidence presented by barristers and witnesses speaking
in favor of or in opposition to the appeal through direct
testimony and cross examination.

In this forum, the persona of the architect came distinctly into view, for of all of the changed circumstances
since 1968, perhaps the most consequential was the fact
that Mies van der Rohe had died in 1969. Despite Mies's
death, the design was still attached to his persona, and in
1984 this attachment assumed a considerable importance
in light of the markedly diminished appreciation for the

1. The Mansion
House Square
Inquiry convened
by Stephen Marks
was held in the
Livery Hall of the
London Guildhall
from May 1st to
July 6th, 1984. The
Inspector's final
report, which con-
tains summaries
of the testimony
and evidence, can
be found in Folder
AT 41/411, National
Archives.

2. Additional papers pertaining to the Mansion House Square inquiry are contained in the RIBA Archives, with John Summerson's testimony included the John Summerson Papers. For an analysis of Summerson's testimony in relation to his concerns about preservation see Michela Rosso, "An Open Space at the Constricted Centre of the City: Summerson and the Artificial Inflation of Victorian Values," in *Summerson and Hitchcock: Centenary Essays on Architectural Historiography*, ed. Frank Salmon (New Haven: Yale University Press, 2006): 155-169.

3. Report by Inspector Stephen Marks, Section 10.88, page 56. [National Archives, folder AT 41/411]

4. John Harris, "Was the design by Mies van der Rohe?," *Financial Times* (30 April 1982)

5. In a minor controversy during the inquiry, the Inspector was told that Dr. Ludwig Glaeser, curator of the Mies archive

proposed development on the part of planning authorities. In order to make their case, Palumbo and his supporters—Richard Rogers, Colin St. John Wilson, James Stirling, and the historian John Summerson were among them—placed the person of Mies van der Rohe at the center of their argument. They pointed to his stature as one of the most important architects of the century and to the widespread appreciation of his realized works as evidence of the importance and value of this prospective tower.[2] They argued, in essence, that the City had an opportunity to build a building by Mies van der Rohe, and the price to be paid was a collection of Grade II listed buildings by lesser-known architects.

While proponents of the scheme affirmed its architectural value by reference to its architect, opponents of the scheme sought to undermine precisely this argument, first by stating that the architect's reputation was less a historical determination than a "myth [that] had nothing to do with the actual quality of his buildings;"[3] and second, by suggesting that the design could not be attributed to Mies van der Rohe with any certainty, due to the architect's death and the absence of indisputable evidence of his hand in authoring the design. Where were the sketches or original drawings, asked John Harris, historian and founder of SAVE Britain's Heritage.[4] The building was one more weak derivation of Mies' iconic Seagram building suggested Philip Johnson and Arthur Drexler. The historian Henry-Russell Hitchcock also indicated to the inquiry that Mies' involvement could only have been a preliminary stage.[5]

In short, the opponents argued that the building was not definitively bound to the person of Mies in biographical terms, and therefore did not possess in aesthetic terms the superior value attributed by its advocates. Forced to rebut this line of argument, Palumbo's barrister brought to the inquiry Peter Carter, who had worked on the Mansion House Square scheme as the job architect and who had continued the development of this and other projects in the firm after Mies' death. Carter assured the inquiry that the building had been designed with the full involvement of the famous architect, whose typical working method left little in the way of sketches and original drawings. He testified that Mies had known and approved of the revisions pending following the first application in 1968, and any subsequent changes were minor and had no effect upon the appearance of the design.[6]

This dispute was not the only point of evidentiary contention during the Mansion House Square inquiry—much of which focused upon questions of conservation, heritage, and urban experience—but it is the issue I wish to pursue here. There's no need for further suspense: following the inquiry and due consideration of the evidence, the Inspector recommended that Palumbo's appeal be dismissed, the Secretary of State for the Environment agreed, and the Mansion House Square scheme joined the catalogue of unbuilt work.[7] The evidence presented asserted with rough equality that the design was by Mies and that it was not by Mies, an opposition that, as it took shape through the testimonies before the inquiry, enabled the emergence of a framework in which the architectural person under scrutiny was not the living (or deceased) Mies van der Rohe, but the signature 'Mies van der Rohe.'

An architectural drawing—the evidence of Mies' authorship demanded by John Harris and other opponents—has long been regarded as an extension of the architect's mind, functioning as an expressive object whose attribution enables the recognition of the architect to occur at a remove from a physical building or an actual body. Such distancing mechanisms within design (a list might also include the separation of design from construction, or the collaborative nature of architecture firms) are familiar facts even though they are most often veiled by personality. In 1984, the drawing had seemingly lost none of its standing to invoke the recognition of agency, but Carter's testimony brought to the inquiry an exacting description of the same distancing figured not by the architectural drawing, but by discussion, review, approval, and other habits and conventions of architectural practice.[8] His version, and the argument of non-authorship it aimed to rebut, removed the sphere of reference from personhood into signature.

The cartoonist Louis Hellman cleverly satirized the Corporation's refusal of the scheme in 1982, with a mocking account in which Christopher Wren and his 1666 plan for the rebuilding of London stood in for Mies van der

and a supporter of the proposed tower, had suborned Hitchcock, attempting to induce him to recant this statement. The Inspector did not pursue the accusation formally but surely took note of it.

6. Opponents also argued that the reputation Mies enjoyed was itself a fiction, forged largely by the sustained propaganda of Philip Johnson. Richard Rogers aimed to rebut this claim with an explication of the broad historical importance of Mies' work.

7. The Secretary of State issued his decision on May 22 1985. See Press Notice, "Patrick Jenkin Rejects Mansion House Proposal" [National Archives, folder AT 41/411]

8. See Peter Carter, "The design was by Mies van der Rohe," *Financial Times* (May 5, 1982) and "Expert Witness: Peter Carter," *Architects' Journal* (22 & 29 August, 1984): 24-25.

Rohe and his Mansion House Square proposal. (In Hellman's cartoon, the then Secretary of State, Michael Heseltine, is made into King Charles II, and Peter Palumbo is

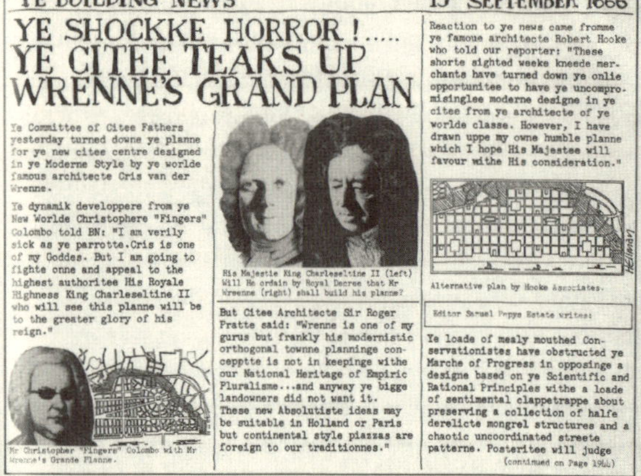

YE BUILDING NEWS   13TH SEPTEMBER 1666

YE SHOCKKE HORROR !.....
YE CITEE TEARS UP
WRENNE'S GRAND PLAN

Ye Committee of Citee Fathers yesterday turned downe ye planne for ye new citee centre designed in ye Moderne Style by ye worlde famous architecte Cris van der Wrenne.

Ye dynamik developpere from ye New Worlde Christophere "Fingers" Colombo told BN: "I am verily sick as ye parrotte. Cris is one of my Goddes. But I am going to fighte onne and appeal to the highest authoritee His Royale Highness King Charleseltine II who will see this planne will be to the greater glory of his reign."

Mr Christopher "Fingers" Colombo with Mr Wrenne's Grande Planne.

His Majestie King Charleseltine II (left) Will He ordain by Royal Decree that Mr Wreenne (right) shall build his planne?

But Citee Architecte Sir Roger Pratte said: "Wrenne is one of my gurus but frankly his modernistic orthogonal townne planninge conceppte is not in keepinge withe our National Heritage of Empiric Pluralisme...and anyway ye bigge landowners did not want it. These new Absolutiste ideas may be suitable in Holland or Paris but continental style piazzas are foreign to our traditionnes."

Reaction to ye news came fromme ye famoue architecte Robert Hooke who told our reporter: "These shorte sighted weeke kneede merchants have turned down ye onlie opportunitee to have ye uncompromisinglee moderne designe in ye citee from ye architecte of ye worlde classe. However, I have drawn uppe my owne humble planne which I hope His Majestee will favour withe His consideration."

Alternative plan by Hooke Associates.

Editor Samuel Pepys Estate writes:

Ye loade of mealy mouthed Conservationistes have obstructed ye Marche of Progress in opposinge a designe based on ye Scientific and Rational Principles withe a loade of sentimental clappetrappe about preserving a collection of halfe derelicte mongrel structures and a chaotic uncoordinated streete patterne. Posteritee will judge

(continued on Page 1944)

the still alliterative Christopher Columbo.) By associating Wren and Mies in this way, Hellman drew attention not simply to the stature of the latter (and the conservatism of his opponents) but also indirectly registered the suggestive presence of signature. For the parody here depends upon transposition—Mies' head wearing Wren's wig— which sets aside the determining details of biography for the more flexible characteristics of signature.

Though signature now inevitably invokes starchitects and their signature buildings, the architect as brand is only one narrow manifestation of signature, which I propose might be understood more usefully as the translation of personhood into a medium other than the actual person.[9] In the case of Mansion House Square, one such manifestation would have been the legal attribution of liability, which had the design been constructed would be assigned not to Mies as an individual person, but to his incorporation as an architectural office or to the licensure of the name stamped upon the working drawings. Other manifestations of signature appearing in the inquiry varied from the irreducible singularity of "genius" to the encompassing breadth of universally legible architectural form. In the former apparition, the signature 'Mies van der Rohe' was an insight or capacity beyond the grasp of

9. An expanded consideration of architectural personhoods can be found in Timothy Hyde, "Notes on Architectural Persons," The Aggregate website (Transparent Peer Reviewed), accessed January 27, 2014, http://we-aggregate.org/piece/notes-on-architectural-persons.

biographical explanation; in the latter, it was the formulation of a timeless classicism. More revealing of the implications of signature were the extensive renditions of the details of the design as the expression of signature, details that both proponents and detractors agreed were the salient elements to be considered. The claim that Mies' buildings were unified by "shared characteristics" was submitted into argument, as was Ludwig Glaeser's detailed explication of the variance by building of module, bay size, and ceiling height in Mies' realized projects.[10] Consisting of both repetition and difference, signature was established here as a cognizance or deliberation within the design indicative of yet independent from the author it embodied.

Understood in this way, as a loosened attachment to personhood, signature forges a particular contract with history, one that acknowledges a relation between a work and its creator at a specific moment, but that also extends that acknowledgment indefinitely forward into the future even in the absence of an accompanying body. The architect, when understood as a person and addressed through the technique of biography, appears with an emphatic presentness, with the reenactment in the present of the prior decisive moment, unqualified and unchanged. This presentness is the repetition of an already determined intention that, although it occurred originally in the past, is being placed again before its audience unchanged as fact. In this sense, personhood forges an isolation from context, with the completed fact reasserted without reciprocation to its newer historical moment. But when understood as signature, the architect is addressed differently through a technique of inquiry that acknowledges the distancing of embodiment and the distancing of time, of duration. Signature moves forward in time, always newly aware of its changing context.

The literary theorist Seán Burke, in an essay on the "Ethics of Signature," described this effect as a "structure of resummons whereby the author may be recalled to his or her text."[11] The signature, Burke proposed, is addressed to the future, it "offers itself to any tribunal which may be subsequently established upon the basis of the signatory's text in relation to as yet unrealized historical circumstances. The signature accedes to this tribunal."[12]

10. Report by Inspector Stephen Marks, Section 10.10, page 40 and Section 10.50, page 48. [National Archives, folder AT 41/411]

11. Seán Burke, "The Ethics of Signature," in *Authorship: From Plato to the Postmodern: A Reader*, ed. Seán Burke (Edinburgh: Edinburgh University Press, 1995): 289.

12. Ibid.

13. The well-known instances Burke references, of Paul de Man and Martin Heidegger and the increasingly de-tailed accountings of their activities before and during the Second World War, are account-ings in both senses of the word; they are inventories of facts and moral assessments. Mies van der Rohe has of course received a similar scrutiny in this regard.

14. Ibid.

Burke elaborated this potential for resummons as an ethical function, whereby, for example, an author could be called to account for his words at some later date. This function might also serve to protect an author from the interpretation of a work, or indeed, to protect a work from the interpretation of its author.[13]

In proposing that signature sets the conditions for a resummoning by a future tribunal, Seán Burke added that the "shape, agendas, and composition [of this tribunal] will necessarily be unknown at the time of signing but [the tribunal's] distinctive form will in some sense be predicated upon the manner of signature and the relation of the signatory to what has been signed."[14] The Mansion House Square inquiry was in quite literal terms just such a tribunal, resummoning the signature to a tribunal of un-expected inclination, and as Burke describes, even though the form of the tribunal was unknown at the moment the signature was produced, the signature nevertheless is fully incorporated into the tribunal's structure of thought. In other words, where the tribunal was simply forestalled in making its biographical address—because Mies was dead, no conclusion could be reached as to his actual involvement—it was freed by the inquisitional address of signature, able to examine and resolve anew the relation of architect, building, and present context.

The tribunal was not thereby arriving at a conclusion as to whether or not Mies designed the Mansion House Square scheme; rather, it was producing an embodiment, an embodiment that enabled it to evaluate the scheme in both its prior and its present context without implicitly privileging one over the other. The testimony heard by the inquiry did not establish points of certainty; to the contrary, that testimony produced an area of uncertainty, in which signature was not a mere personification, but an embodiment of a process of architectural practice. Not a personification of Mies, that is, but an embodiment of the acts and operations of Mies' office and its client. And in this respect, it might be more correct to suggest that the signature stands in for what is actually a complex anonymity.

There is an opportunity in these events, therefore, to consider the consequences for a signature's contract with history when that signature reads 'Anonymous,' a signature fully within history, yet in a particular way unrecognized by history. Michel Foucault, in his essay "What is an Author?", noted that with the modern notion of the author (or what he characterized as the "author-function"), the relation between author and text (or here between architect and architecture) was fixed by signature so that the circulation of illicit or transgressive discourses could be disciplined or curtailed.[15] An author's signature was an acceptance of liability for the undersigned contents, and so in order to evade just that discipline, the signature 'Anonymous' appeared in its modern form.

Anonymity rewrites the contract with history, further loosening—though not severing—the conjunction of work and persona so that any future tribunal can no longer resummon the author to the same standard of presence. When the signature reads 'Anonymous,' no specific body can be entered under judgment. No determined past is announced, and therefore no lineage can be established through the persona and out toward the work. A past exists nevertheless, manifest in the existence of the work, in its embodiment of decisions made and situational potentials realized. But this past cannot be described by the tribunal. It must instead be posited, put forward as a claim, a claim, which burdens more than satisfies judgment.

With the signature 'Anonymous,' the motivation that inevitably accompanies signature initiates a more contingent state, in which motives are assigned provisional attributes rather than being seen to possess definitive personal ones. The anonymous signature would then predicate a different shape and agenda of inquisition of an architectural practice by a future tribunal—whether of historians or lawyers—with the particular relation of signatory to what has been signed a relation premised upon a determinate void, a distance, or a displacement. In effect, motive now attaches not to a person, but to the function of a person, and thus displaced, motive is in a literal sense depersonalized. It does not, however, become abstract or non-human. Rather, the depersonalized condition effected by 'Anonymous' consists of a transfer between attributes of personality and personhood and attributes of institution, system, or technique. Although this signature places such attributes into an embodied

15. See Michel Foucault, "What is an Author?" in *Authorship: From Plato to the Postmodern: A Reader,* ed. Seán Burke (Edinburgh: Edinburgh University Press, 1995):141-60.

form, that form remains inaccessible to biographical interrogation. Instead, the anonymous signature solicits the projection of the tribunal's own motives and intentions and desires.

There is quite a long epilogue to the Mansion House story, but the salient facts are these: following the denial of his appeal, Palumbo conceded that "the Mies scheme is dead," yet did not quit his plans to develop the Mansion House site.[16] He commissioned a new proposal from James Stirling and steered it successfully through heated debate, and yet another public inquiry. The new building—known as No. 1 Poultry and still uncertainly set in the Stirling canon—was completed in 1997. By then, James Stirling had been dead for five years.

16. "Palumbo to commission new scheme," *Architects' Journal* (29 May 1985) 24.

Vapor
Eric Höweler

TRANSCRIPT, FEBRUARY 23, 2014

0:00

We appreciate the challenge or, rather, the dare/risk presented by this conference: to talk about contemporary design practice, relative to questions of origins or originality. Ana [Miljački]'s hunch is that contemporary practice is laced with influences that are more or less explicit. And, as the claims of authorship and originality seem increasingly old-fashioned, our generation of architects ranges between being ambivalent and indifferent to acknowledging their references as the "ecstasy of influence."[1]

We have been asked to shed light on our design process; she has asked us to "fess up" to our influences. Our discipline, we understand, is obsessed with issues of authorship, credit, originality and signature. We've heard various accounts already from historians, practitioners, and theorists with varying degrees of acknowledgement of influence.

1:11

Yet, to succeed in today's image-drenched world still requires some acknowledgement of authorship—or at least attention, if not originality. Architects in search of publicity must still produce works that are attention-worthy. How to stand out amongst the clamor, where the signal is lost in the noise?

1:35

How to find attention in the age of distraction? Our hunch is that the nature of design has changed, not just because of BIM or Grasshopper. Not because of one single tool, device or plug-in, but rather because our culture in general has changed, as has the status of the image, its traffic, and its effects.

Contemporary design does not happen in a vacuum, but rather in a dense atmosphere of references.[2] We work within the context of multiple and overlapping references: varying accounts of the contemporary, with lingering traces of historic references and inferred influence. These references are diffuse and pervasive, appearing at times, almost invisible. The zeitgeist, or Spirit of the Age, is all around us. But the age is awash in images of different temporalities, some historical, some contemporary, and some anticipating possible futures. This is the vapor of the contemporary, a dense cloud of references where histori-cal, cannonical, and trendy merge in equivalence.

2:38

Against this framework, I'd like to present our work as an illustration of a type of self-conscious situational practice, one in which references are part of design methodology, and one that is always already wired into a self-consciousness about design practice. Images of influ-ences, both contemporary and historic, will flash between our project images.[3]

Staring at the gaping hole in [Boston's] Downtown Crossing left by the Filene's Department store, we can't help but think that something is wrong with architecture. The proposed project evaporated when the financing fell through in 2008, and the developer was unable to build. Somehow architecture was too expensive, its financing too fragile, and its ability to respond to markets too slow. For our proposed temporary use, we imagined something quick and agile, something that could be erected quickly, but also dismantled and redeployed. Conscious of 1960s and 1970s references, we developed a modular system of pods that could plug into an armature and re-configure, evocative of Archigram's 1964 Plug-in City, and Kuro-kawa's 1979 Capsule Hotel. However, the design is also indebted to R&Sie's 2007 Olzweg robot-built project. In addition, certainly the program for a algae bio-reactor in downtown Boston is a very contemporary program that relies on a near-future technology.

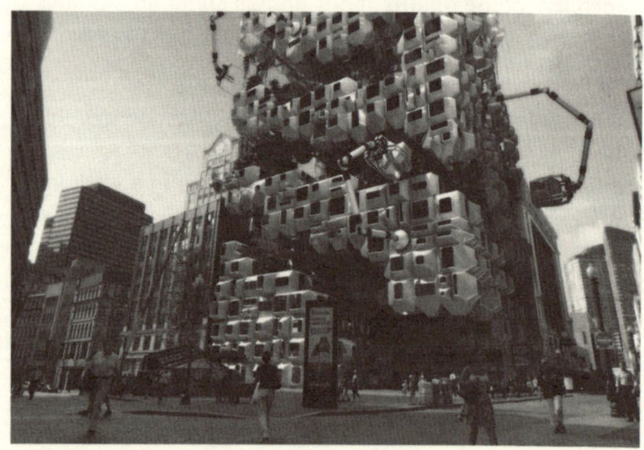

The EcoPods project is both completely contemporary and highly retro at the same time. It addresses contemporary anxieties about energy and the economy by revisiting speculative projects from the recent past to create a new hybrid for the near future.

3:40

The contemporary condition is characterized by having no dominant or master narrative (say, Modernism, Postmodernism, or Supermodernism), and also no dominant disciplinary conflict (white versus gray). It seems to be characterized by a multiplicity of positions, but also a certain kind of ambivalence or permissiveness. We would offer that contemporary practices are not defining themselves for or against a singular position.

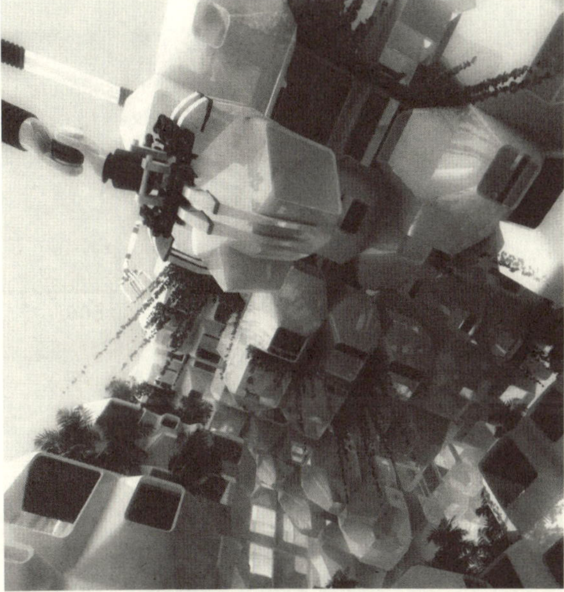

Rather, they are developing a situational stance, a tactical response to specific contexts, dependent on the debit and balance of constraints and opportunities. The discourses and conflicts that characterized previous periods have been distributed and internalized—ingested into the design process itself.

In a context where history has been erased and re-written, China has proved to be a remarkable testing ground for contemporary architecture. Explosive

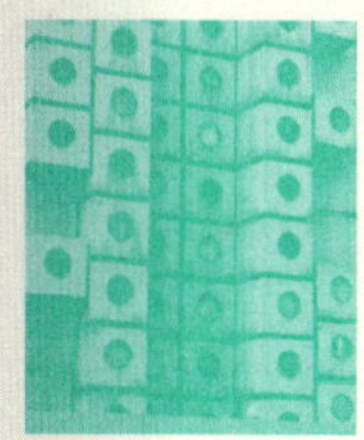

3. The conference presentation is a bit of a performance. The projects were shown rather conventionally, with the 'reference' images interspersed almost subliminally. I didn't refer to the 'reference' images directly, they were only up on the screen for a split second, but they were visible to the audience. I'm interested in pervasive and subliminal practices, but more importantly that is a kind of commentary on our contemporary work milieu. We are surrounded by images, we don't even know, and may not be conscious of. This vapor is made up of contemporary and historic images, without much of a framework, they are rendered ahistoric and equivalent by the overwhelming horizontality

economic development and an insatiable appetite for images of progress have created an arms race of architectural form. Post-Olympics and Post-Expo China has choreographed buildings, and spectacles—and even the weather—to craft the camera-ready scenes flickering across the collective retina of a global television spectatorship. The demands of imaging and the mechanisms of authority have called on architecture to deliver new icons for the highly choreographed urban imaginary.

5:00

This is a proposal [Emporium project] for a pair of residential towers in Shanghai. The towers sit on a podium of retail and common spaces. As residential towers, the common element of design is the residential unit. The façade is characterized by a pattern of balconies.

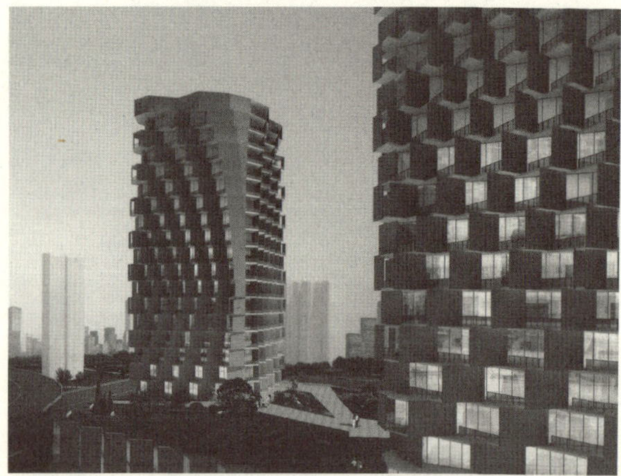

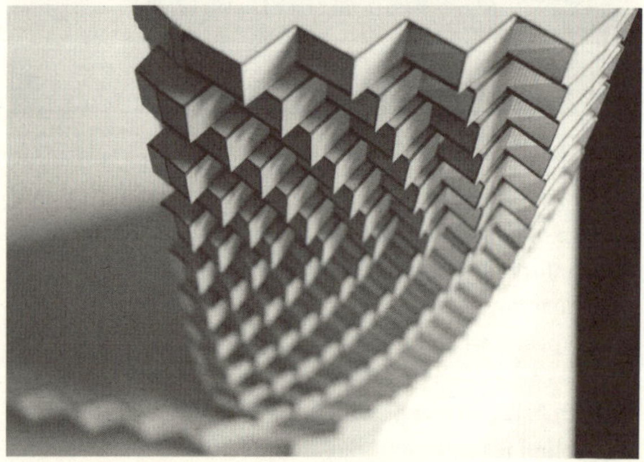

The diversity of unit mix creates a commentary on the lifestyle issues of residential construction. Each floor is packed with a different number of residential units. The oblique views show the units tapering at the corners, and this is a function of the packing algorithm that goes into the stacking of the floors. The pattern of balconies creates the impression of an aggregation of modular forms. The overall tower footprints show the variety of building profiles on the balconies, promising a mixture of privacy and publicity. The unit produces the surface pattern and the massing as a bottom-up logic.

6:00

Even as practices are not fighting a singular fight against a single enemy, they are also not performing for a singular audience of critics or historians (What would Nicolai say about this? Could I show this to my students? How would it play on Dezeen? Or in *Wired*?)

Design work today is produced for multiple audiences, in multiple contexts, and with multiple temporalities. The feedback loop for architectural production and criticism has collapsed. Before the first foundation is cast, it already has a public presence of Flickr and Facebook. The bloggers and the haters have voted well before the historians and the curators. It has a following before it has a retrospective; it is always already posted, commented, liked, forwarded, tweaked and tweeted.[4]

We find that projects have a public life before they are built. Renderings and models are in circulation long before construction. This gives them a public presence and a type of visibility that is different from the presence of a physical building. In some cases, they create an inertia that ensures that they will be built. In some cases, renderings can create a demand for a project in advance of the building. Our renderings of the BSA Space were circulated so widely that the client felt that they couldn't value-engineer the design because the images had already created a foothold in the public imagination about the project.

We are conscious of the fact that contemporary design operates within taste regimes. There are designers working in an anti-aesthetic, redefining notions of beauty through the concept of the grotesque. That is not our project. We are interested in works that may have an

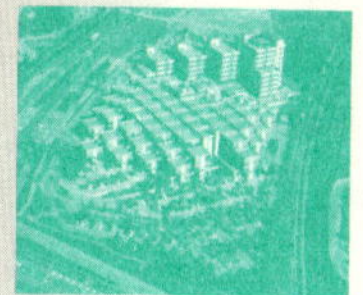

Reference: Central Beheer Office Complex, Herman Hertzberger.

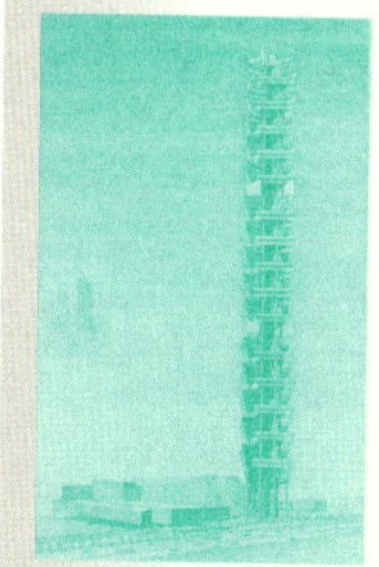

Reference: Library of Congress, Paul Rudolph, section and elevation drawing.(http:// www.loc.gov/ exhibits/british/images/vc161.jpg)

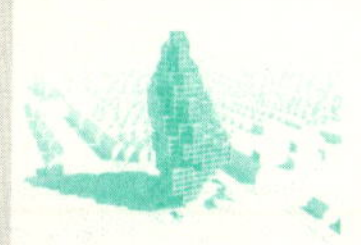

Reference: Sky Village, MVRDV and Adept Architects (http://architizer. com/projects/sky-village/)

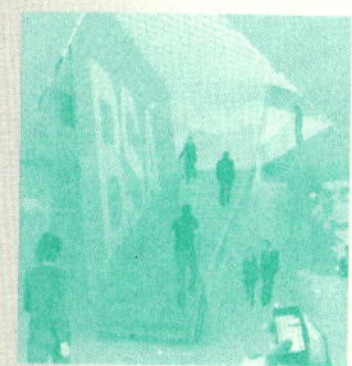

Reference: BSA

4. Ozzy Osbourne was reputed to perform his latest songs in front of a prison audience, in order to test the response to his new material. Presumably if the inmates found it acceptable, then that would validate the album. We've certainly learned not to take comments left on web sites too seriously. The comments section of a web site is not the place for discourse, being too prone to comments like, "My grandma can do better than that," and "this is siiiick!!!" Still, placing work in the public realm invites comments, criticisms and provides a kind of feedback loop early in the design process. Comments and posts represent a prolif-eration of opinions and very little accountability. Like Ozzy's prison performances, it offers a kind of litmus test within a particular target audience.

unconventional beauty, although that is not our goal. For the Emporium Towers, the form emerged from a logic about varied bay widths on each floor. This idea was native to the program—that a residential tower would need to sell a range of different unit types. This diversity of real estate products led us the basic organizational strategy, and the accumulation of that logic created the spiky tower that we presented to the client. It looks kind of like a pineapple. We like that it creates an overall form from the unit, as a bottom-up strategy. The implicit curvature visible on the facade is not imposed from a top-down formal gesture. It emerges from the aggregation strategy.

7:08

Asked to design a 60,000 sq.f "corporate retreat" as part of a compound of seven similar structures, we accepted. The key criteria we had to satisfy were that the building had "to have a sloped roof and it had to be a Chinese courtyard house." After we asked for clarification, we were told that it "must have Chinese feeling." The client sent us a poem by the Tang poet, Li Bai, for inspiration.

The Chinese relationship to history is complex: four thousand years of culture, and ten years of Cultural Revolution. The smashing of 'bourgeois' artifacts and the persecution of individuals with sympathies for the past, created a tremendous gulf in Chinese collective memory, a forceful historical amnesia.

Deng's "One country, Two systems" unleashed an unprecedented wave of construction and destruction. The current building boom in China has produced a profound ambivalence towards contemporary architecture and cultural identity, simultaneously producing the CCTV and the China Expo Pavilion. Herzog and de Meuron's Bird's Nest flickers between the crafted and the contemporary, the local, and the imported. For an emerging upper class, access to history is a privilege and means of differentiation. "Recuperating the past" in the context of China has an entirely different valence than it does in North America or Europe.

The developer of our project in Chengdu insisted that the project should be a contemporary Chinese courtyard house. We designed what we felt was a contemporary interpretation of a courtyard house: a mat building with office and meeting spaces packed around a series of courtyards. The building was on a group site of seven interlocking parcels with seven different architects working together. And our plan took the packing logic and distorted into our irregular shaped parcel.

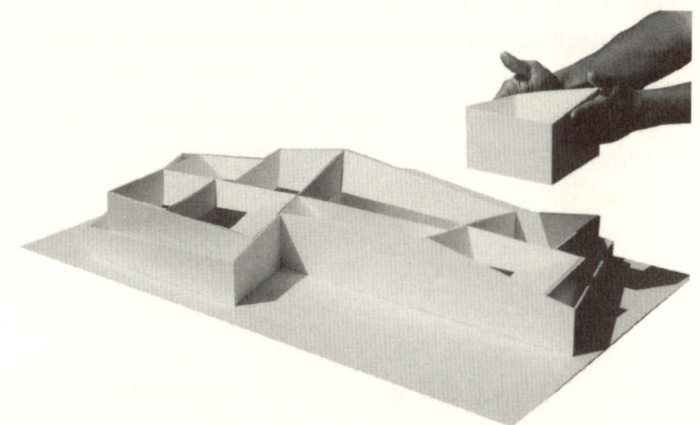

After the first round, our scheme was judged to not have enough "Chinese feeling," and we were sent back to the drawing board.[5] Asking for clarification from one of our Chinese colleagues, he pointed to a view of a Chinese temple covered in a dense fog: "That's Chinese feeling. It cannot be drawn." Our design evolved. The cell packing became less insistent. It also developed a roof of alternating gables and valleys. The twisting geometry of the ruled surface was accommodated by the traditional roof tiles.

During the design process, schedules shifted, programs evolved, and contexts were dramatically reinvented. At some point, the client informed us that the site had been switched. Our building plan had been mirrored to better fit the new site. The program had been changed to an exhibition hall, and lastly that construction had already begun!

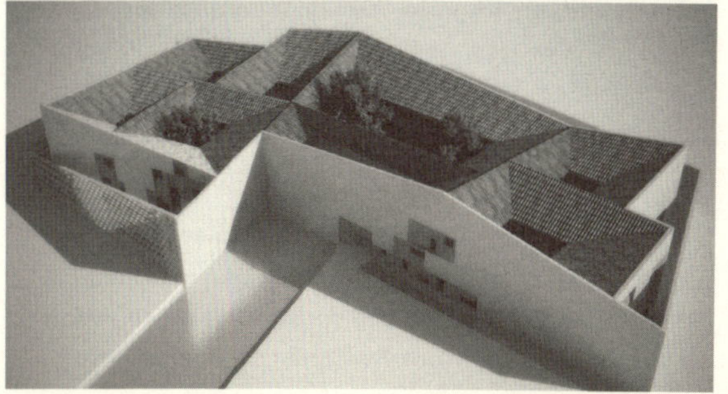

Images: Chengdu, concept model and roof view

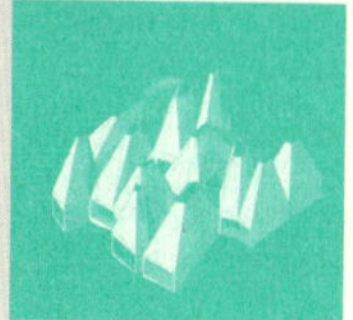

Reference: Ordos 100, #7 House, MOS Architects.

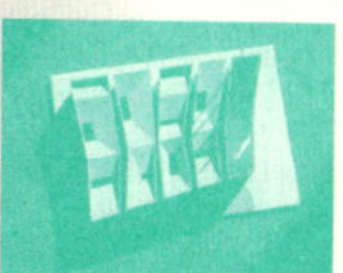

Reference: Qingcheng Mountain Teahouse, Standardarchitecture. (http://waithinktank.com/tag/standardarchitecture/)

5. The Chengdu client was asking for something explicit: a Chinese courtyard house. We struggled with the necessity of that referentiality, trying to develop something new that was very abstractly Chinese. When confronted with the demand for 'Chineseness' we did look at the references that they presented to us: Chinese gardens and patterns. We gained a different understandings of precedent, tradition, continuity and discontinuity. Our design draws on multiple sources

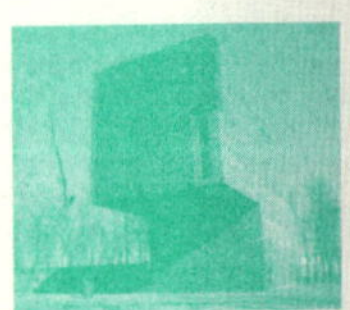

Our design evolved to accommodate the irregular site boundaries. It reconfigured to house the revised program. The façade consists of local bricks laid with a singular orientation throughout the site, so walls built on diagonals become saw-toothed and textured. The windows form a composition of packed indentations, creating a series of taut frames within a rough backdrop of the brick wall.

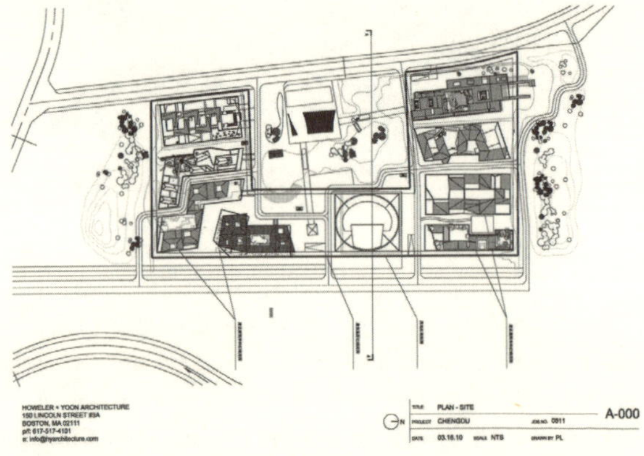

There are obvious references to local building traditions and building techniques. There are also references to contemporary interests in modular structures, aggregation, bottom-up processes, variation and repetition.

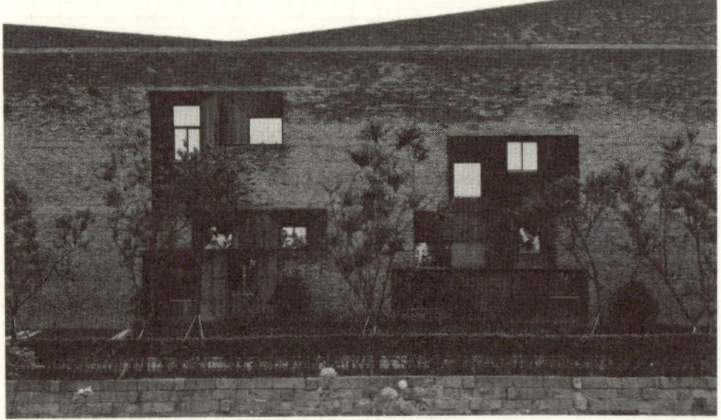

11:18

So, presenting in this interlaced, format I hope to provide a visual context for the work, drawn from a collective archive of historic and contemporary projects: Archigram, Ryoichi Kurokawa, François Roche, Paul

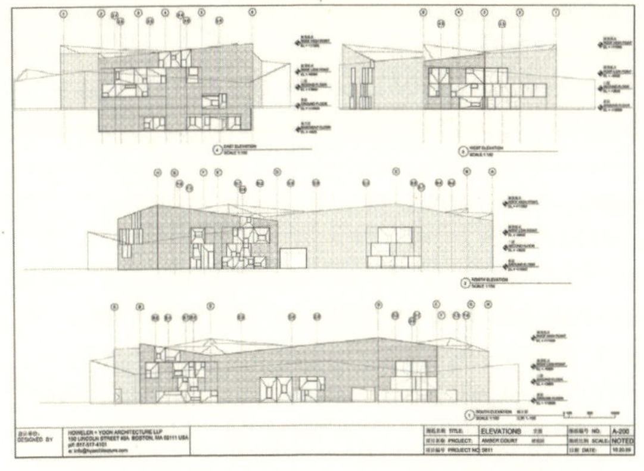

Reference: Silk wall, Archi-Union Architects (http://ad009cdnb.archdaily.net/wp-content/)

Rudolph, Mansilla y Tuñón, and Office dA. These represent the cloud of references that envelops our contemporary design practice. The risk here is that the references may detract from the content and overwhelm the work; the fog may become too thick and the anxiety of influence too strong. The work may lose its aura, diluted by the promiscuity of references.

On the other hand, the parallax between project and precedent may open up new avenues for interpretation and for design. We've found that within our practice, architectural references—the stuff of influence—are less an unacknowledged threat with claims of pure originality and authenticity than an internalized and self-conscious methodology of work in real time, one that acknowledges the information-dense context in which we live and offers new analytical and projective capacities for design.[6]

Images: Chengdu elevation drawings and aerial photograph by Yihuai Hu

6. Originality in the sense of an individual creative genius is vastly overrated, but it is what the public expects of its starchitecture figures. It is a myth and lie on so many levels. The myth of perpetual reinvention, the myth of total discontinuity, the myth of unprecedented newness—a singular unique and original work by the master archi-

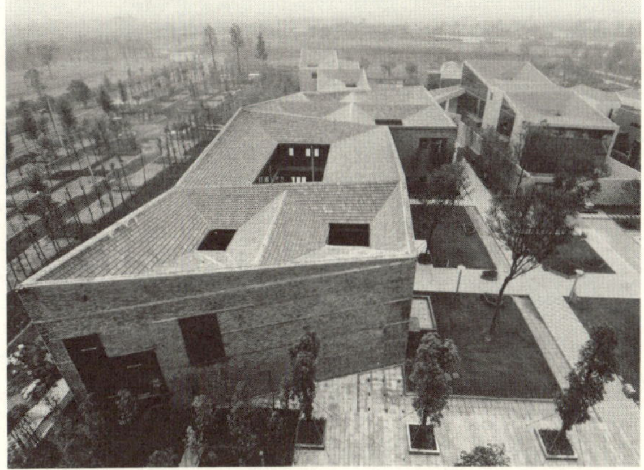

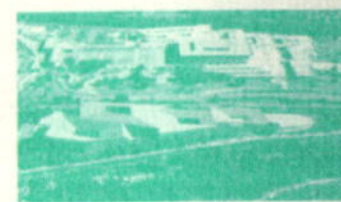

12:28

As a footnote.
We recently received a letter in the mail:


```
Dear Architects,


    So and so architects recently won so and
so competition to design the National Is-
rael Library. The pictures, showing archi-
tect ______'s winning submission is attached,
alongside the Chengdu Skycourts Exhibition
Hall project exhibited on your website, de-
signed by yourselves. A project which won
design awards, your project was completed in
2011, and was shown on Harvard's website
April 2012.


    The project, designed by architect ______
won the National Library design by competi-
tion 6 months later. We believe that no fur-
ther comment is necessary.
```

I responded:


```
To whom it may concern,

We understand that there are claims be-
ing made against ______, award-winning de-
signer for the National Library in Jerusalem,
involving apparent similarities to our Sky-
courts Exhibition Hall in Chengdu China.

As a professional architect, I understand
that we work within organizational systems
and building typologies. The courtyard is a
typology that exists in many cultures. We
understand architecture to be site-and scale-
specific, and while design organizations and
strategies may be shared, an architectural
design is always a unique response to site
and place.

I have seen ______'s design for the Israeli
Library and find it to be an elegant design. I
do not find it be a copy against the Skycourts
design, and I have no claims against him.
```

Further comment may actually be necessary.[7]

Discussion 03
Moderator: Amanda Reeser Lawrence

PARTICIPANTS:
ERIC HÖWELER,
TIMOTHY HYDE,
MARIANA IBAÑEZ,
SIMON KIM,
JOHN MCMORROUGH

0:00 Amanda Reeser Lawrence: It strikes me that the terms examined in our final panel seem the most peripheral, or at least hardest to identify as a set of synonyms for appropriation. Ours is also the panel with the most diverse set of lenses, covering an entire spectrum from historical research to contemporary criticism and practice. So I propose instead looking at this group ('color sample,' 'side effects,' 'signature,' 'vapor') in another way, as expanding the meaning of appropriation, or influence.

Still there are a few things that may connect some of this work, and build upon the conversations we've had earlier today and last night. Picking up on Mario Carpo's talk and the question of non-linearity that he introduced—specifically the idea that we live in a non-linear age—both John [McMorrough] and Mariana [Ibañez] and Simon [Kim], and even Eric [Höweler] circled around the notion of sampling. I think the types of appropriation we are talking about here are much more heterogeneous than in the previous panels, and they are about bringing material together in a highly non-linear way.

Importantly, perhaps both Höweler + Yoon, whose book is entitled *Expanded Practice*, and I/K Studio use the idea of expansion to describe their work and firms. For Mariana and Simon, expansion seemed to refer to an appropriation of techniques from other disciplines (robotics, dance, etc). In your case, appropriation did not just involve relying on a set of samples, it included appropriating other ways of thinking, and other discourses, getting away from a more linear sense of copying that we discussed in the last panel.

I was struck by Timothy Hyde's fascinating notion of disassociating the figure of the architect from architecture via the notion of the signature. My work on Harold Bloom arrives at some of these conclusions, as well. Bloom makes an argument that, for a poet, it is much easier to deal with another poet's poem than with another poet. How would one reference a poet, what would that mean? Bloom gives the example that one can be influenced by Hamlet, but what does it mean to be influenced by Shakespeare? Following from this, and perhaps reinforced by all the "subliminal messages" that Eric showed, is an almost erratic sensibility of the person. Is it John Hejduk that haunts Simon and Mariana, or the particularities of that kind of design? I get the sense—in opposition to Bloom's proposal on the subject—that the answer here may actually be Hejduk rather than any particular project.

Finally, the question about the legibility of the source: does it matter if one both knows and/or acknowledges what the source is? I think question is particularly interesting vis à vis Eric's subliminal messages: getting us to buy popcorn in the middle of the movie without realizing why we're suddenly craving it. The images were up just long enough to tease us, giving us a mere taste of various voices at play. This is the absolute opposite of the approach in which one intentionally elaborates the moves and the references involved, and it results in a more atmospheric sensibility about images, figures, or haunting ghosts of Hejduk.

So those are my general comments. But, let me follow up with a specific question to Timothy since he promised to elaborate on a portion of his talk in the question and answer session. I'm fascinated by the idea, which you stated very elegantly, of translating the person to a medium other than the person. But could you connect that a little bit more concretely to the idea of anonymity?

5:29 Timothy Hyde: When I said I wanted to clarify something later, I wanted to be sure to emphasize the fact that we have used anonymity and anonymous a couple of different times, and I think I'm talking about a slightly different version of it. I'm not talking about anonymous in the sense of the vernacular, or anonymous in the sense of Gideon's "anonymous history," in which there is a form of social consensus that produces stuff. And I should be always saying anonymous, not anonymity, because anonymous is a signature already. You cannot study the 18th century without reading books by Anonymous. And those books were by Anonymous for a set of political and other kinds of reasons and conventions. But anonymous is still a signature; it is just a signature that has been removed from a specific biography. Anonymous is a person, a kind of construction of a person, to which you can assign kind of a motive, and so on. So I want to be clear that I'm not talking about the non-human subject, so, not anonymity of the machine, the script, the algorithm, processes that are acting outside of human agency and are therefore anonymous. Nor am I talking about the social anonymous of vernacular architecture and things that are emerging in that sense. But rather, there is a signature called anonymous, which registers agency and intention and motive, within a sense of displacement or detachment from biography. What fills in the gap, or fills in the vacuum left by biography, is institutional characteristics, economies, the way images circulate, and several other dimensions we have talked about today.

7:14 Ana Miljački [from the audience]: But is this call to anonymity directed at historical work, culture in general, or are you proposing it projectively for those involved in architectural production?

7:28 Hyde: I think both. My emphasis is more on the historical, but I do think it is projective, as well, and I'm waiting for the really strong assertion of anonymous as a signature within architectural culture. I think the kind of recipes for it are there, but there are obviously tremendous hindrances in the construction of the discipline, and the academy, and so on. But I think that it would be relieving if we stopped making the assumption that architects are real people, and we instead understood architects as a construction, and were able to think in those terms, in order to create more fluidity in the discipline. Anonymous would be an extreme version of that, but I think it would be a kind of healthy one to appear. So, yes, my interest in it is projective, in the sense that I'm waiting for somebody to actually do that: sign anonymous.

8:40 Michael Meredith [from the audience]: Has it not been the role of the critic or the historian to bring things together in a way that does not place the person of the architect at the center? Some architects may have actively done it in the past, as well by institutionalizing themselves, and their persona. But it would be great—I think we would all love it—if someone would come along now and do it. Sure, I might hate it if I got left out of certain narratives, but it seems like we need someone who can remove architects from the center of the conversation about architecture, and nobody's doing it.

9:17 Hyde: If you're thinking of it in terms of whose job it may be to instigate anonymity—the architect, the designer, the critic, and so on—I think there's a necessary level of mutuality for it to happen. The work has to come about that's already withdrawn a bit from conventional notions of signature, or that's open to being disseminated it in different ways. A project that simply appears on the web, as opposed to getting posted, for example, would create possibilities of critical narratives about it—for explanations of its meaning that don't end up becoming a kind of hunt for whodunit. So, to me, it's not either/or, your job or my job, it's a kind of mutual recognition of what would be possible and meaningful and what could contribute to some further disciplinary conversation.

10:03 Michael Kubo [from the audience]: I can give an example that might be a counterpart to Timothy's challenge to architectural culture, of the historian analyzing anonymity and waiting for an architect to take this up as a mode of authorship. The story of The Architects Collaborative, the subject of my own work, legitimizes the claim that anonymity can be projective. When it was founded in 1945, TAC was, as far as I know, the first example of an architecture office spelling out an embrace of anonymity (as a result of collaboration) in its name. There are parallels between the differing status of TAC and Walter Gropius, one of its founders, and the aura that Timothy describes surrounding the persona of Mies versus the Office of Mies van der Rohe. But the split may be even more extreme in the case of TAC given that Gropius spent his entire life theorizing and attempting to work against the notion of signature and the "prima donna" conception of the architect. At the same time he understood and, in a very canny way, deployed his own aura, as did the members of TAC, even while they were publishing texts about their faith in collectivity. For example, the only major monograph published by TAC includes separate texts by Gropius and many of the other founding partners, published under their own names, but all discussing collaboration and teamwork; Louis McMillen's for example is titled "The Idea of Anonymity." The problematic of anonymity plays itself out in the reception of TAC's work, for example in the Pan Am building in New York, which devastated Gropius' reputation. Manfredo Tafuri, for example, claimed that in Pan Am Gropius had been "willing to legitimize with his signature" an essentially banal and immoral urban project, debasing himself in the process.

11:43 Hyde: We might point to the mutuality, or lack thereof, between the example and the account of it here, as well. I think TAC is a kind of perfect example of an architectural firm that was trying to move in the direction of intentional anonymity, but with no reciprocation of that on the part of historians or critics, who saw it as Gropius' firm. There was not that corresponding acceptance of the program of TAC or the position of TAC from the side of its critics.

12:05 Kubo [from the audience]: In that sense I appreciate the method that you lay out and the position you find yourself in relative to Mies, partly because I find myself in the opposite situation of yours, working on a firm that tried to develop a collaborative praxis but whose interests were mostly ignored by historians and critics.

12:48 Lawrence: I wonder if we could pose this question of signature and anonymity to Mariana and Simon in relation to their Hejdukian Philadelphia Masque. Are signature and anonymity the terms in which you might describe your relationship to Hejduk as designers?

13:19 Simon Kim: It was really interesting to hear how they refuted the authenticity of Mies as the designer separate from his style. When it comes to Hejduk, it may be best to say that we really like some of his work, but not the man. Because I've never met him, I don't know what he's like. [laughs]. It will never happen. But we are influenced by aspects of his projects. Some parts of the Philadelphia Masque even look like the House of a Suicide. We did have an interesting dilemma working on our Masque, especially when talking about it with students. They had no idea who John Hejduk was when they were working with us. And then when they saw the work they said "Well he's not very good, is he?" So the nature of our relationship to Hejduk does not involve figural resemblance, nothing in our Masque looks like the characters from Riga or Vladivostok, but parts do share narratives that are not explicit.

14:54 Urtzi Grau [from the audience]: Could
we clarify the nature and form of influence operative in
the two last presentations? The brief of the conference is
nicely preceded by a quote on the function of influence
by Jonathan Lethem. Lethem's work is a re-appropriation
of a text by Harold Bloom, which has been systematically
quoted today. Lethem takes references, but also has the
hypothesis that the sheer access to the amount of information that is online and the speed by which one can copy/
paste 'an influence' into their own work has changed fundamentally in recent years. My question is, do you think
that the way you use references today is different from the
various forms of influence described by Bloom in 1973?

16:40 Eric Höweler: I think this symposium has
framed nicely something that is already happening, but
isn't acknowledged. I think everybody working today
is inhaling a kind of image-based culture that I think is
fundamentally different than it was in 1973. Whether it is
computation, Google, or BIM, we are working differently
today, and we may or may not be aware of the way we
incorporate images produced by others. We don't position
our work relative to references, but we acknowledge that
we are consumers, that we have inhaled these references.
I think it is useful to say, as Ana has: "Well let's fess up and
let's talk about the way we work. The students are doing
it, we're doing it, everybody's doing it, but let's talk about
how its being done in explicit ways, without papering over
it or avoiding the question."

17:34 Miljački [from the audience]: I have a
follow-up question directly in response to John's presentation on Girl Talk (thank you for bringing him up). For
me, the mash-up in music, or at least the way that Girl
Talk might explain it, has something to do with particular
expertise in music. Girl Talk is not just inhaling references,
he inhales references that are musical and completely
interpolated through his very deep expertise in music.
So I would love to hear something about architectural
expertise. It's not only that we are bathing in images and
references, but how do they coincide, or engage your own
expertise.

18:38 Mariana Ibañez: Perhaps what I'm going to
say addresses that question, as well as Eric's comment.

I would say, since we are operating in the confessional mode, that when we prepare presentations like these, we repackage the work in a way that intensifies certain things. That packaging involves the production of a fiction that supports an argument or produces a response. I don't think that we need to say much about certain images; we all understand those lineages, and we have certain knowledge that doesn't require any other information to fill in the conversation. So this was, at least for us, a very curated way of presenting the work, showing certain things about it, and specifically not showing other aspects of it.

20:24 Höweler: I would like to say that even though we are awash in images, and we sort of acknowledge certain inheritances, we still believe in invention. And maybe that's what you mean by expertise, that architecture is crafted, and references are structured, organized, and redeployed with a kind of deliberate hand. I think just because we're interested in other people's work and constantly consuming it doesn't mean that we don't think invention is possible. I would not insist on originality, but I do insist on invention.

21:05 Meredith [from the audience]: Also, Girl Talk's expertise is on the technical side. When he talks about how he puts things together he describes trying different things next to each other, so his expertise may be in recognizing the effect of pieces coming together.

21:24 Sam Jacob: I guess there's something special about the sample. It is great that John brought that up as an idea. How does the sample differ from the cover version? And I suppose there's also just the cultural problem of authenticity in general. We should maybe relate this to the idea of signature. I went to see Kraftwerk a couple of weeks ago. Of course, it involved one member of Kraftwerk and some replica Kraftwerk music workers, playing replicas of Kraftwerk's music, which is synthetic work to begin with. You're not quite sure whether this thing is real, or a re-enactment, or a cover version. Is it like those hologram Elvis shows, or is it like going to see Queen with the singer from The Cult taking Freddie Mercury's place? Our contemporary culture is replete with really problematic questions of attribution, where you're not quite sure whether a building is a Mies or not a Mies, whether the chairs are authentic Knoll or rip-off, non-Knoll, illegitimate chairs. Cultural definitions are so complicated that we're kind of lost when it comes to knowing (with any degree of certainty) what things are, or who made them.

22:59 John McMorrough: Well, I think I'm an unwitting outlier in the conversation; I read the 'Under the Influence' differently. It has been a fantastic afternoon talking about the problematic of authorship. For me, the Girl Talk example and the notion of the sample asked a different question.

I just saw a film on remixing that used Girl Talk as an example, as a way to talk about copyright law. It was very fascinating. It was cut with images of people talking about copyright law, next to a dance party that was all about being 'under the influence' of ecstasy.

So the fruitful problem of the sample does not involve authenticity and meaning, but instead, the seemingly unproblematic incorporation of material into the ears of the audience. I am interested in the effects of appropriation. I guess we could go back and think about art post-Marcel Duchamp and about models of lyric poetry and their repetitions, but I think in relationship to these new techniques of proliferation—of which the sample is the most manifest version—what are the possible effects on an audience? What are the new cognitions that are going on? I brought up the digital sample and color in order to read those two analogically next to each other, and then return them back to architecture as a way to think about a notational affective dimension of architecture opening up the field to new pluralities. For me, the promise of a new mode coming out of the contemporary proliferation of images and information might be new appetites, or new possibilities and reception.

Fair Use:
An Architectural Timeline[1]

Producers:
Ana Miljački
Sarah Hirschman

Team:
Kyle Barker
Christianna Bonin
Kyle Coburn
Daniela Covarrubias
Erioseto Hendranata
Juan Jofre
Nicholas Polansky
Kelly Presutti

Ana Miljački &
Sarah Hirschman

FAIR USE EXHIBITION

First exhibited: February/March 2013 at the Keller Gallery at MIT Architecture, Cambridge, MA.

Exhibition contents:

1. Timeline: 500+ 10"x10" cards in browsing console

2. "Moves": 40 3D-printed models of "fair use" architectural moves arrayed within custom built, LED-lit cases on IKB felt pads.

3. Handout: 10"x20" double sided, accordion folded includes key to the "Moves" and condensed timeline

Fair Use is a timeline of historical instances, characters, trajectories, theories, and court cases that together begin to describe the realm of appropriation in architecture. It was compiled during the Fall 2012 research workshop, *4.184 Appropriation: The Work of Architecture in the Age of Copyright.* The three colors in the timeline codify the material in three broad categories: technologies of reproduction, theories of appropriation and legal issues pertaining to ownership of architectural ideas.

The term 'Fair Use' is a loophole in the copyright law that safeguards culture from the monopoly of use of its particular and particularly authored elements. Fair Use law makes parts of this exhibit possible, by literally authorizing the use of some of its material in an academic setting, but Fair Use is also the polemic of this exhibit. Appropriation is as much part of the architectural unconscious as the expectation of novelty, and is therefore at the very core of architecture's disciplinarity. Architecture advances via comment, criticism, parody, innovation, all squarely defined as Fair Uses.

Fair Use *Moves* are this exhibit's particular offering, registering some of the contemporary architectural ideas in circulation. Identified through repetition and variation in at least three contemporary projects each, the *Moves* are abstractions made possible by Fair Use, now copyrightable by the 4.184 workshop, but given back to you for Fair Use.

UNIVERSAL COPYRIGHT CONVENTION (UCC)

1952, INTERNATIONAL, LAW

The *UCC* is one of two principal conventions protecting copyright. It was developed by the *United Nations Educational, Scientific and Cultural Organization* as an alternative to the *Berne Convention* for those states which disagreed with aspects of the *Berne Convention*, but still wished to participate in some form of multilateral copyright protection. These states included most of Latin America, the United States, and the Soviet Union (which thought that the strong copyright protections granted by the *Berne Convention* overly benefited Western developed copyright-exporting nations). The United States and Latin America were already members of a Pan-American copyright convention, which was weaker than the *Berne Convention*. The *Berne Convention* states also became party to the *UCC*, so that their copyrights would exist in non-*Berne Convention* states.

The United States only provided copyright protection for a fixed, renewable term, and required that in order for a work to be copyrighted it must contain a copyright notice and be registered at the *Copyright Office*. The *Berne Convention*, on the other hand, provided for copyright protection for a single term based on the life of the author, and did not require registration or the inclusion of a copyright notice for copyright to exist. Thus the United States would have to make several major modifications to its copyright law in order to become a party to it. At the time the United States was unwilling to do so. The *UCC* thus permits those states which had a system of protection similar to the United States for fixed terms at the time of signature to retain them.

See Exhibit 082 for more information. Source: House Report No. 94-1476 in connection with Title 17, United States Code, Section 104

Fair Use

Ana Miljački &
Sarah Hirschman

249 FAIR USE

1976, UNITED STATES, LAW

17 USC § 107 - Limitations on Exclusive Rights: Fair Use

Notwithstanding the provisions of sections 17 U.S.C. § 106 and 17 U.S.C. § 106A, the fair use of a copyrighted work, including such use by reproduction in copies or phonorecords or by any other means specified by that section, for purposes such as criticism, comment, news reporting, teaching (including multiple copies for classroom use), scholarship, or research, is not an infringement of copyright.

In determining whether the use made of a work in any particular case is a fair use the factors to be considered shall include:

1. The purpose and character of the use, including whether such use is of a commercial nature or is for nonprofit educational purposes;
2. The nature of the copyrighted work;
3. The amount and substantiality of the portion used in relation to the copyrighted work as a whole; and
4. The effect of the use upon the potential market for or value of the copyrighted work.

The fact that a work is unpublished shall not itself bar a finding of fair use if such finding is made upon consideration of all the above factors.

See Exhibits 319, 344, 379, 384 & 409 for more information.
Source: www.copyright.gov/fls/fl102.html

1965
1975
1980
275
STUTTGART STAATSGALERIE
1984, GERMANY, JAMES STIRLING
James Stirling designs the Stuttgart Staatsgalerie, which contains elements of his unrealized projects, the neoclassical museum next door, the Roman Pantheon, and the Guggenheim Museum in New York.
See Exhibits 254–256 & 415 for more information. Source: Malpas, Simon. The Postmodern, Routledge, 2005

2000
2005

420   BOATHOUSE BUILT

2009, UNITED STATES, FRANK LLOYD WRIGHT

Originally designed for a Wisconsin lake
in 1905, Frank Lloyd Wright's boathouse is
constructed in Buffalo, NY to appear as if it
were built in the 1930s.

See Exhibits 95, 192 & 241 for more information. Source: wrightsboathouse.org/

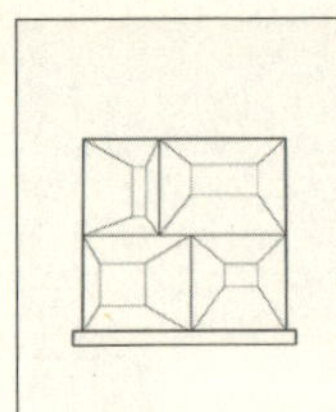

PYRAMIDAL WINDOWS

Chapel of Notre Dame du Haut
Le Corbusier, 1954
Leon Concert Hall
Mansilla + Tuñón, 2002
Mission Bay Block 27 Parking Structure
WRNS Studio, 2009
Sky Courts
Höweler+Yoon Architects, 2011

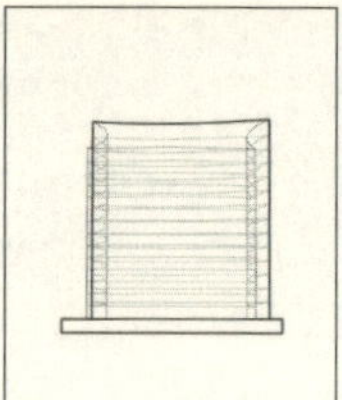

CONVEX FACADE

Laban Dance Center
Herzog & de Meuron, 2005
Galleri Orsta
Claesson Koivisto Rune, 2010
EMU Sports Hall
SALTO, 2010

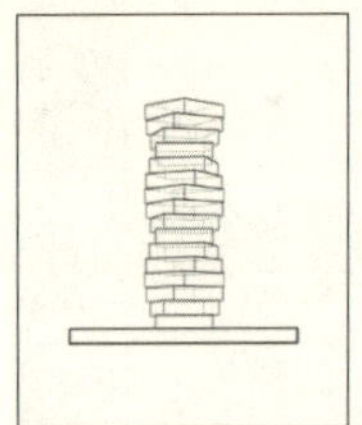

JAGGED TWIST

Coco Towers
BIG
MahaNakhon
Ole Scheeren
Landmark Project
3XN

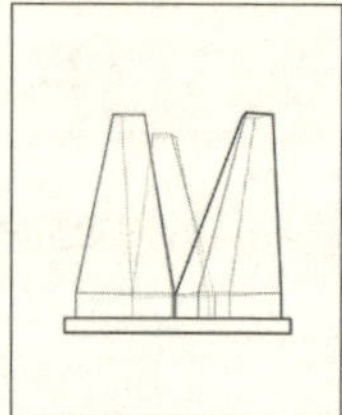

AGGREGATED CHIMNEYS

Museum of Cantabria
Mansilla + Tuñón, 2002
Parish Church of Santa Monica
Vicens & Ramos, 2009
Ordos House
MOS
C-House
Dot Architecture &
Soc-Arc, 2012

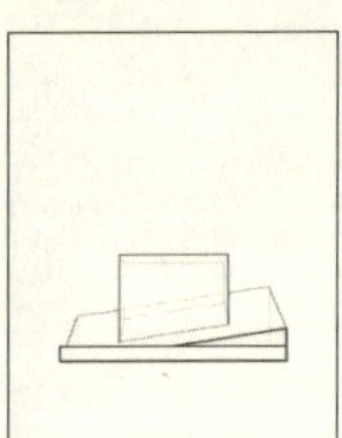

DECLINED ROOF

TU Delft Library
Mecanoo Architecten, 1997
Norwegian National Opera
Snøhetta, 2008
Railyards Cultural Center
3XN

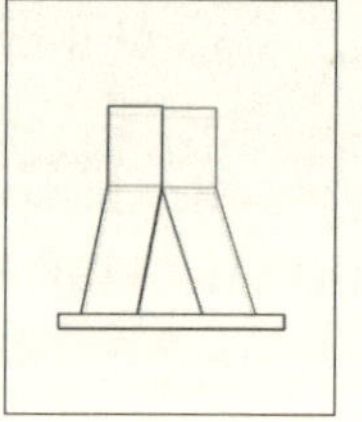

PANTS

People's Building
PLOT, 2004
Torres Siamesas
Alejandro Aravena, 2005
East Tower
RMJM, 2013

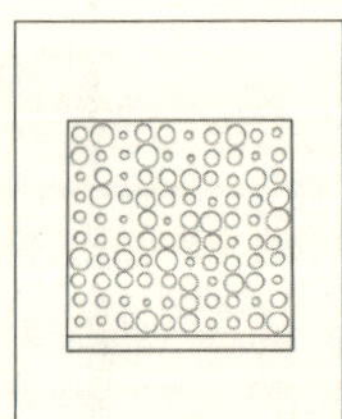

POINT-ATTRACTOR

West Diaoyutai Tower
Bernard Tschumi, 2004
Sinosteel International Plaza
MAD Architects, 2006
O-14
Reiser & Umemoto, 2007

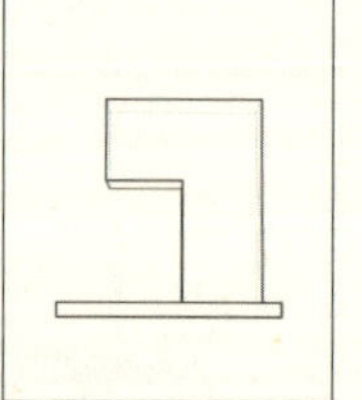

L-SHAPED CANTILEVER

Peckham Library
Will Alsop, 2000
Tongxian Gatehouse
Office dA, 2003
Shipping & Transport College
Neutelings Riedijk, 2006

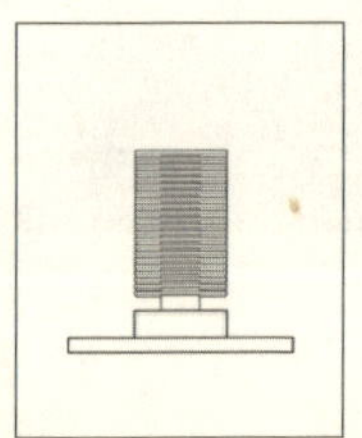

BOXY TOWER

Lever House
SOM, 1952
Seagram Building
Mies van der Rohe, 1958
Gebouw Delftse Poort
Abe Bonnema, 1992

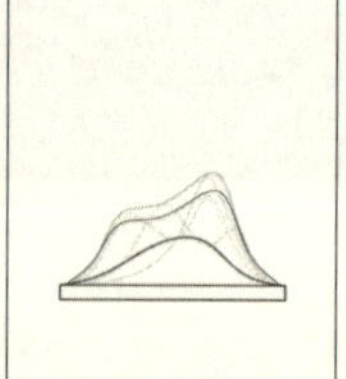

RIBBONS

Opera House
Bernard Tschumi, 2005
City of Culture of Galicia
Eisenman Architects, 2011
Drents Museum
Erick van Egeraat, 2011
BOOM! Palm Springs Housing
Diller Scofidio + Renfro

Ana Miljački &
Sarah Hirschman

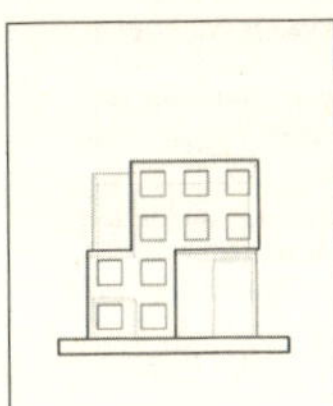

ERODED VOLUME

Simmons Hall
Steven Holl, 2002
Mirador Housing
MVRDV, 2005
Stadskantoor
OMA, 2009
ROC Mondriaan LAAK II
LIAG, 2011

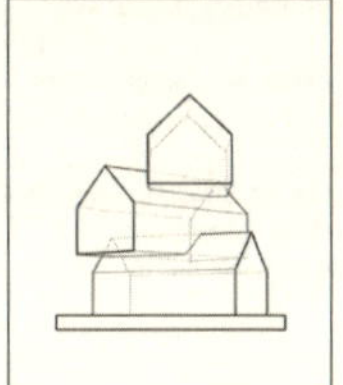

PILE O' HOUSES

Tokyo Apartment
Sou Fujimoto, 2010
VitraHaus
Herzog & de Meuron, 2010
Inntel Hotel
WAM Architecten, 2012

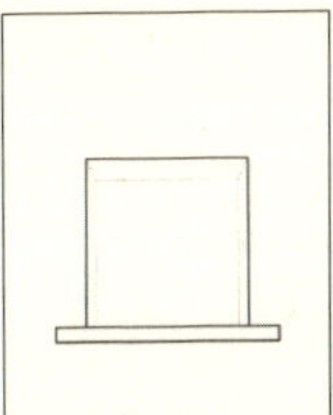

CUBE

*Phillips Exeter Academy
Library*
Louis Kahn, 1972
San Cataldo Cemetery
Aldo Rossi, 1984
*Zollverein School of
Management*
SANAA, 2006

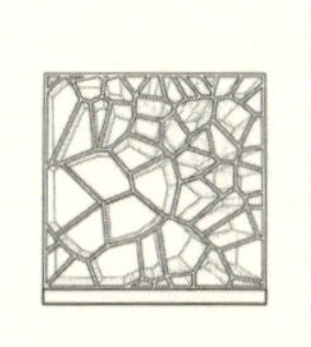

VORONOI

Airspace Tokyo
Thom Faulders, 2007
Olympic Aquatic Center
PTW Architects, 2008
*Campus Restaurant &
Event Space*
Barkow Leibinger, 2008

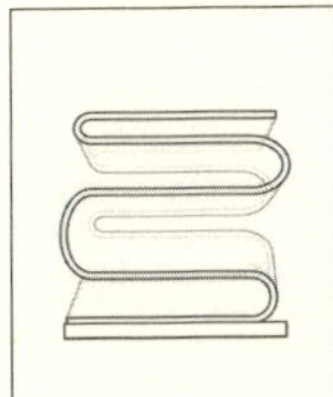

SINGLE SURFACE

Educatorium
OMA, 1997
ICA
Diller Scofidio + Renfro, 2002
Villa VPRO
MVRDV, 1997

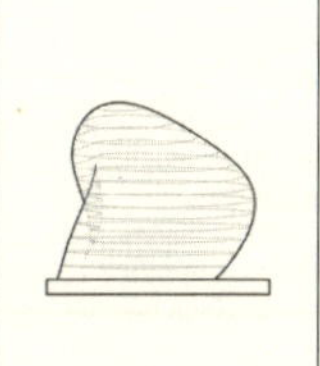

AMORPHOUS BLOB

Selfridges
Future Systems, 2003
Kunsthaus Graz
Peter Cook, 2003
Admirant Entrance
Massimiliano Fuksas, 2010
Galaxy Soho
Zaha Hadid, 2013

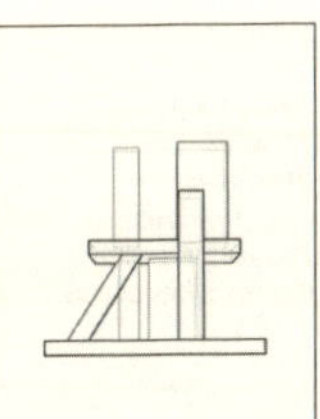

HYPER-BUILDING

Hyperbuilding
OMA, 1996
Museum Plaza
REX, 2013
Cross #Towers
BIG

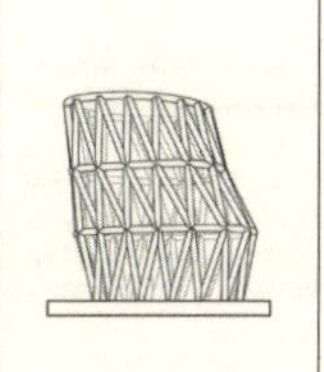

DIAGRID

Swiss Re Headquarters
Foster + Partners, 2005
Prada Epicenter
Herzog & de Meuron, 2006
CCTV Headquarters
OMA, 2012

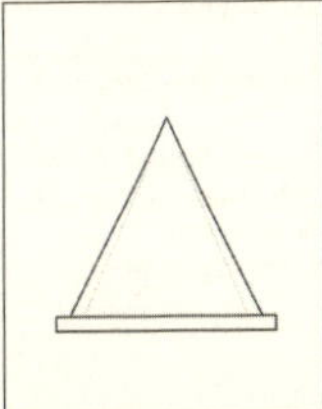

PYRAMID

Great Pyramid of Giza,
2540 BCE
Louvre Pyramid
I.M. Pei, 1989
Le Projet Triangle
Herzog & de Meuron, 2017

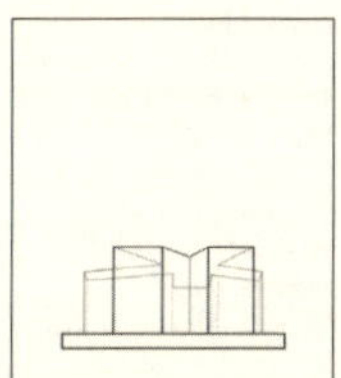

RADIATING BARS

Helsingor Psychiatric
PLOT, 2006
BMVR Library
OMA, 2010
UN City
3XN, 2013

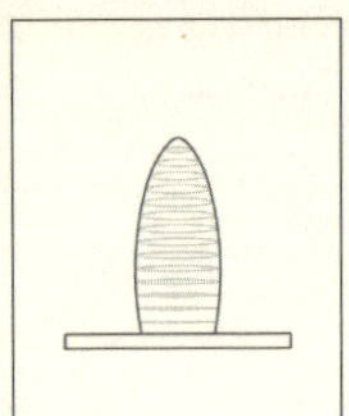

HEROIC PHALLUS

Swiss Re Headquarters
Foster + Partners, 2003
Torre Agbar
Ateliers Jean Nouvel, 2004
Doha Tower
Ateliers Jean Nouvel

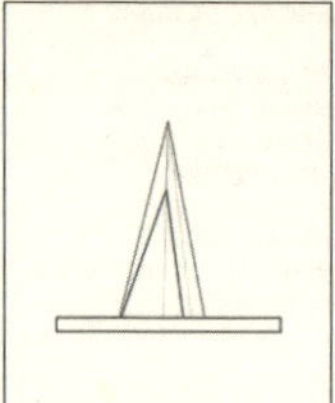

PYRAMIDAL TOWER

Transamerica Tower
William Pereira, 1972
The Shard
Renzo Piano Building
Workshop, 2012
One World Trade Center
SOM, 2013
Ryugyong Hotel, 2014

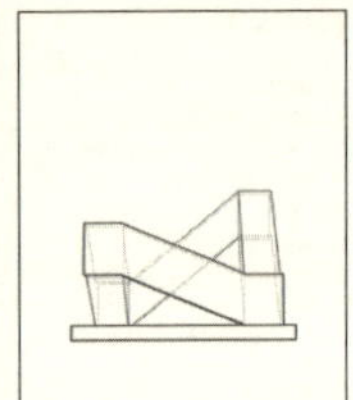

TORQUED LOOP

The Whale
Architecten Cie, 2000
Two Seasons Hotel
JDS Architects, 2010
8 House
BIG, 2010

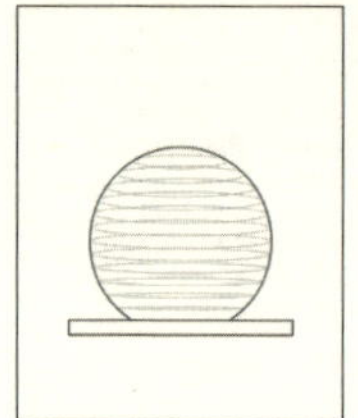

BIG BALL

Cenotaph for Newton
Étienne-Louis Boullée, 1784
House of the Forestry Guard
Claude-Nicolas
Ledoux, 1789
*RAK Convention &
Exhibition Center*
OMA, 2007

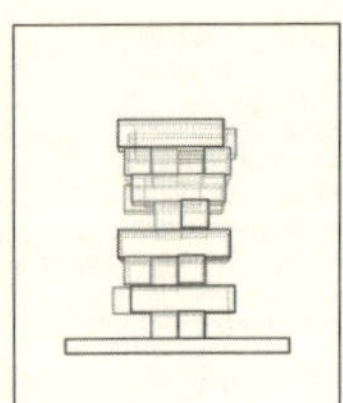

JENGA

Nakagin Capsule Tower
Kisho Kurokawa, 1972
Final Wooden House
Sou Fujimoto, 2008
BUMPS Tower
SAKO Architects, 2009
56 Leonard Street
Herzog & de Meuron

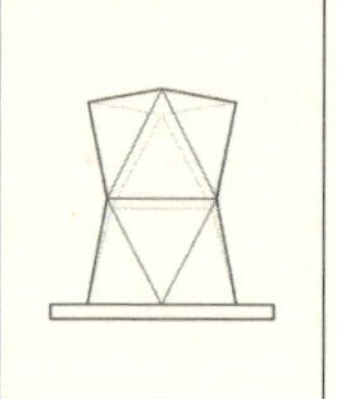

MEGA-FACET

Art Tower Mito
Arata Isozaki, 1990
Hearst Tower
Foster + Partners, 2006
*Yongsan International
Business District Tower*
SOM, 2013

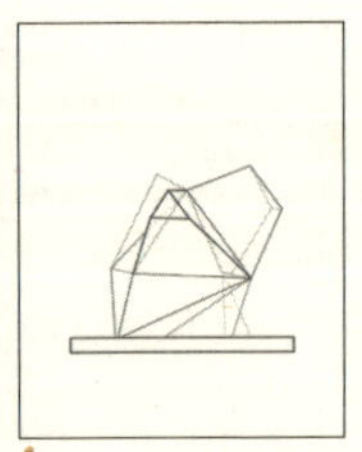

CRYSTAL

Gateway Center & Plaza
Predock Frane, 2000
UFA Cinema Center
Coop Himmelb(l)au, 2001
Royal Ontario Museum
Studio Daniel Libeskind, 2007
Victoria and Albert Museum
REX

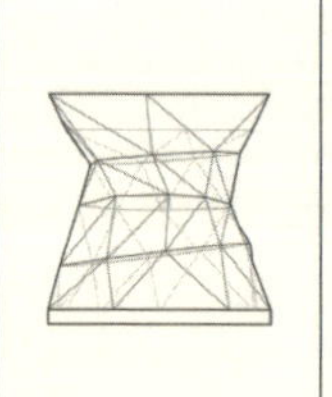

TRIANGULATION

Helios House
Office dA, 2007
BMW Welt
Coop Himmelb(l)au, 2007
Datong Library
Preston Scott Cohen, 2013

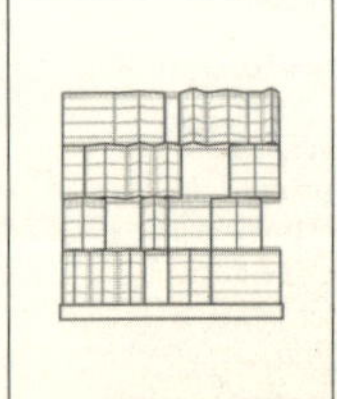

SHUTTERS

*149 Rue des Suisses
Apartments*
Herzog & de Meuron, 2000
Carabanchel Housing
FOA, 2007
Passive House
Karawitz Architects, 2009

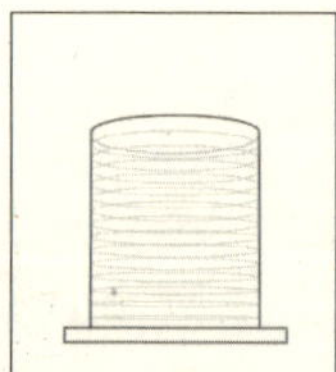

CYLINDER

Stockholm Public Library
Erik Gunnar Asplund, 1928
National Assembly of Dhaka
Louis Kahn, 1962
Palazzo Botta
Mario Botta, 1990

Fair Use

Ana Miljački &
Sarah Hirschman

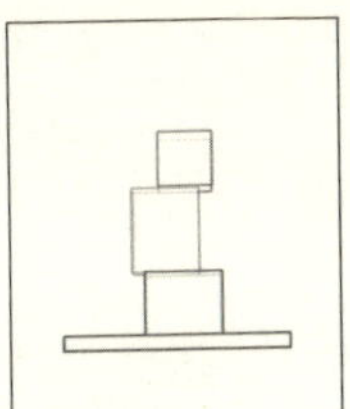

STACK O'BOXES

New Museum
SANAA, 2008
Perm Museum XXI
Valerio Olgiati, 2008
111 First Street
OMA

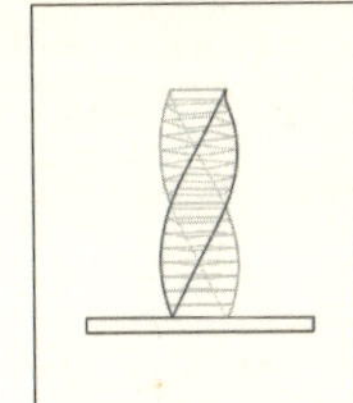

SMOOTH TWIST

Twisting Torso
Santiago Calatrava, 2005
Infinity Tower
SOM, 2008
Guangzhou TV &
Sightseeing Tower
Info Based Architecture, 2013
Scala Tower
BIG

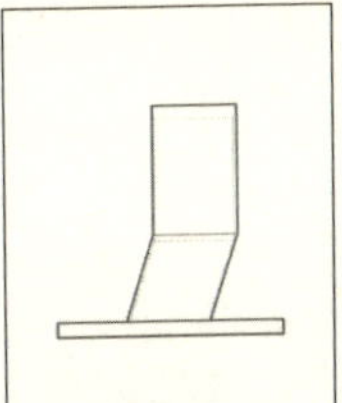

LEANING TOWER

Blue Residential Tower
Bernard Tschumi, 2007
Phillips Business Innovation
Center
Mecanoo Architecten, 2007
Walter Towers
BIG
23 East 22nd Street
OMA

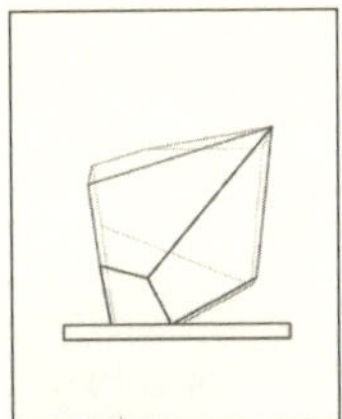

BOULDER

Casa da Musica
OMA, 2005
Theater Agora
UN Studios, 2007
Cultural Center
Bernard Tschumi, 2010

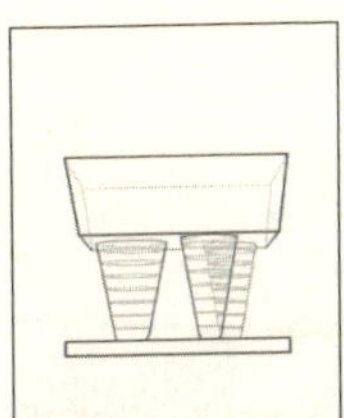

ELEVATED VOLUME

Grand Egyptian Museum
nArchitects, 2002
Phaeno Science Center
Zaha Hadid Architects, 2005
Giant Interactive Group
Campus
Morphosis, 2012

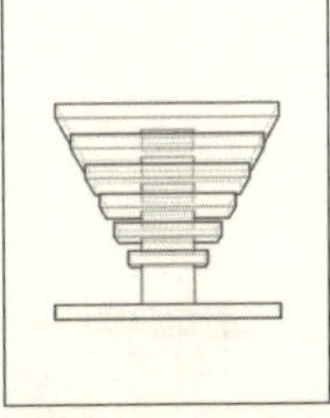

UPSIDE DOWN PYRAMID

Clusters in the Air
Arata Isozaki, 1962
Expo 67 Canadian Pavilion
Rob Robbie, 1967
Slovak Radio Building
Štefan Svetko, Štefan
Ďurkovič & Barnabáš
Kissling, 1983
America's Cup Pavilion
David Chipperfield, 2006

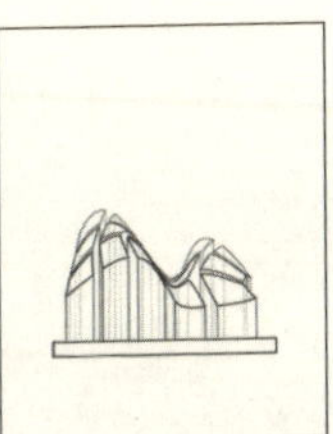

PARAMETRIC URBANISM

One North Masterplan
Zaha Hadid Architects, 2003
Taiyuan Drum Tower
Traditional District Planning
Preston Scott Cohen
Tainjin Green Business
District
Henning Larsen Architects

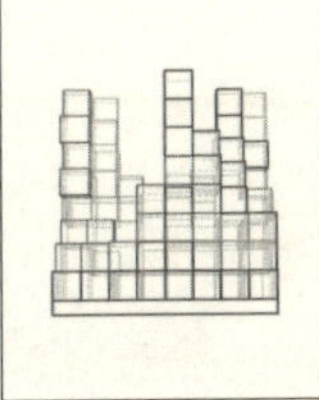

PIXELATED MASSING

Lego Towers
BIG, 2007
Nursing Home in Alcácer
do Sal
Aires Mateus, 2007
Rodovre Sky Village
MVRDV

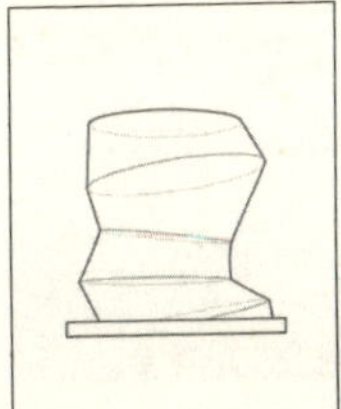

LOFTED SLABS

Small House
Kazuyo Sejima, 2000
Maison Go
Périphériques Architectes,
2003
Samitaur Tower
Eric Owen Moss, 2010

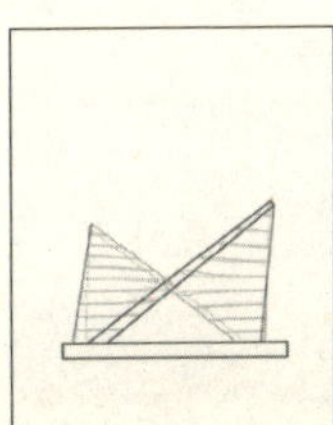

HYPAR

Chapel of San Jose Obrero
Felix Candela, 1959
Saint Mary's Cathedral
Kenzo Tange, 1964
Hypar Pavilion at Lincoln
Center
Diller Scofidio + Renfro, 2011

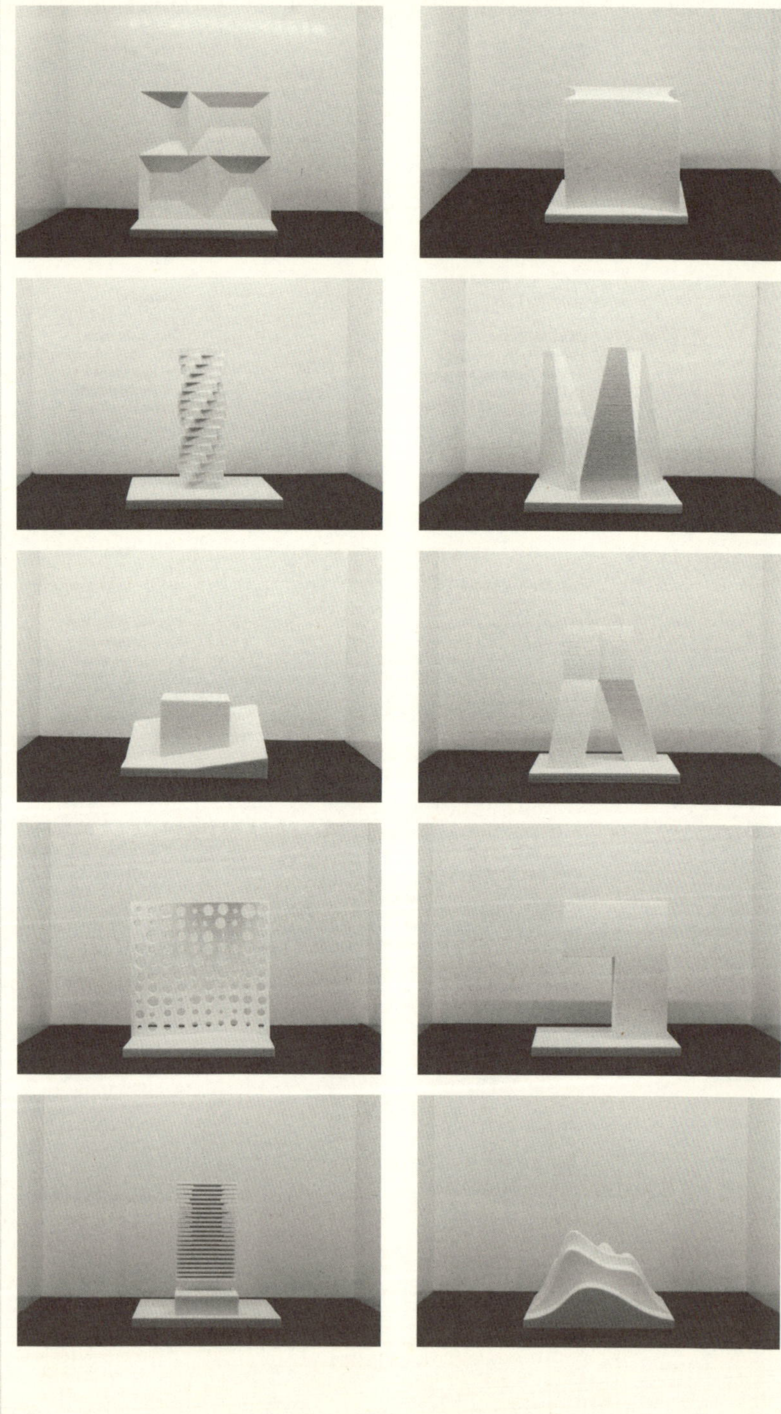

Fair Use

Ana Miljački &
Sarah Hirschman

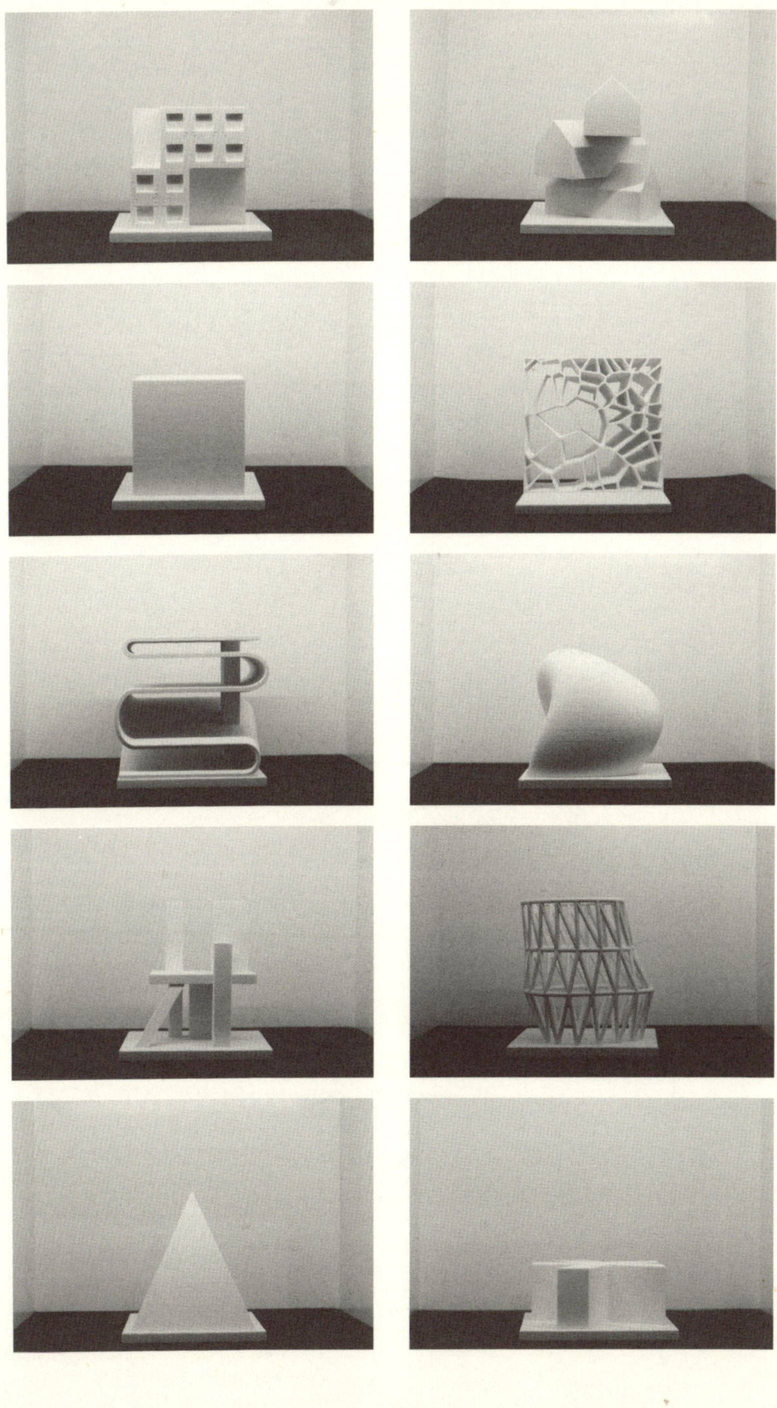

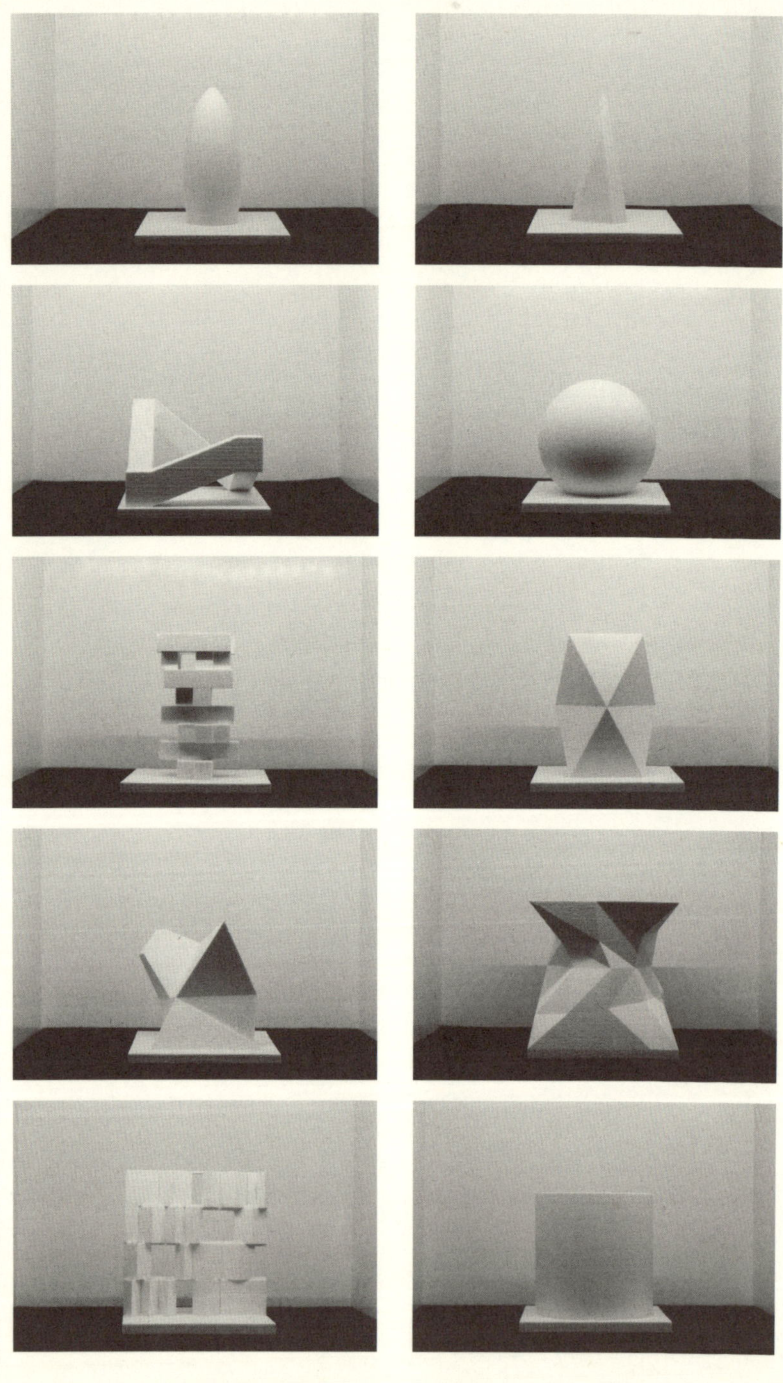

Fair Use

Ana Miljački &
Sarah Hirschman

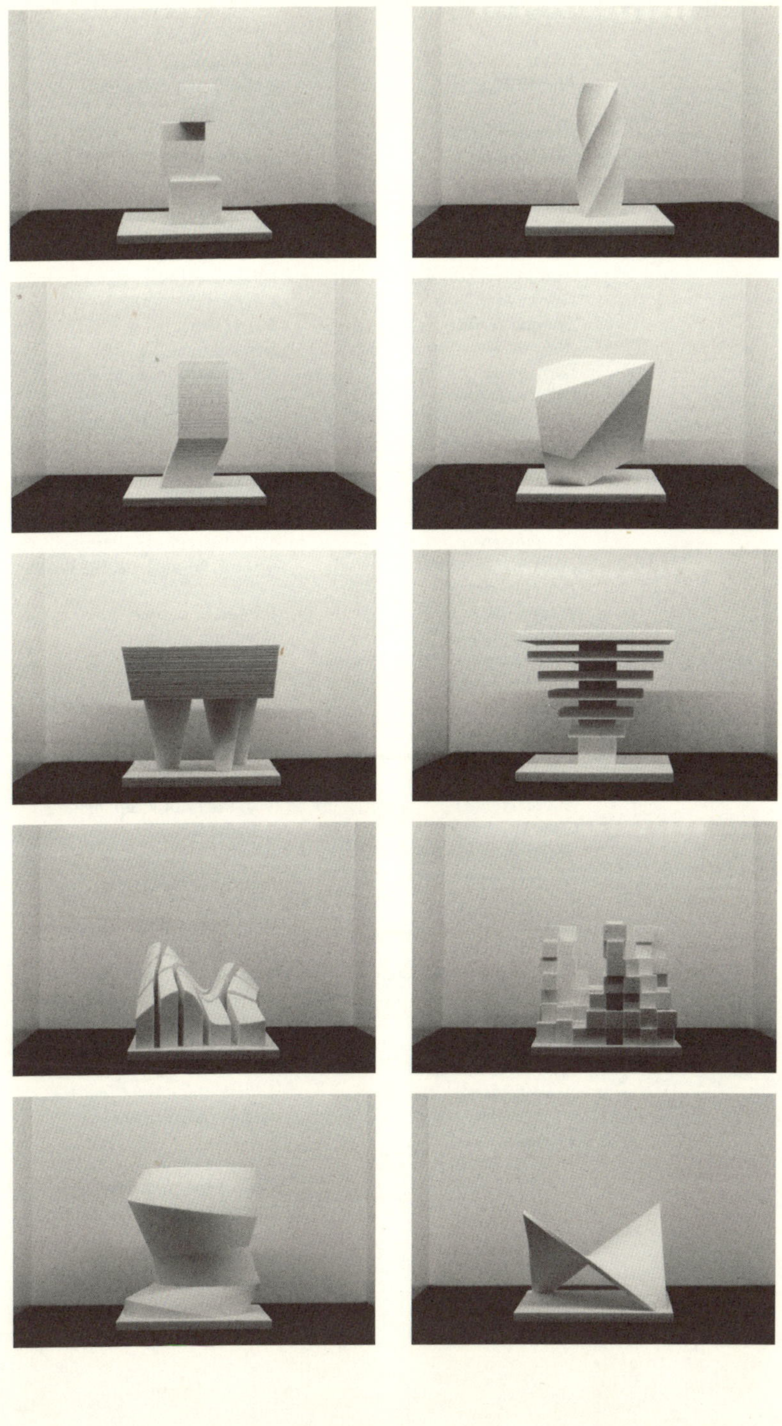

Under the Influence

Editor
Ana Miljački

Assistant Editor
Irene Hwang

Contributors
Nader Tehrani
Mario Carpo
Alexander D'Hooghe
Florian Idenburg
Enrique Walker
Michael Meredith
Sam Jacob
Cristina Goberna
Urtzi Grau
Amanda Reeser Lawrence
Ines Weizman
Mariana Ibañez
Simon Kim
Timothy Hyde
John McMorrough
Eric Höweler
Meejin Yoon
Michael Kubo
Kyle Barker
Sarah Hirschman
Hilary Sample

Editorial Collaborators
Philam Nguyen
Mariel Villeré
Sara Brown
Trevor Herman Hilker
Gideon Schwartzman

Design
TwoPoints.Net,
Hamburg, Barcelona

Publisher
Actar Publishers,
New York, Barcelona
www.actar.com

Printer
Gráficas Campás, S.A.

Distribution
Actar D, Inc. New York,
Barcelona.

New York
440 Park Avenue South,
17th Floor
New York, NY 10016, USA
T +1 2129662207
salesnewyork@actar-d.com

Barcelona
Roca i Batlle 2-4
08023 Barcelona, Spain
T +34 933282183
eurosales@actar-d.com

Indexing
English ISBN:
978-1-948765-15-2
PCN: Library of Congress
Control Number: 2019930029

Printed in Europe
Publication date:
April 2019

Photo Credits
*Pages: 104, 106, 109: Canadian
Center for Architecture; 153:
Scott Covert; 158:* Louis
Hellman; *169: Herman
Hertzberger, Aviodrome
Luchtfotografie; 172, 173:
Yihuai Hu*